MUTINY

D1374112

WRITING AS DAVID HAGBERG

TWISTER

THE CAPSULE

LAST COME THE CHILDREN

HEARTLAND

HEROES

WITHOUT HONOR

COUNTDOWN

CROSSFIRE

CRITICAL MASS

DESERT FIRE

HIGH FLIGHT

ASSASSIN

WHITE HOUSE

JOSHUA'S HAMMER

EDEN'S GATE

THE KILL ZONE

BY DAWN'S EARLY LIGHT

SOLDIER OF GOD

ALLAH'S SCORPION

DANCE WITH THE DRAGON

THE EXPEDITER

WRITING AS SEAN FLANNERY

THE KREMLIN CONSPIRACY

EAGLES FLY

THE TRINITY FACTOR

THE HOLLOW MEN

FALSE PROPHETS

BROKEN IDOLS

GULAG

MOSCOW CROSSING

THE ZEBRA NETWORK

CROSSED SWORDS

COUNTERSTRIKE

MOVING TARGETS

WINNER TAKE ALL

ACHILLES' HEEL

WRITING NONFICTION WITH BORIS GINDIN

MUTINY: THE TRUE EVENTS
THAT INSPIRED THE HUNT FOR RED OCTOBER

MUTINY

THE TRUE EVENTS THAT INSPIRED *THE HUNT FOR RED OCTOBER*

DAVID HAGBERG
AND
BORIS GINDIN

A TOM DOHERTY ASSOCIATES BOOK

NEW YORK

MUTINY: THE TRUE EVENTS THAT INSPIRED
THE HUNT FOR RED OCTOBER

Copyright © 2008 by David Hagberg and Boris Gindin

All rights reserved.

Book design by Ellen Cipriano

A Forge Book
Published by Tom Doherty Associates, LLC
175 Fifth Avenue
New York, NY 10010

www.tor-forge.com

Forge® is a registered trademark of Tom Doherty Associates, LLC.

The Library of Congress has catalogued the hardcover edition as follows:

Hagberg, David.
    Mutiny : the true events that inspired the hunt for Red
October / David Hagberg and Boris Gindin.
        p. cm.
    Includes bibliographical references.
    ISBN-13: 978-0-7653-1350-8
    ISBN-10: 0-7653-1350-2
    1. Mutiny—Soviet Union. 2. Storozhevoï (Ship) 3. Soviet
Union—History, Naval. 4. Soviet Union—History—1953–1985.
I. Gindin, Boris. II. Title.
    DK274.H244   2008
    359.1'334—dc22

                                                    2008006492

ISBN-13: 978-0-7653-1351-5
ISBN-10: 0-7653-1351-0

First Hardcover Edition: May 2008
First Trade Paperback Edition: August 2009

Printed in the United States of America

0 9 8 7 6 5 4 3 2 1

For Laurie

David Hagberg

*This book is for my lovely wife, Yana, with special
thanks. It was she who inspired me to tell this story.
And for my granddaughter, Alexandra Gindin.
My wish is that this book will always remind her of the
immense love I and the rest of the family have for her.*

Boris Gindin

CONTENTS

CONTENTS

ACKNOWLEDGMENTS

I would like to thank Elizabeth Winick, who knew that this was a story that must be told. She had the vision and foresight to take on an improbable project and see it through to completion. Also Tom Doherty, the publisher who took on a Russian immigrant with a story to tell. Without him none of this could have been possible. And to Bob Gleason, a remarkable editor.

Boris Gindin

A special thanks to Larry Bond for his kind help with technical matters. The mistakes are mine.

David Hagberg

AUTHORS' NOTE

Some of the names have been changed.

PREFACE

DAVID HAGBERG

In the fall of 1975 most of the crewmen of the Soviet antisubmarine warfare ship FFG *Storozhevoy* mutinied. The captain was seized and confined belowdecks, and those officers and men who did not want to participate were placed under house arrest.

The dangerously idealistic ringleader of the mutiny sent a message to Moscow telling the Brezhnev government that he was taking the ship in order to give a message to the Soviet people, that their government was corrupt and needed to be changed.

The officer thought it would be a wake-up call not only for Russia but for the entire world that the Cold War was spinning dangerously out of control toward global thermonuclear war.

Within hours after the *Storozhevoy* left the port of Riga, which at the time was part of the USSR, and sailed into the Baltic Sea, Moscow ordered that he be hunted down and killed. The ship, the officers, and the men were all to be destroyed and the entire incident be covered up.

Which very nearly happened, but for the heroic efforts of a few of the officers and crew who saved the lives of everyone.

And the cover-up was complete except for an obscure report of the incident written by a U.S. Navy officer studying at the Naval Postgraduate School in Monterey, California, who managed to piece together the various bits and pieces of the story.

A couple years later Tom Clancy came across the report, which inspired him to write *The Hunt for Red October,* an edge-of-the-chair thriller that was exciting, entertaining, and highly successful.

Writing a nonfiction account of the mutiny through the eyes of one of the officers was supposed to be a natural extension of a career I've made chronicling the Cold War in several dozen novels. I have spent three decades studying the Soviet Union, its government, its military organizations, and its secret intelligence services, including the KGB, as well as its people and places.

I had the real-life, up close and personal story of a key player in the drama. Nothing could have been easier. The book would practically write itself. Boris Gindin would tell me the story, and I would fix up his grammar.

But this was, after all, the stuff of real life.

Which meant that if I came across something I didn't like I couldn't change it for the sake of the story. If some of the facts were messy and not pleasant, I couldn't doctor them up to suit the narrative flow.

I might be able to invent some dialogue and interior monologue that, according to Boris Gindin and my own research, was likely to have happened. But I couldn't change the facts.

Rather than relying on poetic license and clever plotting, the story of the *Storozhevoy* told itself because it is an edge-of-the-chair thriller.

If truth can sometimes be stranger than fiction, then certainly truth can and most often is even more exciting.

PREFACE

BORIS GINDIN

Readers have the right to know why, after thirty-two years, I decided to tell this story. It was not an easy decision. I still have a lot of fear of how the new KGB will react. My only hope is that Russia has taken a course toward democracy, in which *perestroika*—openness—actually means something.

I think that I'm doing the right thing, telling the real story behind the mutiny aboard the *Storozhevoy* in November 1975, because it was one event in a long chain of events that heralded the beginning of the end for the old Soviet regime, of thought police and gulags and the ever-present danger that confrontation with our enemy the United States would result in a global thermonuclear war.

Besides, I owe it to my crewmates to set the record straight.

I was born to a middle-class family who would struggle to make a decent living and educate their children. I grew up with an older sister during the Khrushchev-Brezhnev era, which was marked with pain and frustration for Russians. We thought of that time as the dark ages. People were fed up with lies from their government that a better life was just around the corner. Moscow was spending our money for military weapons, while our grocery stores were almost always empty!

Yet, when I was seventeen, I entered the St. Petersburg Military Engineering Academy because I believed the lie. I wanted to serve and defend my country and build a better future for myself. I wanted my parents to be proud of me. The academy was one of the most prestigious schools in all of Russia, and I wanted to use it to build a career in the navy.

And I did well enough in school, finishing in the top half of my class, so that I was sent to the Baltic Fleet, ending up, by the time I turned twenty-four, serving as an officer on the new Krivak-class warship *Storozhevoy*.

It was a great honor. But at the time I had no way of knowing that one of my fellow crewmen would mutiny, that Moscow would order us hunted and sunk, that the KGB would shoot the idealistic young officer behind the mutiny—a man who only wanted a better life for himself and all Russians—that the careers of many good men would be permanently ruined, and that an American author would make his career writing a novel inspired by the mutiny.

After the incident was over and all of us were under arrest, even those who opposed the mutiny—it made no difference to Moscow—my eyes opened to the way things were. And I began to ask myself questions. Why didn't my government recognize the true heroism? Why were the punishments so harsh and unjust? How could the Politburo send the order to sink the *Storozhevoy* and kill all her crew? How could my government swear me and the others to absolute secrecy on pain of death?

There were to be no disclosures. No discussions to help us get through the pain. No getting it off our chests, not even to relatives, not even to our wives.

Do I regret that I studied at the military academy and wanted to dedicate my life to serving my country and my people? No, I do not.

Do I regret my blind dedication and firmness in following my orders, something that the Soviet government drummed into its people's heads from the time of birth? Yes, I do.

After the mutiny, the crew of the *Storozhevoy* signed a KGB document promising never to tell what happened. Everything was buried. For the old Soviet Union, truth had always been the enemy. In some ways I expect that mind-set may still be the case in Moscow.

So why have I written this book? And, maybe more important, should I have told the true story?

I left Russia and I'm no longer bound to keep my promise to the secret police. I'm an American citizen now.

The mutiny was a significant event, and the facts should not be lost to history.

The men and officers who with me opposed the mutiny have had to live with the consequences. Moscow unfairly blamed them, as well as the mutineers, and their lives and careers were irreparably ruined.

With this book I hope finally to set the record straight, to clear their good names and reputations.

MUTINY

THE MUTINIES

1905–07

On the fourteenth of June 1905 the crew of a brand-new Russian battleship that was engaged in a live fire exercise off the Black Sea island of Tendra murdered the captain and most of the officers and took over the ship. This was at a time in Tsarist Russia in which the people were in open rebellion against their government. Fighting was going on in all the major cities in the east. And in Moscow, St. Petersburg, and Odessa workers were on strike.

The ship had taken on a load of rotten meat, crawling with maggots, and the men refused to eat it even after the doctor said it was okay. The captain ordered the crew mustered on deck, where he picked out several of the men to use as examples. He was going to have them shot to death for betraying a direct order.

The first mate ordered the guard to open fire, but he refused and the bloody mutiny began.

She was the battleship *Knyaz Potemkin Tavrichesky*, of which a famous movie was made in 1925. But hers wasn't the only navy crew to mutiny during that year and the next two. There was the battleship

Georgiy Pobedonosets, the training ship *Prut,* the cruisers *Ochakov* and *Pamyat Azova,* and the destroyers *Svirepy* and *Skory,* among others.

The real reason behind all those mutinies was the same, and it wasn't rotten meat. It was a rotten government. Change was coming.

What do a handful of men and officers aboard a warship think that they can accomplish against an entire nation, even one in turmoil?

Do they expect that their actions can make a difference?

The mutiny of the battleship *Potemkin* signaled the beginning of the end for the Tsarist Russian government, just as the mutiny aboard the frigate *Storozhevoy* signaled the beginning of the end for the Communist Russian government.

It was a rebirth of sorts for the crew, for the ship, and for the nation.

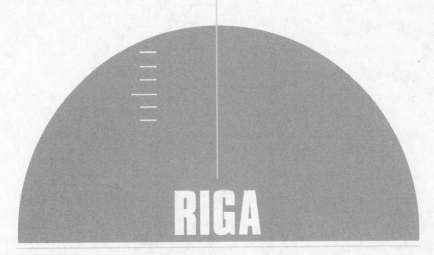

RIGA

NOVEMBER 8, 1975

**Reason's icy intimidations
and records of a heart in pain.**

ALEXANDER PUSHKIN
EUGENE ONEGIN

RIGA

THE RIVER

The morning of the mutiny the northern winter frost rides heavily on the stiff ocean breezes in the harbor. Not many people are up and about along Eksporta Iela Krastmala Street, which runs along Riga's waterfront on the Daugava River. Yesterday throngs of people lined up to see the ships of the great Soviet navy on parade to honor the fifty-eighth anniversary of the Bolshevik Revolution, but on this chilly pre-dawn all of Riga, it seems, is sleeping.

Moored in the middle of the river are fourteen Soviet warships: submarines, destroyers, cruisers, tenders, and frigates, all in parade formation, all respectful of the law and order, peace and prosperity, that serving the Motherland—the Rodina—guarantees. It's a brave new world over which lies a morning haze of wood and coal smoke from the chimneys of homes of people lucky enough to find fuel to waste in late fall merely for heat.

Aboard the frigate *Storozhevoy*, moored practically on top of an Alpha-class submarine, reveille has sounded. It is time for the two hundred men and officers to rise from their slumbers, dress in trousers and *telnyaschka*, the long-sleeved blue-and-white-striped undershirts that sailors wear no matter the time of year, and muster on deck for exercises. But yesterday was a holiday, and the mood this morning is almost universally one of indifference toward routine, yet there is a strange undercurrent of anticipation that has permeated the ship, though only two men know the reason.

The *Storozhevoy* is a low-slung, sleek warship that even tied up at his* moorings looks like a greyhound at the starting block, ready at a moment's notice to charge forward, to do battle. At over four hundred feet on deck, he is a third longer than a football field, but with a narrow beam of only forty-six feet, flaring bows, a low-slung afterdeck, and midship masts bristling with radar and Electronic Surveillance Measures (ESM) detectors rising seventy-five feet above the water, the ship looks lean and mean. And dangerous.

Down two decks and aft through three sets of watertight doors, open now, and just forward of the engineering spaces, before the midshipmen's mess, Ordinary Seaman Pavel Fomenko is sound asleep in his bunk while all around him in the cramped, smelly compartment, called a *cubrick*, his sixteen crewmates are bustling to get dressed and report on deck.

It is 0700, still pitch-black outside. Standing above Seaman Fomenko's rack is his boss, chief of engineering, Senior Lieutenant Boris Gindin.

At twenty-four, Gindin is a well-trained officer aboard ship, but he's young and relatively untested. The new men among the seventeen in his gas turbine section do not know him yet. He has a set of ground rules he learned at the academy and on his other postings, but he hasn't explained himself. He hasn't proven himself. He will stand up for them and defend them if the need should arise. But he wants to know that they will behave themselves, that they won't get drunk, that their uniforms will be neat at all times, and, most important, that they will obey orders.

*Russians use *he* and *his* for ships.

Riga is still asleep. But the crews aboard the other warships moored in the river are coming awake. From here the city's most famous structure can be seen. It's the wooden tower of St. Peter's Church in Vecriga, the old city. Dating back to the fifteenth century, it used to be the tallest wooden building in the world. Even now, rising seventy-two meters above street level, it gives a view all the way out to the Baltic Sea to the northwest. Tourists climb to the top to see the sights, and lovers make the pilgrimage for luck. For the Soviet sailors the tower represents nothing more than another authority figure. It's always something or someone, towers or officers, looking down on them, ordering them about, sometimes fostering a resentment in a man that can run deep.

Like today.

His crew needs to obey Gindin, but they do not have to know that he comes from nothing more than a middle-class family from Leningrad. Certainly not rich by any standards, certainly not well connected, certainly not favored by the Politburo or the Communist Party.

They don't have to know he's a Jew.

Every morning Gindin is up before his men, so that he can make sure they are ready for their mandatory exercises. In the academy, where he learned gas turbine engineering, he was on the weight-lifting team. He is five-feet-nine and stocky, with the round but pleasant face of a Great Russian, obsidian black hair, and blue eyes. It's obvious that he's in better physical shape than most of his men, especially Seaman Fomenko, in part because of the luck of the genetic draw but also because Gindin continues to work out and because officers aboard Soviet warships eat much better than enlisted sailors.

Gindin kicks the man's bunk. "It's time to get up."

Fomenko opens one eye and gives his officer a baleful look. He cannot get up with the others. "My father is an alcoholic and I have a hangover, so you see I cannot get up."

"I don't appreciate your joke," Gindin tells the man. "Get out of bed now."

Several of the seaman's crewmates have remained behind to watch from the open door. It is the officer against the new troublemaker.

"I have told you that my father is an alcoholic and I have a hangover. Now go away and let me alone." Fomenko turns over in bed. He means to disobey a direct order.

Gindin glances at the men watching the unfolding drama. He is not a hard man. He does not have a bad temper, as some of the other officers do. He does not treat his men harshly. But he does expect his orders to be obeyed. This is important to him, and to the ship, and especially to the Soviet navy, to which he owes his entire future.

Gindin throws back the thin blanket, grabs Fomenko by the collar of his shirt, hauls him roughly out of bed, and slams him against the wall. "Do you feel better now?"

"No," the seaman says. He is provoking Gindin to take the situation to the limit or leave him alone, in which case the men will have won a small battle against an officer.

Gindin smashes the seaman against the steel bulkhead again, this time with much greater force. "How do you feel now?" Gindin asks.

"Better but not good enough."

Gindin lifts the man's feet completely off the floor and smashes him against the wall again, his head bouncing off the steel. "How about now?"

"I feel much better, sir," Fomenko says. He is ready to go on deck for morning exercises.

The seventeen men from the motor turbine division make their way topsides, where they join their comrades. Thirty minutes of exercise every morning, seven days per week, at anchor or at sea, rain or snow or shine. Curiously, despite the bland, monotonous food in the crew's mess and despite the fact that no matter the weather the men dress only in trousers and cotton shirts, no one gets a cold or the flu. These boys are healthy, most of them from the farms or small towns across the Soviet Union, with iron constitutions.

Every morning after exercises the enlisted men are served kasha, which is a gruel made of hulled buckwheat, and a couple thin pieces of bread with a little butter, while the officers are served a special kasha made of processed oatmeal, cheese, kielbasa sausages, and as much good bread and butter as they can eat.

After making sure that his men show up for their exercises Gindin walks forward to the officers' dining hall on an upper deck. It's about twenty-five feet long and half that width, with three long tables and two big windows. It is a bright, airy room, something Gindin appreciates, since his duty station is belowdecks in the machinery spaces. The table to the left is for the skipper, Captain Second Rank Anatoly Potulniy; his *starpom*, executive officer, Captain Lieutenant Nikolay Novozilov; and the *zampolit*, political officer, Captain Third Rank Valery Sablin; plus any visiting VIPs.

This is the end of a six-month cruise, which has taken them as far around the world as Cuba, to show the flag, to show support for a friendly nation. Tomorrow the *Storozhevoy*, which in English translates very unsexily into "large patrol craft," is scheduled to sail to the Yantar Shipyard in Kaliningrad, where he will undergo two weeks of repairs, and then back to base at Baltiysk, fifty kilometers away.

Gindin's family lives in Pushkin, about twenty-five kilometers south of Leningrad, and it'll be good to get home on leave, because he's just lost his father, Iosif, with whom he was very close. His dad's death was a real blow, which he is having a hard time dealing with. He wants to be morose, but he can't let himself slide into self-pity and still do his duties. But two weeks will not be soon enough for him to be with his mother, Yevgeniya, and sister, Ella, who need him.

Boris's roommate, Senior Lieutenant Vladimir Firsov, is at the breakfast table when Gindin walks in and takes his place. The captain's not here this morning, but Zampolit Sablin is, and it looks as if he has a fire in his belly.

"Good morning, Boris," Sablin calls with a lot of bonhomie. "It'll be a fine day, don't you think?" He's got dark hair, a good build, and the kind of face that is always smiling.

Gindin remembers an incident when the ship sailed down to East Germany for a celebration of the thirtieth anniversary of the end of World War II. A parade had just passed by, and everybody on the pier was happy. Gindin and Sablin and some of the other officers went down on the dock, and Sablin scooped up one of the children and held the kid high in the air with a big smile. Everyone was laughing and singing. Sablin was married and had a child of his own, and he liked all children. But Gindin wasn't married, had no children, and didn't understand. Except that Sablin has the same happy, excited look on his face this morning as he had in Germany that day.

"What's with our good *zampolit*?" Firsov asks. He's five-nine, with blond hair, a mustache, and a wicked kick on the soccer field. He's a bright guy. He and Gindin have hit it off.

"He's always like that," Gindin says. "He thinks he's here to save us."

"From what?" Firsov asks. "Our crazy crew?"

Gindin looks sharply at him, thinking that he was the only one who'd noticed that something strange was going on. Things felt different somehow. It promised to be a bright, crisp weekend, and there was nothing to spoil it. Yet coming up a companionway from belowdecks he ran into some sailors who were in a huddle, having a serious conversation about something. When they spotted an officer coming their way, they broke off.

It was a holiday, when people normally smile and laugh and have happy faces. But this morning Gindin has not seen any smiling sailors; he's heard no jokes, no laughter.

Only sullenness.

Except from Zampolit Sablin.

The mess steward comes with Gindin's food. All the officers contribute an extra twenty-five rubles a month for good food, but Gindin has a special relationship with the cook because he controls the ship's water. It's the same on all Soviet warships. Some systems in the military seem to work better than others, and this is one of them.

Another involves a pure alcohol, called *spirt*, which Gindin uses to clean his equipment. It's 96 proof and when distributed to a friend or to anyone you would like to curry favor with is part of another system that works well.

"After duty we'll have some *spirt*," Gindin suggests to his roommate. "Maybe we'll figure out what bug Sablin has up his ass."

Firsov is quick to laugh, and their *zampolit*, out of earshot, nods his approval. Sablin likes to see his men happy, especially his officers. He has a seemingly genuine interest not only in the crew's comfort and morale but, curiously, in the ship's systems as well. All the ship's systems, mechanical and electrical.

But this morning his mood seems somehow contrived. Maybe false. As if he were afraid of something.

Of what? Gindin wonders.

THE ACADEMY

1967

When Boris Gindin turned sixteen it was time for him to apply for his internal passport, which all Russians need to travel inside their country. It's also a form of national identification and classification. His mother and father were both Jews. But under "Nationality" her passport was marked "Jewish," while Iosif's was marked "Russian." It meant that Gindin had a choice—to declare himself a Jew or a Russian. His father told Boris to put down "Russian" because when it came time to make a career, life would be much easier for him as a Russian than as a Jew. He was rightfully afraid that the next year, when he was thinking about joining the Soviet navy, he would not be accepted because he was a Jew, unless he followed his father's advice about the passport. Not that a religion would keep Boris out of the service; it's just that he knew a Jew would never get into any of the prestigious academies that were necessary for advancement.

Go into the service as an enlisted man and any sort of a real career was impossible. It was a life he did not want to contemplate.

His father, a man whom Boris adored, was an engineer. Boris was going to follow in his father's footsteps. But not as a civilian. Iosif was the sole breadwinner in the Gindin family, and even as an engineer he was barely making 160 rubles per month. That was scarcely enough to pay the rent on their small apartment and put food on the table. At first the Gindins shared a small apartment with several other people, the three of them living in one room. The Gindins never had good things; the furniture was shabby and primitive, their clothing hand-me-downs from relatives, they never had a vacation, and when Iosif had to go into the sanatorium for his failing health a difficult life got even tougher.

"You want to be an engineer, I can get you into the academy," Boris's brother-in-law, Vladimir Simchuk, said one evening over dinner.

"Gas turbines," Boris said. He'd already been having the dreams.

The St. Petersburg Military Engineering Academy is in Pushkin, but the locals call it Tsarskoye Selo because the last tsar had his summer residence there. It's a lovely little town whose palaces and gorgeous parks, which are especially spectacular with the changing leaves in the fall, were created in the eighteenth century by the empresses Elizabeth and Catherine the Great.

Vladimir was in his fifth year at the academy and was doing very well. His grades were good, he was on the school's weight-lifting team—a sport that Gindin had practically made a career of in high school—and, best of all, the head of Vladimir's *rota*, or company, Captain Third Rank Spartak Svetlov, agreed to put in a good word for Boris.

The academy, which only dates back to a few years after the revolution, is located on a few acres of prime parkland near the Catherine Palace and was home in those days to fifteen hundred engineering students taking the five-year courses.

In order to be accepted out of high school, Boris had to take and pass five tests: verbal and written mathematics, verbal physics, literature, and sports fitness, plus an extensive physical exam. Dumb, sick students are not accepted. This is *the* elite school. He gets a decent mark in physics and does very well on the other four. His grades are good enough to ask for any five-year course of study he wants. Steam Turbines, Diesels, Submarines, or the newest, most glamorous, sexiest course of all, Gas Turbines. With gas turbines his advancement in the navy will be rapid, and once he retires his career as a civilian will also be all but guaranteed.

That was the easy part. The second, biggest hurdle was meeting with Admiral Nikolaev, who was the head of the academy, and two of his officers: the faculty commander and the assistant for military training.

It was mid-August in Pushkin, pleasant, not too hot, the fall colors already beginning to show, when Gindin showed up for his interview in the school's Administration Building. It was a big conference room with three large windows through which the sun streamed. Immediately to the left was a long table, behind which sat the three officers.

"You did well on your exams, Comrade Gindin," Admiral Nikolaev complimented Boris. The admiral is an old man, in his mid-sixties, with a longtime active navy career behind him. The students think of him as a father, because he is stern but warm and friendly. If you have a problem, the admiral will listen.

The other officers on the interviewing commission weren't so nice; in fact, the colonel who was Admiral Nikolaev's assistant for military training had never served in the active navy and was a mean, condescending man. Everyone in the school knew that if you happened to meet him on the street, you'd better cross over to the other side before he noticed you, because he was sure to find some fault and send you to your *rota* captain for disciplinary action.

The main thing the admiral and his two officers want from Gindin is the promise that he is ready to dedicate his life to serving his country. That means dedicated to *giving* his life for the Rodina, Mother Russia. Shedding his blood for the Soviet Union if need be.

Gindin is young, just seventeen, the navy is the glamour service: prestige, an impeccable reputation. Its officers are considered to be a part of the Russian elite that got its start with Peter the Great, who established the navy and, therefore, Russia as a world power.

This moment is the very beginning of Gindin's life.

"Da," he enthusiastically responds. Yes, he will dedicate his life to the Rodina; he will shed his blood for the Motherland if called upon to do so. As a gas turbine engineer, taking care of the power plants aboard the newest, most modern ships anywhere on earth.

But he had not counted on one fatal flaw. Despite his Russian passport, the admiral and his officers know that Gindin is a Jew. It was his first, though not last, experience that being a Jew in the Soviet Union meant fewer choices. Here at the academy it meant that sometimes you had to step out of someone else's way so that his career could advance.

"We have no room for you in Gas Turbines, Comrade Gindin," the colonel says, with a smirk. "You will be joining the diesel facility."

Gindin nods dumbly. No other choice is open for him, not really. The diesel curriculum is easier, but it has less prestige and less opportunitiy than gas turbines. And since the gas turbine major is tougher, only the guys who did the best on the exams get chosen. This knocks the wind out of Gindin's sails, because he knows he did very well. But he keeps his mouth shut because no one here is interested in his side of the story. He figures that he should consider himself lucky that he was accepted at all. Lucky and grateful.

"Da," he will faithfully serve and defend the Motherland as a diesel engineer.

But two weeks later someone has pulled some strings, probably Gindin's brother-in-law, and without any explanation he is suddenly transferred to Gas Turbines. He never questions the change in orders, but for the first few days he floats a few centimeters above the ground.

COLD WAR CONSIDERATIONS

1968

The period between the end of WWII and the early nineties, when the Soviet Union finally collapsed, was called the Cold War because the USSR and the United States were not shooting at each other. But both sides were constantly on alert for the hot war to begin. That meant Soviet missile forces were drilled 24/7 to launch their ICBMs against targets in the West. It meant that Soviet pilots stood by their interceptors and nuclear bombers. It meant that the vast Soviet armies were poised to pour across the border into West Germany. And it meant that the navy was almost always training for the big day.

The idea of Mutual Assured Destruction, MAD, that in the event of a global thermonuclear war no one could survive, was all that prevented a third world war. The Soviets, like the Americans, depended on what was called the triad: nuclear weapons delivered by long-range bombers, nuclear weapons delivered via silo- or train-launched ICBMs, and nuclear weapons launched by submarines.

It was to this last leg of the triangle that the navy and its Anti–Submarine Warfare (ASW) vessels, such as Gindin's ship, the FFG *Storo-*

zhevoy, were so important. A submarine could sneak to within spitting distance of the Russian coast and launch its missiles so that no warning would be possible. By the time the military defense forces knew that an attack had begun there would be absolutely nothing to be done. Innocent people would die. The Rodina would be wounded. Possibly mortally.

Sailors aboard ASW platforms, as they are called, were filled with a holy zeal. If submarine-launched missile attacks could not be defended against, then the submarines themselves would have to be detected and destroyed *before* they could launch.

Boris Gindin was especially filled with the Rodina. He had never been a devout Jew, but now out of the academy and in the fleet he'd fully replaced his Jewish religion with the religion of the state. He was on a holy mission, as were many Soviet officers. He wanted to do well so that he would be noticed. He wanted to have a life for himself. To get married, to have children, to have a nice apartment, maybe even a summer house, that most Russian of retreats, the dacha.

As a Soviet navy officer Gindin is allowed to shop in the Albatros or Bereska special stores that are stocked with imported goods.

As a Soviet navy officer he can smoke American cigarettes. Walking down the streets of Leningrad with a package of Marlboros in his pocket makes him feel nine feet tall. It sounds stupid, and maybe even foolish, but in '75 people had nothing, so some little luxury gave you a sense of self-worth and an enormous satisfaction with the lifestyle you could afford.

Gindin will do anything to defend the Rodina and protect this life. He loves his father but won't end up in the same boat, earning a lousy 160 rubles per month, when it costs more than 110 rubles a month just to keep food on the table for four people! Which means he's going to do a good job in the academy, then go out into the fleet, where he will distinguish himself.

In exchange for a five-year education, the Soviet naval officer has one term of enlistment, and it is for twenty-five years. There's no getting around it. But it's not a hardship, because navy officers are privileged.

They stand among the high priests of the Communist regime.

In the summer of 1968, after his first year at the academy, Boris leaves from Kronshtadt aboard the T-58-class large patrol craft *Kirov*, a different vessel than the WWII heavy cruiser or the late eighties battle cruiser. But this ship, as old as he is, is good enough to train first-year students.

Except one night, sleeping on a hard cork mattress, Gindin is awakened to the screams of Jurij Kotovshhyk, one of the cadets in his *cubrick*. A gigantic rat is sitting on the boy's chest, calmly grooming itself.

When the lights come on, dozens of rats scurry away into the dark corners. It's Gindin's first taste of the *real* navy with which Moscow expects to defend the Rodina against the soft Americans.

But it won't be his last on this summer cruise in 1968.

One morning the captain announces over the ship's intercom that the people of Czechoslovakia are about to start a revolution. They want to overthrow the Russian brand of Socialism. The *Kirov*'s crew is issued with Kalashnikov assault rifles and ammunition. They are to sail from their base at Kronshtadt to Czechoslovakia to put down the revolt.

"I was excited and scared all at the same time," says Gindin. "I ned on to defend the Rodina with my life if need be. I'd promised admiral. We'd all made the promise. But not one of us ever be- d it would really come to this. Not like this. Not so soon."

indin and the other cadets aboard are just eighteen, and as they out into the Baltic to head southwest, maintaining their ship- outines as well as cleaning their weapons and going over mili- ics with their division commanders, no one seems to take note hoslovakia is a country that is completely landlocked.

becomes a moot point twenty-four hours later, when the iounces that the revolt has already been put down by Spe- (Spetsnaz), Russian Green Berets. Boris is there with Vik- his best friend from the academy, and Sergei Strogonov, mmander of their class, none of them certain whether they should cheer that the revolt has been put down, so they won't have to fight after all, or be disappointed that they won't get the chance this time of living up to their oaths to defend the Motherland. But the *Kirov* is ordered back to base. Boris Gindin has taken the first step to becoming an officer in what he fervently believes is the finest navy on the planet.

EN ROUTE TO HAVANA

FEBRUARY 1975

Gindin is on his second rotation aboard the *Storozhevoy,* regular military duty in the Mediterranean Sea, in Februrary 1975 when the crew gets word that they will cruise south to Cuba, where they will spend one month. This is just eight months before the mutiny, and almost no one aboard has the least premonition that their lives are soon to be ended or altered forever. There isn't an officer or jack-tar aboard who isn't over the moon. Cuba, at the time, meant not only sunshine and warmth but also the possibility of visiting ashore for fabulous food and luxuries almost beyond imagination—the girls are said to be beautiful, even if they are out of reach. Whenever the men were allowed off the ship, it was always in a group; even so, visiting ashore was nothing short of wonderful.

The KGB doesn't maintain a strong presence in Havana. In fact, the only KGB representative the officers and crew will have to contend with on the trip is Captain Lieutenant Sergey Drankov, the dour military intelligence officer assigned to the ship.

Among other things the *Storozhevoy*'s crew means to do in Havana, besides eat, drink, and sightsee, is provide a little entertainment for their Cuban allies. Gindin figures that it is some gesture of gratitude that the Soviets have a military base there and that the two governments are friends.

One of the plans is for the crews of the *Storozhevoy* and his brother ship the *Silyni,* also en route to Havana, to put on a concert of singing and dancing. Capain Potulniy orders the *Storozhevoy* to come to all stop to wait for the *Silyni* to rendezvous. They are in the middle of the unpredictable Mediterranean Sea, but the captain means to send a contingent of sailors across in a launch so that the two crews can practice. He wants everything to be just right when they get to Cuba. The USSR is like a big brother, there to show its allies how a world-class navy operates.

The transfer of crewmen goes without a hitch, the three-hour practice is a success, and the little entertainment is ready. The only problem is the weather, which has piped up to 30 knots of wind, with mounting seas rising well above four meters. The *Storozhevoy*'s crew must be retrieved, but operating a motor launch in those conditions is difficult. Potulniy orders his ship to come around to the windward side of the *Silyni* to temporarily block the wind and waves for long enough to put the launch over the side, retrieve the crewmen, and make it back across the hundred meters or so of troubled sea.

"The situation went all to hell almost immediately," Gindin recalls. He is with his men in the engine spaces, taking increasingly desperate orders from the bridge. The two ships are drifting together at an alarming rate, and there simply isn't enough sea room or enough engine power to stop the *Storozhevoy* from slamming into the side of the *Silyni* with a sickening, ship-wrenching crash. The *Silyni*'s massive anchor breaks loose, some of its enormous chain pays out, and the three tons of metal begin swinging wildly like a wrecking ball bent on destroying everything in its path.

The first damage is a hole three by six meters punched into the *Storozhevoy*'s hull, thankfully above the waterline. Stanchions and lifelines on deck are the next to go, along with a section of deck plating where the ship's rockets were loaded aboard.

KGB captain Drankov, sitting at his desk, feels the tremendous crash. He jumps up, throws open the porthole in his cabin, and sticks his head outside, just as the huge anchor swings past, missing him by centimeters. The joke among the crew later is: Too bad he didn't stick his head out a little farther.

Gindin is at the main board where the monitors and controls for the main engines as well as the fire and drain pumps are located. It is his normal posting. When the first collision occurs he is thrown violently across the compartment, where he smashes into a steel bulkhead.

This is a modern Soviet warship on his first rotation, but Potulniy and his officers know what they're doing. They've trained for emergency situations. No one loses his head.

Gindin is back at the board, and between him and the captain they somehow manage to regain enough control to back away from the *Silyni,* get some sea room, and retrieve their crew, all without any serious injuries or loss of life.

For most of the crew the navy is a necessary evil of life in the Soviet Union. For many of the officers it's just a rotten job that happens to pay well. But for Potulniy, who loves everything about the service and his position as captain, the accident is totally unacceptable. He has no one to blame except himself, and he knows that although sea duty aboard a Soviet warship, any warship, is by nature extremely hazardous, at times even deadly, Moscow does not reward failure of any kind, for any reason.

The *Storozhevoy* is ten days from Cuba, and Potulniy is in a tough spot. He can't sail into Havana with a damaged ship. Nor can he call for help. His ship must be repaired. He must be repaired by the crew aboard with the materials at hand, no matter how impossible that might be, and he has to be repaired before they reach Cuba. So Potulniy turns to the one man aboard who shares his nearly holy zeal for the ship and the navy—Gindin.

"This is something I trained for," Gindin says. He is in love with the navy and with his job and, most of all, with the Rodina. "I was going to fight capitalism if it got in our way. We were going to live better lives than our fathers and grandfathers, because they fought fearlessly to protect us and our country. It was up to us to continue the same traditions to make sure we continue to be the greatest, strongest, and most powerful country in the world. And I understood this almost from the beginning: Octebryata in first grade when we learned about Lenin; the Pioneers in grades four and five when we learned about the October Revolution and what it meant to the people; then the Komsomolez in the eighth grade where we learned more about Lenin and about Marx and Engels. Our education was neverending. Even now in the military it was up to our *zampolits* who made us understand what was expected of us.

"Serving our country was the most noble and honorable thing any Russian could do."

So, when Captain Potulniy calls Gindin, his chief of the gas turbine section of BCH-5, to fix the damage, he naturally agrees. In fact, he completely agrees, because he well understands the fix that not only the captain is in but the entire ship.

Potulniy wants Gindin and his people to heat the deck plating at the rocket-loading hatch and pound it back into shape. Gindin has a hell of a time convincing the captain that such a fix is impossible at sea but has an idea that might work. The area of mangled deck is cut away with acetylene torches, the gaping wound is covered with plywood and canvas, and the entire patch is painted burgundy to match the rest of the deck.

But that's the easy problem. The major damage done by the *Silyni's* anchor is the huge gash on the starboard side of the hull, just aft of the bow but, thankfully, enough above the waterline that the pumps are taking care of the water that rushes in every time the ship plunges into a trough between waves.

Gindin is a packrat. Every time they are at home port at Baltisk or the Yantar Shipyard in Kaliningrad he hounds the port masters for spare parts, anything he can get his hands on; he even uses his supplies of *spirt* to bribe anyone who can help. Parts for the engines and the pumps, electrical wires and parts to repair the motors, nuts, bolts, screws, piping and joints, grease and lubricants, wire and cabling, even plywood and metal plating. Anything, in short, that will allow the *Storozhevoy* to be repaired at sea without having to call for help. That's a lot of extra weight for a warship to carry.

A few months before they head out on this rotation, they're still tied to the dock at Yantar when Potulniy calls Gindin off the ship down to the pier. The *Storozhevoy's* waterline is nowhere to be seen. "Look what you've done with all the junk you've brought aboard. We're never going to get out of here, let alone get back to base."

"Captain, I think we're getting ready for another rotation, which means six months at sea," Gindin points out respectfully.

"That's right, Boris."

"Do you want to make it back on your own? Without asking for help, no matter what happens?"

"Of course."

"Or maybe get towed back to base in shame?"

"Out of the question," Potulniy fumes.

"Then, sir, I don't see why our missing waterline should be a problem."

Gindin is allowed to keep his junk, and ten days out of Cuba the stuff comes in handy.

The first problem is the electrical cable runs, which have been severed and partially ripped away from the inner hull. It's no good trying to get at them from inside the hull; too much equipment and too many bulkheads would have to be cut away, and there's no time for it. Gindin's roommate, Senior Lieutenant Vladimir Firsov, who's in charge of BCH-5's electrical systems, will have to go over the side and do the job himself. If his lifeline doesn't break, sending him into the sea, where there is virtually no chance of ever getting him back aboard, if the towering waves and motion of the ship don't dash him against the hull, crushing the life out of him, and if the edges of the jagged tear don't rip his body apart, he's faced with the almost impossible task of identifying and splicing as many as one hundred electrical cables. But he's a Soviet navy officer, filled with nearly the same zeal as Potulniy and Gindin. Firsov does the job, and when he's hauled aboard three hours later, drenched with seawater and sweat, his body battered and bruised, *every single circuit that he had spliced works.*

"I would call it an extreme situation, and one tough job to do," Gindin says. "But it was our duty, and no one looked at us like we were some kind of heroes."

The storm calmed down, but the waves are still very high when Seaman Semyon Zaytsev, the ship's best welder, is sent overboard to patch the hole with metal plates. Another seaman is sent overboard after him with a bucket of gray paint. "By the time the whole thing was done the ship looked like new. We spent a month in Cuba and no one ever noticed that we ever had any damage," Gindin says. But this is the typical bond between Soviet sailors. You get into a tough situation, and you pull through, no matter what. "As simple as that," Gindin says. "I'm still very proud of my crew for what they did that day, and how they did it."

THE FINEST NAVY ON THE PLANET

In 1984 Tom Clancy published his first novel, *The Hunt for Red October,* very loosely based on an article about the *Storozhevoy* mutiny that appeared in *Seapower Magazine* and the master's thesis of an officer at the Naval Postgraduate School in Monterey, California. The *Storozhevoy* was an ASW frigate, while *Red October* was a new Typhoon-class ballistic missile submarine with a nearly silent propulsion system. Aboard the *Storozhevoy* a few of the officers and crew arrest the captain and stage a mutiny because they believe the Soviet system under Brezhnev is rotten. Aboard the *Red October* the captain and a few of his officers fool the crew into trying to defect to the West with the submarine because they believe that the Soviet system under Brezhnev is rotten and that with boats such as the *Red October* a global thermonuclear war is not only possible but likely. Clancy starts his story with the *Red October* sailing out of the submarine base at Polyarnyy, in the Arctic north, under the command of Captain First Rank Marko Ramius, on the sub's maiden voyage. They are to test the sub's silent drive against submarines of his own fleet and then return to base for an evaluation. If the submarine is as silent as his designers hope him to be, he will be able to sneak to within spitting distance of the U.S. coast and fire his nuclear missiles anytime he wants and there would be no warning. Millions of Americans would die, and a World War Three from which no one on the planet could survive would begin.

But soon after they submerge, Ramius murders their *zampolit*, Captain Second Rank Ivan Putin, because he is the one man aboard who could stop the mutiny in its tracks. Ramius makes it look as if the *zampolit*'s death was an accident so that the part of the crew not in on the plan will not become suspicious. It's Ramius's intention to sail his boat out into the open Atlantic, eluding detection by his own navy until he can somehow make contact with the U.S. Navy, ask for asylum for him and his crew, and offer his boat as a prize. The story hinges on a letter Ramius posted to his uncle Admiral Yuri Pedorin back in Moscow before *Red October* sailed, stating his intention to defect to the West. This, of course, leads to the massive hunt for *Red October* by Russian as well as U.S. and British military forces.

But as all good stories must, Clancy's hinges on the personalities of the crew. Among them are the first officer Gregoriy Kamarov, who would like to marry a round American woman, live in Montana, and raise rabbits; his chief engineer, who is a chain-smoker and a mechanical genius; the ship's surgeon, the timid Dr. Petrov, who believes they should turn back; and a KGB ringer who works undercover as an assistant in the galley.

So it begins, Ramius thinks to himself, as must the mutineer aboard the *Storozhevoy* that morning after the parade in Riga, because this story also hinges on a message sent to Moscow and on the personalities of the crew. Every Russian warship has its *zampolits,* its chief engineers and first officers and captains and ordinary seamen, each with his own story, which, taken as a whole, as Gindin maintains, are the links that forge the bonds among them.

Even under a rotten system that nearly everyone in the Soviet Union hates, guys like Captain Potulniy and Firsov and Gindin, who love the Rodina and are perfectly willing to give their lives in her defense, are not uncommon. And that's a double-edged sword, a crying shame, because the Communist government is an omnivorous psychological monster that not only depends on this nearly religious devotion but also feeds off it, even nurtures it. Russians place great faith in their families, because for most of them little else is of constant value in their lives. They can depend on almost nothing. Most of the officers get married right out of the academy, because they want the comfort of their own family, but this usually is a mistake, because Soviet sailors go to sea on six-month rotations and when they're in port they're humping their butts working on base. Junior officers have very little time for their families, so the divorce rate is very high. This leads to widespread alcoholism, low morale, and wholesale cheating at every turn. Hell, the system is cheating them; why not cheat back? Nothing else makes much sense.

Because of this, Soviet officers are just about like officers every-where, always thinking about getting drunk and getting laid, both at the same time, if possible. The big difference is that Soviet officers, probably more than officers of any other country, also think about their families and Mother Russia, both at the same time.

Gindin remembers that in the summertime he and his father used to go mushroom picking. Boris was nine or ten years old the first time. The factory where his father worked would pick up its employees around four in the morning to take them a couple hours outside of Pushkin into the woods. Boris's mom packed their lunches and sent them each off with a kiss, because they would be gone the entire day.

"I remember the feeling when we broke for lunch, dead tired from getting up so early and spending four hours looking for good mush-rooms, opened our bags, and found boiled eggs, bread, kielbasa, toma-toes. It tasted so unbelievably good, even with our hands dirty from mushrooms."

Those days were the happiest of his life, and standing at the rail on the *Storozhevoy*'s deck in Riga the morning of the mutiny he can't help but remember. Unlike most of his academy classmates, he hasn't gotten married yet, so he's not pining for a wife and children, only for his father, Iosif, who died four months ago.

"When we came back home, I would go to bed exhausted, but my mom would stay up most of the night sorting the mushrooms, getting them ready to cook and pickle and marinate and dehydrate to make into soup later." It makes Gindin melancholy that he'll never see his father again. "We would bring back several buckets of mushrooms in those days. My mom used to fry them with potatoes for us. I loved those trips with my dad. I loved being with him. It was fun."

Scratch a Russian, so the proverb goes, and you'll find the dark, rich soil of the land just beneath his skin and flowing in his veins.

The Gindins had a small piece of land not far from where they lived, which was given to them by Iosif's employer, where they planted potatoes and some other vegetables. In the middle of September they would harvest several bags, each about thirty kilograms, which lasted them at least through the winter until spring. There wasn't much meat, so suppers of herring and boiled potatoes were the norm, but no one complained.

It was the Russian way.

This was in the sixties, when in the West the Beatles were coming to America, Detroit was turning out millions of big-finned, massive, gas-guzzling cars, McDonald's was going head-to-head with A&W, and JFK and Jacqueline were creating a Camelot in which the young president told his fellow Americans not to ask what your country can do for you but ask what you can do for your country.

In the meantime, life in the Soviet Union was a harsh reality. What's truly sad for Boris is that his father had worked hard all his life but had practically nothing. A small apartment, outdated furniture, hand-me-downs, and even if he had worked for ten lifetimes, he would never have been able to buy a car.

But Boris is basically a happy person. Nobody else had anything, so the Gindins never worried about it. In those days they couldn't know that a lot of teenagers in the United States had cars, but even if they did it wouldn't have mattered. It was all propaganda anyway. Soviet sailors were the best sailors on earth. Their navy was the best equipped, the best-run military service on the planet, with the finest officers, the most dedicated men, and therefore the highest morale.

"Besides, we were defending the Rodina."

Despite all that, Boris is not a stupid man. Even as a kid he understood that his only path out of the grinding poverty in which he was raised was to get accepted in a military academy and become an officer. The pay was very good, and the privileges were fantastic. As a civilian, no matter his profession, his pay right out of college would only be 100 to 120 rubles per month. It didn't matter if he became an engineer or a doctor; the pay was all the same. But Gindin's pay in the service is 300 rubles per month, plus free meals aboard ship, free uniforms, and when the ship visits any international port the officers are paid in hard currencies.

Nor were Soviet women stupid. They knew that if they married an officer, they could have lives of luxury beyond the reach of most civilians.

At the academy where Boris studied engineering for five years, girls paid to get into dances on campus, trying to snag a young cadet. Some of the girls weren't so good-looking. It was sad to see the same ones year after year not able to convince a cadet to marry them. But the prize was worth the effort.

He and his friends went over the fence from the academy whenever they got the chance, risking a lot of trouble by going *samovolka,* or AWOL, because the girls in town would do literally anything to get officer candidates to marry them. If you wanted to get laid you went *samovolka,* because the dances on school grounds were closely supervised. No alcohol, no hanky-panky, everything aboveboard. No fun whatsoever.

Boris is in his fifth year at the academy and will be graduating as a lieutenant in a few months. A dance is going on over at the club, but he's not interested. It's just the same old shuffling around. He wants sex right now, not marriage, which will come when his career is well established. He'd been caught going *samovolka* and is confined to academy grounds for a whole month, so he's in the dayroom watching television when one of his classmates comes running in all out of breath. Something interesting is going on over at the club. The power is down, and everybody is in the dark with the girls.

"I was bored to death, so I decided it might be fun. Better than sitting alone watching TV," Gindin says. When he gets over to the club the place is almost pitch-black. Only a few cadets on patrol are walking around with candles, trying to keep the order until the lights come back on. The whole place smells like sweat and cheap perfume. It's hot and the air is stifling, but no one is complaining. The dancers can plaster their bodies against each other and nobody is going to stop them.

Boris is standing near the door, wondering what's going to happen next, when someone or something brushes up against his arm. At first he thinks he must be mistaken, but then someone *is* there in the dark beside him, touching his uniform sleeve. He grabs an arm and pulls the person close enough so that even in the dark he can tell she's a girl.

"What are you doing?" he wants to know.

She's feeling for the hash marks on his sleeve to find out what year he's in, and she's not embarrassed to admit that she doesn't want to dance with a second- or third-year cadet because they're stuck at the academy most of time. But if she gets a senior she knows that he can get time off to come into town and spend the night with her.

If Boris wants some steady sex, clearly this is the girl for him. But her honesty turns him off. Maybe it's because the hunt itself is sometimes more exciting than the conquest. Or maybe it's because now that he's so close to graduating and going out into the fleet, he's that much closer to meeting the right girl and settling down.

"I told her that I'm not interested," Boris says. "'Don't waste your time on me.'"

Looking across the river at the city of Riga and all the ships lined up at their moorings, Boris is finally just about ready to settle down. Once they get back to base at Baltiysk, Captain Potulniy has promised to write him a letter of recommendation for a shoreside job working as military liaison and inspector at a shipyard. There'll be no more six months of sea duty separating him from his family. Just a few more weeks and he'll visit his mother and sister and then start looking for a wife.

But something is pulling his thoughts back to the academy and that girl in the dark, so desperate to find a fifth-year student to marry.

"I suppose that living in the academy did some mental damage to most of us," Boris says. "We lived in a very strict environment. Everything was regulated; every minute of our days and nights was monitored. We felt deprived of the love and affection that our parents and relatives gave us when we lived at home. Remember that we were only seventeen or eighteen when we enlisted, and five years is a very long time for a kid that age. This was why lot of students got married as soon as they graduated, and why eighty to ninety percent of all those marriages didn't work out."

Boris never wanted to suffer that same fate. He wants to follow in his father's footsteps as an engineer with a loving wife and children. Only Boris wants to do it as a naval officer and not a poor civilian. But for reasons he cannot know at this moment, he's already developing a bad feeling, an itch between his shoulder blades as if a sniper is pointing a high-power rifle at him from some great distance and nothing he can do will change it. Some of the other officers feel the same way as he does, and that fact is even more unsettling to him this morning than his own misgivings.

It's their *zampolit*, Valery Sablin; not only was he in an odd mood this morning at breakfast, but he had been even stranger yesterday morning when he came down to the mechanical room, where Gindin was checking the gas turbines and every other piece of machinery that he's responsible for.

"Good morning, Boris," Sablin said. He was more than full of his usual good cheer. "How is everything going in Gas Turbines?"

"Good, Comrade Captain," Gindin replied. He was a little busy just then, but Sablin was the *zampolit*.

Sablin took Gindin aside, out of earshot of the other men. "Are you happy down here, Boris?" he asked.

The question just then struck Gindin as odd. But he nodded. "Yes, sir."

"Tell me, are you satisfied with the seventeen sailors in your section? Do they know their jobs?"

Again Gindin nodded, but this time he was a little wary. What the hell was the *zampolit* looking for? "They're good boys. They know their jobs."

"Good. That's very good." Sablin started to leave, but then he turned back all of a sudden, as if he'd forgotten something important. "I have some extra time now in case you would like a little help with your political lectures. You know, I could fill in. Give you a little extra time off."

"Sure," Gindin readily agreed.

Sablin ranks just below the captain, so he's important aboard the *Storozhevoy*. He almost always has a smile plastered on his face that sometimes seems just a little forced, like now. He is married and has one son, but more important, Sablin comes from an important, well-to-do family and attended the Frunze Military Academy, the most prestigious military school in all of Russia. You'll never make it to the top in the navy unless you've graduated from Frunze. This is where all the officers of the line went to school, but instead of opting for a command position, Sablin chose to become a political officer. Ideologues, these guys are sometimes called. They're almost always the ones with the cobs up their asses, who've swallowed the Party line and whose one mission in life is to shove it down everyone else's throats.

"But he's a very social guy," Gindin says. "Always talking to the sailors and officers about their families." Once, when Gindin comes back from a vacation to Leningrad, Sablin wants to know how people are getting along in the city, what their mood is, what they're talking about, and whether they are generally happy with the way things are or seem to be dissatisfied. Those are strange questions to be asking a young officer, but even stranger this morning is Sablin wanting to know the procedures for the emergency start-up of the gas turbines. Normally it takes a full hour to go through the necessary steps to safely bring the engines on line from a cold start. But if the captain is in a big hurry the engines can be started and brought up to full speed in as little as fifteen minutes. It's a dangerous procedure and has to be done just right to avoid any sort of problem. Sablin also wanted to know if Gindin's sailors knew these procedures. In a real emergency, if Gindin was injured or unable to reach his duty station, could his men do the job? Of course they could; Gindin has trained them well.

That strange conversation sticks in Gindin's mind this morning. From the day Sablin was assigned to the *Storozhevoy* he took a great interest not only in the men and their personal lives but also in the operations of the ship: the electronics and navigation systems, the weapons and their computers, even the pumps and mechanical equipment. So it should come as no surprise that he is interested in the gas turbines.

But later that same morning, after the parade in town, Sablin is even more animated than usual, Gindin recalls. "Asking me how I liked the parade and how everything went. He also asked me if everything was okay on the ship, the engines, the mechanical systems. I got the feeling he was putting so much emphasis on this day that something personal and significant must have happened in his life. Or was about to happen. But he was kind enough to ask about my mother's health and her condition after my father's death." It touches Gindin deeply that someone cares.

Still, as Gindin is standing at the rail, everything that's happened in the couple of days since they came up from Baltiysk adds up to an odd foreboding.

DEFENDING THE RODINA

The Russian navy has been continuously at war for nearly its entire history and, since the end of WWII, preparing for the mother of all wars with the United States. A lot of ships have gone to the bottom since the late 1500s and early 1600s, and with them tens of thousands of sailors.

The Russians have fought the Swedes, the Danes, the Finns, the Italians, the English, the French, the Chinese, and the Japanese, but mostly the Turks, with whom they battled from 1575 until the end of 1917, when Vladimir Lenin's new government ended the war, dissolved the Russian navy, and created the Workers' and Peasants' Red Fleet.

In the early days the Slavic Cossacks sailed in tiny ships called *chaikas*, which meant "seagulls," because they could fly across the water so fast. Scarcely fifty feet at the waterline, the open boats could hold as many as seventy warriors, who would crouch down beneath the gunwales, which were bordered with twisted cane for extra buoyancy and protection. These were ships completely open to the weather, and the Cossacks terrorized the Ottoman Turks and Crimean Tatars no matter the season. Slavs and Russian sailors, then and now, were a tough lot not to be taken lightly.

An old Russian proverb sums up the three hundred plus years of war until the Bolsheviks took over: *In Moscow they ring the bells often, but not for dinner.*

But it wasn't until the mid-1600s that the situation for the Russians really began to heat up. In fact, historians call those years the Time of Trouble, just before the Romanovs took over and imposed the death penalty against the sailors aboard any foreign ships caught off their northwestern Arctic coast in the White Sea, especially Dutch and British merchantmen hunting fur seals up there.

When Tsar Mikhail Feodorovich commissioned the first real warship to be built inside Russia, christened the *Frederick,* the floodgates were opened and Russian sailors began losing their lives in droves. On the ship's very first voyage on the Caspian Sea, the three-masted *Frederick,* with 247 hands on board, was overcome by a fierce storm and the ship went down with all hands. They rang the bells in Moscow.

Of course that didn't stop the Russians from building ships and sending men and boys to sea to make war on their neighbors.

In 1656 the Russian military attacked and took over a couple of Swedish forts and immediately started building ships on the spot to make war in the Baltic. But the Swedes were just too tough, and in 1661 Russia was forced to sign a peace treaty and give back the forts they had taken, plus all the ships they had built. This was at the cost of a few hundred more good Russian men and boys. Once again the bells in Moscow were rung.

Even that couldn't hold the Russians back. They had the bit in their teeth, and the tsar concentrated next on the Volga River and Caspian Sea, where in two years four ships were built, including the twenty-two-gun galley *Oryol,* which means "Eagle," only this time it was the Cossacks who turned rebellious, grabbed the ship, ransacked it, and sank it in the Volga.

It was about this time, near the end of the 1600s, when Peter Alekseevich became Tsar Peter I at age ten. Even at that tender age the new tsar was fascinated with ships, shipbuilding, navigation, and naval warfare, so a miniature shipyard, for which tiny replicas of famous Western warships were constructed, was set aside for him and his pals to stage their mock battles.

Peter I was hooked. As soon as he was old enough, he ordered a real shipyard be built in the White Sea, which almost immediately began cranking out warships. Next he turned his attention to the Baltic and the Black Sea in the south, built a couple of shipyards, and by the spring of 1696 two warships, twenty-three galleys, four fireships, and more than thirteen hundred small vessels were crewed and got ready to do battle against the Russians' old friends, the Turks.

It's not that the Russians or the Cossacks had anything against the Turks, except for Turkey's strategic location in control of the very narrow Bosporus and even narrower Dardenelles. Beat the Turks, and Russia was free to break out into the Mediterranean Sea and, from there, the open Atlantic. The entire world would be theirs, something that was difficult to achieve from Arkhangel'sk, up in the Arctic, which at the time was their only port.

The first step was to take control of the Azov Sea, from which Russian ships would have access to the Black Sea. This was done by June of that year, with the help of forty Cossack boats. The bells were rung in Constantinople as well as in Moscow.

But in October the tsar ordered that a permanent well-stocked and well-funded Russian navy be created in the Sea of Azov. Peter I went down there and lived in a tent to be in command of the Russian navy, while Chief of the Admiralty Alexanter Protasyev oversaw the construction of the base and the ships, which was done by several thousand serfs under the direction of hundreds of shipwrights and officers imported from Western Europe.

In 1697 Peter I sent sixty of Russia's young noblemen to Europe to study shipbuilding and navigation and went himself to Holland to study advanced nautical sciences while working as a common ship's carpenter.

When he returned to Russia he was a certified shipwright, and he'd brought back hundreds of books, charts, tools, and even ship models from which the new Russian navy would be designed and built.

In 1698 he opened the Nautical School and Maritime Academy for future seamen and the Nautical School of Mathematics and Navigational Sciences in Moscow.

The very next year, a Russian fleet of ten ships of the line, armed with 366 guns and a crew of more than two thousand officers and men, plus two galleys and sixteen smaller boats, broke out into the Black Sea and headed toward Constantinople. The Turks were so impressed they surrendered without a shot ever being fired. It was one of the very few times that the bells did *not* ring in Moscow.

With the northern fleet set at Arkhangel'sk to take care of business on Russia's Arctic coast and the southern fleet in the Black Sea to mostly keep the Turks at bay, Peter I turned his attention next to his second most hated enemy, Sweden.

Although the northern fleet had successfully defended the realm against the Swedes trying to attack over the Northern Route, the tsar figured the only way to beat them was to have a Baltic fleet. If he could pull that off, Russia would not only present a serious threat to Sweden but could also take a run at Poland, Lithuania, Latvia, and Estonia, not to mention Finland and even Denmark. The only problem was that Sweden had thirty-nine ships in the Baltic and Russia didn't have one. Nor were the Swedes about to leave the Russians alone long enough to build such a fleet.

Thus in 1700 began the navy's part in the twenty-year Great Northern War, when a fleet of seven Swedish ships attacked the Arctic port at Arkhangel'sk. The Russians not only beat them back but also followed them, capturing strategic Swedish territory and even a couple of Swedish ships that had tried to come up the mouth of the Neva River to St. Petersburg. The bells in Moscow rang again, but everyone who survived got a medal with the inscription: *The unprecedented has happened.* The Order of St. Andrew the Summoned was created.

Even more important, on May 16, 1703, Peter I ordered the building of St. Petersburg Fortress at the mouth of the Neva and Fort Kronshlot in the Gulf of Finland to protect a new admiralty on the left bank of the Neva where the Baltic fleet would be built.

One year later a second Swedish attack against St. Petersburg was beaten back, and in the summer of 1705 a much smaller Russian fleet sent the Swedes packing after a fierce sea battle that lasted several days. The Russians didn't have a modern navy yet, but they were sure heading that way. And no one could fault the Russian sailors, officers, and crewmen alike for lacking courage and sheer tenacity. As a result the Moscow bells never seemed to stop ringing.

The great northern struggle finally came to an end. Peter I died in 1725, and for a couple of decades the Russian navy fired no shots in anger. Waging war was an expensive business, and Russia needed to refresh its coffers.

The Nautical School and Maritime Academy continued to crank out midshipmen who went on voyages of exploration and mapping along the Arctic Circle in the Pacific, looking for a passage to India and China. Among the Russian navigators were Ivan Fyodorov and Mikhail Gvozdev, who accurately charted the route of Captain-Commodore Vitus Bering, who discovered the narrow passage that was named after him, between the Asian and North American continents, at the top of present-day Alaska. In fact, many of the seas and gulfs above the Arctic Circle are named after Russian naval explorers of the era: the Kara, Laptev, and Chuckhi seas and even the Sea of Okhotsk, north of Japan. Russian explorers made it all the way south to Japan, thus finally circumnavigating, and therefore mapping, the entire Russian empire. Not only that, but the Russian Alexey Chirikov, along with Captain-Commodore Vitus Bering, explored well down the west coast of the North American continent.

But the peace for Russian sailors did not last long, and in the fall of 1769 the bells in Moscow began ringing in earnest, when the sixty-six-gun *Yevstafy* broke out into the Mediterranean Sea to help the Greeks whip the Turks.

In July 1773 Russian ships attacked Beirut, in present-day Lebanon, because the territory had for a long time helped fund the Turkish military.

In 1783 the Russian naval presence on the Black Sea was strong enough that the Crimean Peninsula, along with most of the coastal territory around the entire sea, was annexed and the city of Sevastapol was founded.

By 1788, with another war against Sweden looming on the horizon, Russian ships of the line were being refitted with new, more powerful guns that fired shells instead of cannonballs, copper sheathing was installed to help protect hulls from damage and increase speed, and each year one hundred new officers graduated from the Naval Academy, now called the Naval Cadet Corps.

In 1798 just about everybody became allies, including Russia and her old adversary Turkey, to fight Napoléon. But by 1826 Tsar Nicholas I ordered his navy to switch sides, this time becoming allies of the French and English, to help the Greeks fight the Turks. Of course the Turks hired as their chief naval adviser a Frenchman by the name of Letellieu, which in due course led to the Russian-Turkish War of 1828–29, and this time plenty of bells were rung in Moscow.

In the first half of the nineteenth century Russian warships under sail were among the best in any ocean, but then, with the invention of the steam engine, the entire world was turned upside down. The Russians managed to build four steam frigates and a twenty-three-gun screw-propeller frigate, the *Archimede,* by 1849. And they managed to successfully wage war against Egypt, which was trying to invade Turkey, and against Prussia, which was trying to grab as much territory from Denmark as it possibly could.

Even more bells were rung in Moscow, but it was nothing compared to what was on the horizon with the start of the Crimean War, in which Great Britain and France as allies came to the aid of Turkey. That was in 1853, and that fall the allies began a siege of the Russian town of Sevastopol that would last six long, bloody months, which most historians regard as one of the most distinguished events in Russia's military history, even though the Russians lost. The entire Black Sea fleet was destroyed; three admirals, more than one hundred officers, and nearly four thousand sailors were killed defending the town. And more than fourteen thousand were wounded.

Eventually the Russians lost not only the battle for Sevastopol but the entire war. A treaty was signed on March 18, 1856, by the new tsar, Alexander II. Russia's Black Sea fleet and coastal fortifications were taken away, but in exchange the shattered remains of Sevastopol were returned to Russian control.

Every bell in Moscow rang continuously for the entire two years. Medals were awarded, new naval academy midshipmen were graduated, and Russia, as did the rest of the world, entered the age of the ironclads, starting with eighteen steam-powered ships of the line and ten frigates as a new, modern Baltic fleet.

The fight was not over.

By 1876 the Russian navy was ranked number three in the entire world, and one year later Russia began another war with Turkey using torpedo boats, a brand-new innovation so effective that the Turks pulled almost all of their forces from the Black Sea.

Disaster loomed just on the horizon for Russia's Pacific Fleet, which responded to a growing threat from Japan. But the path to that war was complicated by alliances that seemed to ebb and flow with the tides. First Russians and Chinese moved to the verge of war, before the Chinese backed off. Next the Japanese were building a powerful army and navy because they wanted a foothold on the Asian mainland. Russia, now allied with France and Germany to help China resist the Japanese, sent its Pacific squadron to the region, and Japan backed off. For the moment.

But war was coming, and everybody knew it, so the Russians started building ships at a breakneck pace, which they based on the Kwantung Peninsula, which they leased from the Chinese. That included a fortress at Port Arthur.

On the morning of January 27, 1904, the main body of Japan's naval forces, under the command of Vice-Admiral Togo Heihachiro, appeared like an apparition out of the darkness off Port Arthur, very much like their surprise attack against another enemy less than forty years in the future. Nineteen months later the war was over, with Russia the loser in more than one way. More than five thousand Russian sailors were killed and six thousand taken prisoner.

And so it continued right up through World War I, with more good Russian men and boys going to the bottom of the sea, until the new Bolshevik regime declared peace with Germany, and for a brief period the bells of Moscow were silent.

But in the years that followed, under the Communists, *babushkas* and mothers and wives and sweethearts who had marched off to church to weep and pray for their sailors lost at sea could only cry silently and pray in their hearts, because God and churches were no longer permitted. A darkness began to settle over the land. Maybe the sailors who had given their lives for the Rodina were the lucky ones after all.

AT THE READY

Standing at the rail, Gindin finishes the last of his cigarette and flicks it in a long arc down toward the dirty water between the *Storozhevoy* and the Alpha sub moored just below them. He's having some trouble shaking off the sense of foreboding he's been getting all morning, with Seaman Fomenko's defiance in the *cubrick,* with the group of sullen sailors huddling in the corridor, and with Sablin's strangely animated mood in the officers' dining hall.

Gindin hesitates a moment longer in the crisp morning air before turning and heading belowdecks and aft to his machinery spaces. It's his day off, but he's restless. Anyway, there's not a day goes by that he doesn't check in with his engineering crew and machinery. He helped build the ship and, like Captain Potulniy, feels a sense of, if not ownership, at least pride.

Gindin has also been working on a maintenance and repair plan for when they get to the Yantar Shipyard in Kaliningrad tomorrow. They'll have a couple of weeks there to get the *Storozhevoy* ready for his next six-month rotation, and Gindin wants to make sure not only that everything in engineering that needs to be fixed, rebuilt, or replaced is done, but also that he can get all the spare parts he needs. This time he doesn't think Potulniy will offer any serious objections if the ship rides below his waterline.

After those two weeks they'll dock at Baltiysk, their home base, for regular shoreside duty until it's time to head to sea again. Gindin will get some time off so that he can see his mother and sister and try to put his father's death in some kind of perspective. But that will be tough, and the more Boris thinks about never seeing his dad again, the tougher it gets for him.

Gindin comes around a corner belowdecks and practically runs headlong into Sergey, who is one of his crewmen. He's a tall, dark guy with a mustache who usually kept everything to himself. If Boris needed something, Sergey would never volunteer, even though he had good mechanical skills. He was a loner and didn't talk much. And this morning, when Gindin comes around the corner, Sergey looks up like a frightened animal caught in headlights, hesitates for just a second, and then turns on his heel and tries to get away, but Gindin stops him.

Sergey is supposedly on duty right now, so Gindin is more than a little concerned. "What's going on?" he asks.

Sergey doesn't want to look up, let alone answer any stupid questions. He is clutching something in his left hand, and it looks as if he is on the verge of tears.

"Look, I'm your superior officer," Gindin says mildly. "I want to know what's wrong, and that's an order."

"I just got a letter from my mother," Sergey says. He's having real trouble not bursting into tears. "She says Larissa is going around town with some other guy." His eyes are wide. "We're engaged to be married, Senior Lieutenant."

It's the next thing to a Dear John letter, the kind that half the sailors in the fleet either have gotten or will get at some time or another. The normally tough, antisocial Sergey can hardly hold his emotions in check. Gindin feels sorry for him, because he didn't deserve something like this. He was just a young kid, far away from his family, carrying out his duties, maybe getting only four hours' sleep a day, working like a dog, and then he gets this letter. He is grief stricken, and the more Gindin talks to him the worse it gets. Maybe he'll actually do harm to himself; it's happened before.

"You're young," Gindin tells him. "You have your entire life ahead of you. This girl doesn't deserve a guy like you, out here serving his country."

Sergey isn't buying it.

Gindin is trying to convince his sailor that all the men in the turbo/motor division are friends and crewmates who respect him. He doesn't need to be treated this way by any girl.

Being away from home puts a lot of emotional stress on the crew, especially the sailors who are just kids, mostly eighteen or nineteen and from small towns or farms out in the country. They're capable of doing some really stupid things, and it's up to the officers to make sure nothing bad happens. Gindin spends fifteen or twenty minutes talking with Sergey, trying to put some good perspective in his head and make sure the kid will be okay. But watching Sergey head back to work, Gindin isn't so sure that he's helped very much. The sailor mumbled his thanks, but that was it. The mask was back, leaving an unreadable expression. They could have been discussing the weather.

Standing alone for a moment, listening to the sounds of the ship tied to a mooring, engines off, Gindin thinks that already this day is dragging when it's supposed to be relaxing. He and Firsov agreed at breakfast that this evening they would get together with some of the other officers for a few drinks, maybe swap some jokes. Tomorrow it would be back to work for all of them, so this was their last day to relax. But for some reason the day seems to stretch; every minute seems like an hour. No one aboard ship is having any fun; everyone is long faced, down in the dumps.

Just forward of the machinery rooms, Gindin runs into Firsov and Sergey Bogonets, who is a senior lieutenant of the BCH-3 torpedo systems section. The two of them have hatched a practical joke on Senior Lieutenant Nikolay Bogomolov, in charge of the BCH-3 rocket systems section. He and Bogonets are roommates, and practically no one aboard ship likes Bogomolov. He's sneaky, and whenever he sees somebody doing something wrong—officer or crewman—he immediately runs to tell the captain. Bogomolov has tried to build a friendship with Gindin and Firsov, but it can't work because they think he's a *stukach,* a snitch.

It's less than ten hours before the mutiny, and there's a growing edginess throughout the ship. Ordinary military discipline isn't exactly flowing out the hatches, but nothing seems right. Just after breakfast Gindin spots one of his sailors lugging a heavy wrench, about the length of an umbrella, forward as if he were on an urgent repair job. A half hour later the same sailor is scurrying aft with the same wrench and the same determined expression on his face. And just a few minutes later the sailor is heading forward again, the wrench over his shoulder. The boy isn't on any repair mission; he's trying to *look* as if he were busy to avoid any real work. But the wrench was really heavy, and the last Gindin saw of the boy, sweat was pouring off his forehead. The kid was doing more work trying to get out of work.

The same look of determination is on Firsov's and Bogonets's faces. They want to play a practical joke on Bogomolov. Unless the *Storozhevoy* is tied up at a dock and connected to shoreside utilities, water is so scarce aboard ship that the men are allowed to take very few showers. Many of them go weeks or even a month without a shower. That includes the officers. Part of Gindin's job is control of the water pumps and steam heat. In other words, anyone who wants to take a shower needs Gindin's cooperation.

"Let's give Nikolay a shower he'll never forget," Bogonets suggests, his face lit up, and Gindin immediately understands just what kind of a shower these guys have in mind.

Topsides, in officers' territory, Sergey and Vladimir hold back out of sight as Gindin offers to let Bogomolov take a shower. It's a gesture of real friendship that Nikolay appreciates. He rushes back to his room for his soap, towel, and clean clothes and hops into the shower room, giving Gindin a big grin.

Of course, Gindin turns off the steam right in the middle of Bogomolov's shower, so that the water immediately switches from hot to ice cold. Nikolay lets out an ear-piercing screech and scrambles out of the shower, his body covered in soapsuds, a towel hastily wrapped around his waist. Gindin, Firsov, and Bogonets are all standing in the passageway laughing so hard that tears are streaming down their cheeks. But this is the kind of stuff that happens at the end of a six-month rotation at sea. The only problem is that the crew will have just time enough to get the *Storozhevoy* back in shape, take a short leave to see families, and it'll all start over again.

It's the Cold War, against the North Atlantic Treaty Organization (NATO) and especially the Russians' main adversary, the United States, that could turn hot at a moment's notice. They'll be ready. Gindin and other officers just like him will make sure of that. *At least that's what most of them believe in their hearts this mid-morning, moored in the middle of the Daugava River, near downtown Riga.*

THE *STOROZHEVOY*

IN CUBA

NATO war planners describe the *Storozhevoy* as a Krivak-class frigate, which means his size is somewhere between two thousand and six thousand tons, and his main job should be as an offensive surface warship. But the Russians designed the Krivaks as defensive ASW ships. That's a big difference in how each side sees the class. In the West the ships were viewed as just another example of the Soviet Union's aggressive military posture, while Gindin and his fellow officers thought of their ship as a last-ditch stand against Allied submarines.

The *Storozhevoy* is 405 feet long on deck, carries two hundred men and officers, and can cruise forty-five hundred nautical miles at 20 knots or, if he's in a hurry, less than seven hundred nautical miles at 32 knots. He was built in 1972–74 in the Yantar Zavod 820 shipyard in Kaliningrad and was outfitted with an impressive number of weapons systems. In addition to quadruple torpedo tubes amidships port and starboard, his most effective ASW platform is a four-tube launcher for the SS-N-14, which is backed up by missile launchers for the radar-guided SA-N-4 SAMs, plus a variety of 30mm Gatling and three-inch guns, the usual complements of mines, and a pair of twelve-barrel RBU-6000 ASW mortars forward of the bridge. This last weapons system is deadly effective out to 3.3 nautical miles and is automatically loaded. As fast as the weapons officer, who happens to be Senior Lieutenant Bogomolov, pushes the button, the RBUs will fire until they run out of missiles.

The ships are equipped with state-of-the-art electronics including the Head Net C search radar, a pair of Eye Bowl radar systems to control the SS-N-14 missiles, Pop Group radars for the SA-N-4 missiles, plus Owl Screech radar for the guns, Don Kay, Palm Frond Surface Search Radars, and the usual array of VHF and IFF radio communications systems, and a complete suite of ESMs equipment to detect any sort of electronic noise from a submarine or any other ship.

In Gindin's mind, and in the minds of Captain Potulniy and most of the other officers, the *Storozhevoy* epitomizes what a modern navy warship should be. He and his brother Krivaks are the largest ASW ships in the Baltic and provide the last line of defense against any NATO submarine attack on the Rodina.

There may have been better captains in the Soviet navy, but none could have been so proud of his position as was Potulniy. He was assigned to take command while the ship was still under construction in 1973, so he could help supervise the building. He'd been executive officer on the *Bditelny,* the first of the Krivaks, so he knew how the ship was supposed to be put together. He was only thirty-seven at the time, and although he called all of his officers by their first names, he was generally more preoccupied with the needs of *his* ship than the needs of his men. He practically lived on the bridge, and while at sea he was always on duty, day and night, leaving the care of his crew to his *zampolit,* Captain Third Rank Sablin. It was an arrangement that both men felt comfortable with but one that Potulniy would regret for the rest of his life.

The two men couldn't have been more different. Although they both graduated from the prestigious Frunze Military Academy, which put them on a fast track to command positions, Sablin opted to become a political officer. That in some ways is professional suicide, because *zampolits* never become ship captains and therefore promotions are few and far between. Also, political officers are generally not liked very much by the officers or the crew. They're the ones whose job it is not only to force-feed the standard Marxist-Leninist doctrine down everybody's throats but also to sugarcoat the latest Party orders no matter how stupid they are. The captain is the absolute ruler aboard his ship, while the political officer is the Party hack. Every sailor must attend political classes every two weeks. Normally the *zampolit* supplies the lesson materials and the officers teach the sailors in their sections.

On the one hand the captain should be close to his crew, know their names and backgrounds, know who can be trusted to come through in a tight situation and who will probably fold. After all, the safety of the ship depends on his men. On the other hand, the *zampolit* is just the guy who dishes out the propaganda that no one ever wants to hear.

But the situation on the *Storozhevoy,* this crisp November day in Riga, is different. Potulniy really does seem to care more about his ship than he does about his officers and men. He is an aloof man who goes strictly by the book. He is young, and he has a lot to prove. Being the captain of an ASW ship is just the start; it's a stepping-stone to much bigger and better things. But Sablin is everybody's friend—officer, midshipman, and ordinary sailor alike. He takes time to talk to the men, find out about their towns and their families, about their fears and ambitions. He's not afraid to talk about a sailor's dreams and what they might mean or help a sailor figure out his love life, or lack of love life. Sablin is there to be a friend and to act as the father figure, a role that the captain should be playing. But the *zampolit* is kind to the other officers as well, offering to take over their political classes when they are too tired or bored. And he's always cheerful, always ready with a pat on the back, ready to lend a hand, and always genuinely interested in what a man's job is and how he does it.

Like this morning at breakfast.

Gindin has some vague premonitions this morning, but he does not connect them to the captain or to Sablin or to the marked differences between the two officers. He just has this unsettling feeling of unrest, and he thinks that most everyone else aboard feels the same way to one degree or another. But he can't put his finger on it.

When he tried to talk to Potulniy about his fears a couple hours ago, the captain dismissed him out of hand.

"Stick to your duties, Boris," the captain said. "Do your job correctly, supervise your crew, make sure that they're physically and mentally fit, and everything else will take care of itself."

It's as if the captain is so distant from his crew that he doesn't know what's really going on aboard his own ship. But that's not true, either.

They were on their way down to Cuba, and Gindin, like every other officer aboard, did normal duty rotations, which were four hours on, four hours on standby, and four hours off. The rotations were changed each month, so you didn't always get the same shifts.

On this night, Gindin had the midnight to 4:00 A.M. rotation with two gas turbine specialists, two motor/diesel men, one steam/fuel sailor, and one electrician. These were all young kids, and with nothing much happening on the graveyard shift and their last meal at nine in the evening, they would get hungry. And as stomachs growl, ingenuity increases.

Gindin's crew wants to know if he'd like something to eat. Of course he says yes, and he's led aft to the machinery room, where two of the gas turbine engines are turning over. Somehow the men have gotten some potatoes from the galley, some oil, and a frying pan. Each turbine develops a hot spot on its upper casing and they are using one of them to fry up the potatoes. Gindin knows he's supposed to put a stop to this business, and his sailors know it, too. They're all standing there, looking at him expectantly, waiting for the shoe to drop, but the smell of the frying potatoes is almost too much to bear.

Anyway, Gindin is not much older than his men, it's the middle of the night, there is no safety issue to worry about, the engines are running normally, and he's hungry, too. So he says, "Sure," and the meal is nothing short of fantastic, almost as good as the kinds of snacks he'd had with his dad, picking mushrooms in the woods.

A couple of days later Gindin is called up to the bridge. "We have a small problem, Boris," the captain starts out pleasantly enough, but Gindin's stomach does a slow roll. He has a pretty good idea what's coming next. The cook has been complaining to Potulniy that potatoes keep disappearing and he doesn't know where. Every night Gindin's inventive sailors sneak up to the pantry area where the potatoes are kept under lock and key. These are the engineering crew, so it's no trouble for them to break into the locked boxes, steal some potatoes, and then fix the locks so no one can tell what's happened.

The only bad luck was that the captain was wandering around the ship in the middle of the night and passing the machinery room smelled the frying potatoes.

"They're young boys and they were hungry," Gindin admits. "And I had some, too, sir."

Potulniy barely smiles. "It will not happen again, Boris. Do I make myself clear?"

"Perfectly, Captain," Gindin replies.

So the captain *was* aware of what was going on aboard his ship, but the difference between him and Sablin was that the *zampolit* would have understood and probably would have joined the men for an early-morning snack of fried potatoes if for no other reason than to find out how the crew was doing.

But there's something about Russians that's fairly well universal, if not practically eternal: They're usually more complicated than they seem at first glance. Certainly after four and a half centuries of hardships and deaths, naval officers may be the most complex of Russians. All along they've had to balance their jobs of protecting the Rodina, whether it be from Turkey or Sweden or Germany or the United States and NATO, with protecting themselves from their own government, whether it be run by a tsar or a Communist Party Secretary.

Potulniy is no exception. On the one hand, he is aloof from his men, while on the other, he understands they are all his responsiblity. The *Storozhevoy,* his ship, includes his men, and he'll never blame his crew for his own mistakes.

It was 1974 when the *Storozhevoy* was ordered out of his base at Baltiysk for a short training cruise of just a few hours. It was a fairly common occurrence between deployments, mostly to maintain crew efficiency and check on repairs and new equipment. The *Storozhevoy* is fitted with four gas turbine engines. Two of them, called marching engines, produce 18,000 horsepower and are used for normal cruising. The other two are boost engines developing 36,000 horsepower and are used for battle conditions when more speed is needed.

One of the boost engines was down, and the mechanical crew was having trouble finding the problem. At the time, Captain Lieutenant Alexander Ivanov was in control of all BCH-5, but the engines were Gindin's responsiblity. Ivanov reported the downed gas turbine to Potulniy and, according to regulations, to the assistant division commander on shore, who gave the go-ahead for the brief mission anyway.

The shakedown cruise goes without a hitch until they head back and are about fifteen minutes from the dock, when both marching engines break down and neither will restart.

It's Gindin's rotation and as the ship loses control he reports the situation to the captain, who orders the anchor to be immediately lowered. They are in the narrow cut leading to the base, and the wind is shoving them toward the land. When the anchor bites, the *Storozhevoy* turns broadside, completely blocking the ship channel.

Gindin starts the boost turbine, which is the only operational engine left, so that they will have power, and he and his crew attack the problem with the stalled marching engines. Twenty minutes later they get one of the engines started, and shortly after that the second, which puts them where they began—with two marching engines but with only one boost turbine.

He radios Potulniy on the bridge. "Captain, I have the two marching engines on line again."

"What about the boost engines?" Potulniy demands, and Gindin can hear the strain in his voice.

"Only one of them is working. The other one is still down."

"How soon will it be operational, Boris?"

"I don't know," Gindin has to admit.

In this instant Potulniy's career is on the line. The Soviet navy high command is not forgiving of its officers who make embarrassing mistakes. Of course the problem with the boost engine could be blamed on the gas turbine crew, and the problem returning home from the short cruise could be blamed on the assistant division officer. In any navy it's called covering your ass, *prekrit cvoju zadnicu,* and Russian ship captains know how it's done.

But right now Potulniy is faced with staying where he is and blocking the narrow ship channel or getting under way in the hopes that the marching engines won't quit again.

He opts to stay put and call for the gas turbine manufacturer's rep on base to be brought out to the ship to fix the problem. It takes the expert all night to resolve the issue, and in the morning the *Storozhevoy* makes his way into base with all his engines up and running. And there were no repercussions from Division Headquarters. In this instance Potulniy acted as a man of steel, taking complete responsibility for everything and everyone aboard his ship.

Yet six months later, on their cruise to Cuba, Potulniy shows a completely different side. More a man of cotton than steel, Gindin thinks. The Cubans expect a representative from the ship. This is a social occasion with everyone in dress uniforms, and it's a holiday—International Women's Day—and on the list of dignitaries the Russian representative will have to meet is the wife of Fidel Castro, the wife of the commander of the Cuban Fleet, and the wife of the minister of defense. It's a big job, one that the captain should take responsibility for. But this time Potulniy shrugs it off. Maybe he's too shy.

He calls Gindin up to the bridge first thing in the morning after exercises and breakfast. "I have a big job for you, Boris," he says. "An important one, representing our ship."

"Sir?"

"Take it easy; you'll do just fine," Potulniy assures a totally mystified Gindin. "The Cuban government is sending a car for you at eleven hundred sharp. Dress in your holiday uniform and get something to take to the ladies."

By now Gindin's palms are cold and sweaty and his heart rate is up. Fixing a ship in mid-ocean after a collision is one thing, but what the captain is asking him to do now is downright nerve-racking. "Something for the ladies, sir?"

Potulniy waves it aside. "Go see our *zampolit;* he'll know what you should bring."

Gindin wants to ask the captain why Sablin shouldn't be the one to go, but by now Potulniy has turned away to deal with some minor problem with *his* ship. Who knows? Maybe the captain's palms are even wetter than Gindin's. And maybe the captain figures that Gindin isn't shy and his easygoing, social personality makes him the best man aboard ship for the job.

Of course Sablin knows exactly what to do, and when the car comes for Gindin at precisely 11:00 A.M. he's carrying flowers for the wives, as well as Russian nesting dolls, chocolates, Russian champagne, and vodka.

It was ninety-eight in the shade that day, the car was not air-conditioned, and although Gindin does not have to wear a uniform coat he does have to wear a tie with his white shirt and a jacket showing the three stars of his rank, black trousers, and a cap with gold embroidery. And he's a Russian. What does he know about this kind of weather? Besides that, he's very nervous and the translator, sent along to make sure he pronounces names correctly, is relentless.

Their first stop is the villa of Castro himself. He's not at home, but his wife, Dalia Soto del Ualle Castro, greets them at the door with a big smile. She is young and beautiful and charming, and Gindin is speechless at first.

The Cuban translator smooths over the first few minutes until Dalia Castro offers them something to drink. Turns out she doesn't care for wine, she only drinks straight whiskey or rum, and the only food she serves is some nuts and crackers on a tray. With the translator's help, Gindin and Mrs. Castro chat about Russia and Cuba and their warm relations and even about Gindin's family, all the while drinking straight whiskey. By the end of the visit, Dalia Castro is inviting Gindin to stay with her and her husband in the big house the next time he comes to Cuba.

"We have plenty of room for you. You'll see."

Gindin remembers later that he felt as if he were in some kind of a wonderland. He'd never seen such a magnificent place in his life, beautifully furnished and decorated with impeccable landscaping; flowers, trees, lawns, everything so perfect.

His next two stops are at the houses of the commander of the Cuban fleet and the minister of defense. The husbands were gone, but the wives give Gindin and his translator the same warm welcome that Castro's wife had given them. And, like Dalia Castro, they drank only straight whiskey or rum. Gindin is given a few shots at each house, to celebrate the holiday, and how can a mere senior lieutenant refuse such offers?

After Gindin has handed out the gifts and visited the three wives and drunk their whiskey, it's about three in the afternoon before he gets back to the ship. The translator, who was drinking shots right along with Gindin and is half-drunk by now, grins and says the trip was a smash hit, Gindin is a swell Russian, and the translator hopes he will come again soon.

When Gindin makes his way up to the bridge to report to the captain, he is about ready to go to bed, which is just what Potulniy suggests. Later, in the sober light of day, Gindin realizes that maybe the captain hadn't been shy after all. Maybe he knew what was in store for the officer who visited the important wives, and if someone were to drink a little too much and make a fool of himself, it would be better if it were a junior officer rather than the captain.

But that afternoon is just a memory now, as Gindin heads back to his cabin to write a letter to his mother. He's also getting flashbacks from his father's funeral. The entire workforce of the factory where Iosif worked showed up to pay their last respects, telling Boris and his mother how much they respected and would miss their friend. Boris desperately wants to be with his family today—even more so today than other days, for some reason—so he hopes that the letter will put his mind at ease. In any event, they will head to the shipyard tomorrow and after that it'll only be a couple of weeks until he is on leave with his family.

Or so he thinks.

THE BALTIC

Moscow . . . how many strains are fusing
in that one sound, for Russian hearts!
What store of riches it imparts!

ALEXANDER PUSHKIN
EUGENE ONEGIN

EVENING OF THE MUTINY

Dinner has come and gone, the sky is starless, there is a cold breeze stirring, and traffic along the waterfront is sparse. The holiday is over and the people of Riga are doing their own thing: family gatherings, playing chess, watching television—the Bolshoi Ballet is doing a matinee performance of *Giselle*. Anyway, tomorrow the *Storozhevoy* will leave for the shipyard where for two weeks everything aboard will be put to rights. Already the weapons loads—missiles, mines, torpedoes, and depleted uranium ammunition for the guns—have been taken off the ship, and his fuel tanks are nearly but not quite empty. One of the refit tasks will be to send the smallest sailors through maintenance hatches into the tanks to repaint them. The less fuel there is to pump out beforehand, the quicker the job will get done.

Gindin goes back to his cabin to get another pack of cigarettes— they've been at sea for six months, so he is out of Marlboros until they get back to base; now he has to smoke the shitty-tasting Russian ones, Primas without filters. But he guesses that he really doesn't mind. One of the main reasons he started smoking the much more expensive

American brand was so that he could impress civilians with how good Soviet navy officers have it.

"We were protecting their lives," he says. "So maybe we deserved a few *bogatstvo*, luxuries."

As he's stuffing the pack into his uniform pocket, his roommate, Vladimir Firsov, walks in, a half smile on his pleasantly square face.

"So, Boris, what's eating your ass?" he wants to know. It's like half the ship has come down with the shits or something. Almost nobody is smiling.

Gindin hasn't a clue. He shakes his head. "I don't know," he says. "Something." It's a general feeling that something is right around the corner or that someone is sneaking up behind them. He's developed a case of the *volocy vstali dybom,* the willies.

Vladimir and Boris leave their nine-by-eleven cabin and head back up on deck, where they lean against the rail and smoke. The wind has picked up and now that the sun has gone down it has gotten even colder than this morning. One of the fronts that regularly sweep across the Baltic from the Arctic must have come through in the past hour, because they can see their breath.

"It's cold," Firsov says after a long silence, and Gindin isn't at all sure his friend is talking about the weather just now.

"Havana was better," Gindin replies. They're talking, but it's like they're wading through molasses. It's as if they are drifting, rudderless, without any purpose. Gindin has never felt like this.

They talk about the rotation they're finally coming off and the big repair job they were stuck with on the way to Cuba. There'll be a lot of work for them at the shipyard, but in two weeks they'll be home with their families.

Vladimir is married and has one young kid. Each year Boris helps Vladimir celebrate his anniversary and the birthdays of his wife and son. It's a sweet Russian custom, especially among sailors at sea. The little celebrations tend to make the loneliness more bearable.

Boris is thinking that he won't be able to celebrate his father's birthday next year, or any year after that, when Nikolay Bogomolov gets on the ship's public-address system—the 1MC. He's the duty officer on this shift. It's coming up on 1900 hours, and Nikolay announces that all officers and midshipmen are to report to the midshipmen's dining hall in uniform.

Boris and Vladimir head belowdecks. They've been off duty, so they have to change into the uniform of the day. All the ordinary sailors not on duty are watching a movie in their dining hall. It's *The Battleship Potemkin,* which is the favorite of just about every *zampolit* in the fleet.

Sergey Kuzmin, who's the lieutenant in charge of BCH-3 sonar systems, wants to know what the hell is going on. According to Sergey, this sounds like one of Sablin's little tricks. The *pizda,* pussy, has been sticking his nose into everybody's business for the past five days.

Sergey Bogonets, who'd had Boris help play a trick on Bogomolov, storms out of his cabin, a deep scowl on his dark face. "The bastard wants to get back at us for the trick with the shower," he says. "Just watch: When we get dressed up and back to the dining hall, there won't be any meeting."

But playing this kind of a joke on the ship's officers at the end of a six-month rotation is a dangerous thing to do. There'll be a lot of resentment that might spill over to the next rotation. What is not needed aboard a ship at sea, especially a warship at sea, is a group of officers who are holding a grudge. The safety of the ship depends on the complete and instantaneous cooperation of the entire crew.

But if it's Sablin calling this meeting, then none of them have any choice but to snap to, like dutiful Communist sailors, and at least give the appearance of appreciating his lecture. The *zampolit* is the number-two officer aboard any Soviet warship. That means he answers only to the captain and no one else. And in political matters the *zampolit* is the supreme authority.

Curiously, the officers don't particularly care for Sablin, but the sailors do, because this *zampolit* really listens and really seems to care about the welfare of the enlisted men. He's an officer, but he's sincere. The officers, however, who are educated, can tell the difference between being sincere and being genuinely brainwashed.

"Political classes were a fact of life," Gindin says. "It felt foreign to us even though we'd been hearing the same things all of our lives. The lies we were being told never touched us, never got into our bones, never adhered to us. The classes were distant from reality, in a sense just another obligation."

Most of the people aboard ship or in high school or in college felt stupid and degraded being forced to study this stuff.

Everybody knows it's a lie.

But at the same time everyone lives the lie because it is the only life they know. "You believe in things," Gindin says. "You are ready to put your life on the line for the ideals, and yet somewhere inside, maybe not consciously, but somewhere, you see things differently. But you can't change things and you continue to live the way you are told to live."

The story is that Sablin actually *believes* the Party line. He is an idealist who knows in his heart-of-hearts that a better life is just around the corner for all of them. If they just stick with the basic principles, if they just keep on working, keep trusting in Moscow, everything will work out fine.

"Hey, Boris, what the hell is going on?" Senior Lieutenant Oleg Sadkov wants to know. He's the medical doctor and he's just come up from the dispensary. He's not much older than Gindin, maybe twenty-six, and is married with one daughter. Sadkov has never had a bad word to say about anyone—officers or enlisted—and everyone likes him because he's easygoing, open, and honest. Besides that, he's as skinny as a rail, and with his dark hair and thick mustache he looks like a teenager. No threat to anyone.

Before Gindin can answer, Senior Lieutenant Dimitry Smirnov comes out of his cabin with a deck of cards in his hand and a big grin on his face. He's the chief navigator and commander of BCH-1 and normally keeps to himself, but this evening he's just as puzzled as the other officers. Sablin's called the meeting, Smirnov is sure of it, and he's not going to give the prick the satisfaction of ruining everyone's holiday.

Smirnov holds up the deck of cards. "Maybe we'll have a game and the meeting will turn out okay after all."

Eighteen officers, plus the captain, and eleven midshipmen are assigned to the *Storozhevoy*, but including the ones who were on duty at 1900, plus those few on leave, only the captain, eight officers, and four midshipmen are available for the meeting. None of them are happy.

"That's okay with me," Boris says. "But in two weeks I'm going to be home with my family. If that means sitting through a boring political meeting with our *zampolit* and earnestly enjoying what he has to say, that's exactly what I'll do."

Of course nobody can disobey a direct order. Someone could call in sick, but Soviet naval officers do not operate that way. There's the same sort of discipline in just about every navy. But there's also the same sort of griping, including the Soviet navy.

"There's no reason for this," Captain Lieutenant Victor Vinokurov mutters half under his breath.

Gindin is near enough in the now-crowded corridor to hear this remark. "It's Sablin."

"Maybe so, but the captain has to give his approval for all meetings," says Vinkurov, who is the commander of BCH-2 in charge of artillery. He's a tall, blond guy, very strict with his officers. He wants to be captain of his own ship one day. "This is a holiday. There's no urgency. Nothing has happened to cause such a meeting. It makes no sense, I tell you."

It makes no sense to Boris, either, but an order is an order, and along with the other officers he heads forward to the midshipmen's dining hall. It's one of the largest compartments where the officers can gather on the entire ship. It's on the port side, toward the bow, and right under the upper deck, on the opposite side of the ship from the

Sekretka, the Secret Library, where officers have to go to check out the classified documents, blueprints, and manuals for the weapons and equipment under their responsibility.

Once again Gindin is struck by how unnaturally quiet the ship seems. No engine noises, of course, because they are at a mooring, but there are no crewmen running around, making jokes, talking loudly, arguing perhaps. No officers are in their cabins now, the doors open, drinking *spirt* and telling stories or laughing or debating about something or playing chess, which sometimes can be loud.

Captain Lieutenant Nikolay Proshutinsky, who is in charge of the entire BCH-3 acoustic systems division, storms up the corridor from his cabin. He's Kuzmin's boss, and he slaps Sergey on the back.

"Eb tvoiu mat," Proshutinsky says. It's a uniquely Russian expression, which literally means "fuck your mother," but it's never used in that context. Instead, the phrase means that something is screwed up. Almost like the American GI expression *FUBAR*—Fucked Up Beyond All Recognition. *Eb tvoiu mat,* what the fuck is going on now?

"I don't know, Lieutenant," Kuzmin replies. He gets along well with his boss. "Maybe it's Sablin going to give us a patriotic speech like last year."

Proshutinsky is shaking his head ruefully. "Well, if that's all it is, let's not keep our good *zampolit* waiting." He looks over at Gindin and grins. "Anyway, when we're done Boris has invited all of us to his cabin for some *spirt,* isn't that right?"

They come around a corner and straight ahead is the open door to the midshipmen's dining hall. It's this exact point in time that Gindin will remember for the rest of his life, though he doesn't know it now, but he has developed a very bad feeling. One that he thinks he shares with the other officers. At that moment, for some reason he can't know, he wishes that he could talk to his father for just a minute or two. Boris wants to ask for some advice. But even if he could somehow magically talk to Iosif, Boris wouldn't know what to ask for.

Wherever his future lies, it's just beyond the open door.

SOVIET DOGMA

HOOK, LINE, AND SINKER

When the Bolsheviks took over Russia, one of the first things they did was rename the Imperial Russian Navy, calling it the RKKF—*Raboche-Krest'yansky Krasny Flot*, Workers' and Peasants' Red Fleet. Next it renamed most of the ships. And then almost nothing happened for fifteen or twenty years. Little or no money was given to build the navy, and the midshipmen graduating from the leadership and engineering schools languished in a fleet that had almost nothing to do.

Remember, it was the battleships *Potemkin* and *Aurora* and others that had supported the revolution, but Lenin's new government, as idealistic and egalitarian as it was supposed to be, had a short memory.

And everyone in the world knew that the new RKKF was little more than a rust-bucket joke. During the negotiations of the Washington Naval Treaty right after WWI, when the most powerful nations met to cap the size of the world's navies to limit the possibility of another war, the Soviet Union was not invited to the table. It was a slap in the face that the new Communist government was completely ignored.

They were busy doing other things, like killing the kulaks, their own people, by the millions. In fact, by the end of WWII, when the body count of Jews killed by Hitler topped 6 million, the body count of kulaks, or peasants, killed by Stalin may have topped 40 million, though nobody knows for sure.

During the Winter War in 1939, the Soviet navy saw a little action in the Baltic, but it wasn't until Hitler's 1941 Operation Barbarossa that the Soviet Union finally woke up to the fact that if it wanted to be a world power it needed a modern navy. It was too late to play catch-up in WWII. In fact, most of the Soviet Navy consisted of ex–U.S. Navy Lend-Lease destroyers, and what navy the Soviets had in the Baltic was blocked for the duration in Leningrad and Kronshtadt by German and Finnish minefields. But the seed of an idea had been firmly planted in Moscow.

After the war the Soviets went on an all-out crash program of ship-building, starting with submarines from homegrown designs supplemented by designs liberated from the Nazis and liberated from the United States and other Western nations. Although in the early days the Soviets were almost always one generation behind NATO boats, they were cranking out warships at a furious pace.

Next the Soviets turned to their surface fleet, arming just about anything that could float, no matter what size, with a lot of missiles, including the big cruisers of the Kirov class that displaced 24,300 tons and then in the sixties and early seventies their helicopter aircraft carriers the *Moskva* and *Leningrad,* followed up by the Kiev-class ships. The Soviets could never hope to match the U.S. advantage in super-carriers, so they had to concentrate on their submarine fleet and ship-to-ship missiles. Anyway Stalin didn't really understand sea power and did not want to spend the money on aircraft carriers.

All this was during the heady days of *Sputnik* and Yuri Gagarin and the race into space on which the Soviets had a lock, while the Soviet navy had all it could do to defend its own coasts from attack or invasion along the Atlantic, Pacific, and Arctic oceans and the Black,

Caspian, and Baltic seas. There were four fleets: the Northern, based at Murmansk-Severomorsk, with at one point more than 170 submarines; the Pacific, based at Vladivostok; the Black Sea at Sevastapol; and the Baltic at Baltiysk. Plus by 1975 Soviet flotillas and squadrons were deployed in the Mediterranean Sea and the Indian Ocean with access to supply and repair ports in Cuba, Syria, Libya, Ethiopia, the People's Democratic Republic of Yemen, the Seychelles, and Vietnam.

All of that rebuilding, all of the modernization of the fleet, all of the worldwide deployments, all of the drive for parity with NATO, and especially the United States, and all of the Soviet navy's success belonged to one man, Admiral of the Fleet of the Soviet Union Sergei Gorshkov, who understood two basic facts of life. The first was that the Soviet Union had to become a world naval power, with not just a coastal defense force but an arm of the military that could project its power everywhere on the globe. And the second was that the Soviet Union could never hope to match the U.S. Navy ship-for-ship. There wasn't the time, the money, or the technology to achieve such a dream.

The main threats that the U.S. Navy posed against the Soviet Union were aircraft carriers and ballistic missile submarines. Gorshkov set about building a navy of warships equipped with powerful missile systems that could damage and sink even a supercarrier, and a navy of warships that could find and sink ballistic missile submarines.

But it wasn't easy, especially in a nation whose heroes seemed to go in and out of favor faster than Western women's fashions. His predecessor, Admiral Nikolai Kuznetsov, was around in 1956 when Nikita Khrushchev came to power and decided to scrap most of the navy's big surface ships, which in the Party Secretary's mind were draining the fragile economy. When Kuznetsov objected, he was fired and the forty-six-year-old Gorshkov was appointed to take his place. But the new boss of the Soviet navy knew when to keep his mouth shut, when to slip in through the back door, and when to finesse the Kremlin. In fact, Gorshkov long outlasted Khrushchev.

One of the early examples of how the wily admiral finessed the

Kremlin leadership was the way in which he convinced the Communist Party that a strong navy was not only a necessity but also a bona fide part of the Russian national heritage. The superpowers of the United States, Great Britain, and France had convinced the world that Russia's real power was as a land force. Her great armies were poised to pour across the Polish plains into Western Europe, and nothing but an all-out nuclear war could stop them.

This so-called Land Power Doctrine was imperialistic propaganda and nothing more, according to Gorshkov. The doctrine's only purpose was to keep the USSR from becoming a sea power, yet Russia had the world's longest coastline and Russians have always loved the sea.

"It's the Soviet manifest destiny to go to sea," Gorshkov argued successfully. "Our navy will become the faithful helper of the army." And the admiral's timing was impeccable. It was 1962, in the midst of his campaign, when the U.S. Navy blockaded Cuba, turning the Soviet navy away. Moscow was finally convinced, and one of the most powerful and versatile navies of the world was reborn.

Gorshkov realized that a Russian navy faced three major problems: ice, choke points, and long distances. Once he was given the go-ahead, he attacked all three.

Most Soviet navy bases are up around the Arctic Circle or close to it and are frozen over for much of the year. Arkhangel'sk in particular is blocked by ice six months out of the year. Vladivostok in the Far East is unusable for several months each year, and even the Baltic Fleet at Baltiysk and Riga is closed down sometimes for three months.

Gorshkov partially solved the problem by building the world's most powerful fleet of icebreakers. No longer were the northern ports closed when they were most needed.

The admiral's solution to the other two problems was as brilliant as it was simple. If it came to war, the U.S. Navy could effectively hold almost the entire Soviet fleet close to home by mining and blockading the narrow passages leading to the open ocean. In the Pacific Ocean the La Pérouse Strait, north of Japan, and to the south the Tsushima

Strait are the only ways out for the Soviets. In the Atlantic the so-called GIUK, or Greenland–Iceland–United Kingdom gap, could easily be controlled by the Allies. Then there are passages that are even tougher for the Soviet navy: the Turkish and Gibraltar straits, the Suez Canal, and up north the Skagerrak-Kattegat straits.

The way around this was to deploy Russian warships beyond these choke points, so that if it came to a war, they would not be held close to home. But that was the second part of the problem. In the early days Soviet warships could not be resupplied at sea. They had to return home for that. Admiral Gorshkov ordered the design and building of a fleet of supply ships, and he strongly urged the Kremlin to use its considerable diplomatic skills to set up places overseas where Soviet ships could be restocked. Angola, South Yemen, and Cuba were among the first.

As a result of these policy changes, the Storozhevoy *stayed out to sea for six months at a stretch and stopped at Havana for something more than Gindin's trip ashore to visit with VIP wives.*

Under Gorshkov the navy became not just a stepchild of the Russian military establishment but an extremely important leg in what was called the nuclear triad for deterrence, which consisted of land-launched nuclear missiles, air-launched nuclear missiles, and nuclear missiles launched usually from ballistic missile submarines. The Soviet navy not only operated a fleet of the largest missile subs but also could launch nukes against NATO from a wide range of surface ships, and its ASW platforms, such as the *Storozhevoy*, were very good at what they were designed to do. Namely, to protect the Rodina.

So, starting in the sixties the navy became *the* branch of the military to join, and it attracted a lot of very bright, very ambitious young men into the academies. Which was a great deal. Civilians entering the trades, such as engineering or medicine, would have to work until they were sixty-five before retiring. But naval officers could retire after only twenty-five years of service—which included the five years they spent in the academies. It meant a naval officer could retire around age forty-four or forty-five, a full twenty years earlier than his civilian counterpart. But since the navy was expanding at such a rapid rate, it also relaxed many of the usual Soviet restrictions, such as not admitting Jews to the inner circle. This was exactly Boris Gindin's ticket, though when he signed up he didn't realize how difficult the work would be, nor how it would end for him and the rest of the *Storozhevoy*'s crew.

Once Soviet ships were able to deploy to every part of the world, Groshkov's next job was to establish its missions beyond the vague but important notion of *protecting the Rodina.* In the good admiral's mind there were four basic missions that his navy would have to carry out.

The first and most important was deterrence. Using the fleet, especially its ballistic missile submarines lying just off the U.S. coast, to threaten an all-out attack with no notice and no hope to defend against, the navy was an important tool for preventing a global thermonuclear war from ever happening. Of course Western analysts put a different spin on the issue, looking at the massive Typhoon-class missile subs as offensive, first-strike weapons. It was the same view the Soviets maintained when it came to the U.S. Ohio-class SSBMs.

The second mission was power projection, which the U.S. Marine Corps is so good at. The United States fields 180,000 marines, while the Soviet Naval Infantry only has 12,000 troops. But Gorshkov saw to it that there would be at least one naval infantry regiment in each fleet. It was a start.

The third and fourth missions, for which the *Storozhevoy* was built and his captain and crew were trained, were sea control and sea presence. In the first, Gorshkov wanted to avoid a war with the West, but if one did happen he wanted the Soviet Union to win. In order to ensure victory he built multi-purpose ships that could launch torpedoes to kill submarines, lay mines to stop surface ships, and fire missiles that could take out both subs and carrier battle groups as well as knock down airplanes. It's why the *Storozhevoy* and ships like him carried so many weapons systems and were deployed to every ocean on the planet. Wherever the Americans and their allies planned to deploy their subs and ships and aircraft, the Soviet navy planned to be there waiting for them.

The last mission, that of sea presence, came to Gorshkov via Teddy Roosevelt, who'd promised to "speak softly and carry a big stick." The idea, according to the admiral, was to send his ships—warships and merchant ships alike—to any nation that would have them. During their visits, which generally coincided with some significant military event or holiday, the navy crews would be sent ashore to organize sporting or musical events. Sometimes their officers would be sent on missions to visit with local dignitaries and their families. In Admiral Gorshkov's own words:

> Friendly visits by Soviet seamen offer the opportunity to the people of the countries visited to see for themselves the creativity of the socialist principles in our country, the genuine parity of the people of the Soviet Union and their high cultural level. In our ships they see the achievements of Soviet science, technology and industry. Soviet mariners, from rating to admiral, bring to the people of other countries the truth about our socialist country, our Soviet ideology and culture, and our Soviet way of life.

The admiral, it seemed, bought the Soviet dogma, hook, line, and sinker.

TO THE MIDSHIPMEN'S DINING ROOM

Even the finest, most technologically advanced warship, equipped with the most sophisticated deadly weapons systems known to man, is nothing more than a well-crafted hunk of metal, plastic, glass, and rubber without a crew. Soviet officers are just about the same as the officers in any other modern navy. They're volunteers and pretty well motivated to do their best. Gindin is typical of this class of sailor; he worked very hard to get himself qualified to be selected for a naval academy. And when he got to school he worked ten times as hard to make the grade. For a lot of guys like Gindin, failure is never an option. It's a mind-set that is about to be severely tested this early evening of November 8.

Once a Soviet officer candidate qualifies for training at a specific school he is sent to either a technical institute, like Gindin's St. Petersburg Military Engineering Academy, or a surface warfare school, such as Potulniy and Sablin's Frunze Academy, the most famous of them all in the Soviet Union, very much akin to Annapolis in the United States. As soon as the officer candidate finishes his primary training he's sent out into the fleet to stand watches and learn the responsibilities of his division. That's four hours on, four hours of standby, and four hours off, twice in each twenty-four-hour period. But it's not that easy. Besides learning how to do his own job, the young officer must be a shepherd to his enlisted crew 24/7. That means teaching them the technicalities of each of their jobs and their shipboard responsibilities and duties, such as calisthenics every morning, and giving them their ideological training—the Party doctrine.

On the one hand, if an officer wants to rise to a command position, such as the captain of his own ship, he must master every aspect of every vessel he serves on, learning one or more new jobs each time he goes out on rotation. At the end, when he is finally picked to run his own ship, he first has to serve as an executive officer, *starpom,* and if he survives that duty he is given a series of very rigorous ship-handling tests that are designed to flunk out all but the very best candidates. The Soviet navy does not want to promote average officers.

At least that's the theory.

On the other hand, if enlisted crewmen mostly come from the smaller towns and farms, they're drafted for a three-year term, and except for about twenty-two weeks of shoreside basic training they learn all their skills aboard ship at sea, where just about every minute of their time is rigidly planned. If they aren't in their *cubricks* tending to their uniforms or sleeping, they are supposed to be in training, working, or listening to political lectures. Stuff like hanging out for a smoke and a chat with friends, maybe playing a game of cards or lingering over a cup of tea, is strongly discouraged, though these boys are sometimes pretty inventive and every now and then they do find the time for a diversion, the main purpose of which is to get out of work.

Most of them are eighteen or nineteen when they come out to the fleet and are country bumpkins or unsophisticated rustics, what are called *muzhiks*. And most of them are ignorant, because they've grown up in households with no access to television. They know nothing about life in their own country, let alone the outside world. They are naive kids, *prostofiljas,* and that includes an almost total lack of knowledge about sex. There is no such thing as sex education in Russian schools, nor is the subject ever discussed by parents. Such a thing is simply too embarrassing.

One day a senior sailor from BCH-3 hands a bucket to one of the younger kids and tells him that he has to climb the ladder to the top of the crow's nest, what is called the observation bridge, remove the uterus up there, put it in the bucket, and bring it back. The kid doesn't have a clue what the hell a uterus might be, it's enough that a senior sailor has given him a job to do, and he'll be damned if he'll admit he doesn't know.

"Do you understand your assignment?" he's asked.

He nods. Of course he understands. But the moment the senior sailor goes away, the kid runs back to his *cubrick* to find out what he's supposed to do. By the time he's finally told exactly what a uterus is and what it does, just about every senior sailor aboard ship is falling on the deck with laughter, while all the other junior sailors are wondering when it'll be their turn.

Like when one of the senior sailors from Gindin's section hands one of the new kids a cloth bag.

"Are you aware that there'll be a major disinfection for medical purposes throughout the entire ship first thing tomorrow morning?" the senior asks.

Of course the *muzhik* knows nothing about any medical drill, but he nods. After all the sailors aboard ship have gone to bed for the night, the kid is supposed to collect their toothbrushes in the bag and leave it at Dr. Sadakov's door. The boy does what he's told. In the morning all the sailors aboard ship get out of their bunks to clean up before exercises, but no one can find his toothbrush. What's going on? Dr. Sadakov arrives at his dispensary, where he finds a big bag of toothbrushes with no note, and he has to wonder what the hell is going on.

After all is said and done, the young sailor's boss gives him a very good piece of advice: "Be smarter next time. Try to actually *use* your brain instead of merely carrying it around."

On the other hand, Russians carry their souls just under their skin. It's a common heritage, as an old Russian proverb provides: *We are all related; the same sun dries our rags.*

Mischa Mihailov was one of the typical sailors aboard the *Storozhevoy* in that he was average in just about everything he did. Gindin recalls that Mischa never showed any passion for his work, though he did have some fairly good basic knowledge of the machinery. If he could get out of a job, he would do it without a moment's hesitation.

But Mischa could play the guitar and sing Russian songs until there wasn't a dry eye in his *cubrick*. Whenever he had time off, usually just before bed, the other sailors would beg him to sing. Especially one particular song that back on base was played all the time on the radio:

> *Our duty was tough today, carried out*
> *Far from Russia, far from Russia.*
> *Every day we sacrifice our lives*
> *Far from Russia, far from Russia.*

The song had been approved by the Kremlin just for sailors like those aboard the *Storozhevoy*, and whenever it was played everyone, sailors and officers alike, couldn't help but get a little misty-eyed.

"It was glorifying and praising us for the tough job we did far from home," Gindin says. "It represented the value and the morality of our Soviet system, and what was important and what deserved to be honored.

"It uplifted our spirits, made us proud of what we did far from our homes and families. It gave us an incredible sense of accomplishment that our people and our government knew and appreciated how difficult our mission was."

A warship's mission and the morale of his crew are bound together tighter than anyone who never served in a navy can understand. And both elements come from the top down. Although Potulniy wasn't as close to his sailors as was Sablin, everyone knew that the captain was a first-class officer who understood the ship and his systems better than anyone else aboard.

Potulniy was in his late thirties when he was assigned to the *Storozhevoy,* and he was very proud of his position. He spent most of his time either on the bridge or wandering around his ship to make sure that everything was working the way it should be and that his crew was doing their jobs. His personality and style of command was actually a perfect balance between Sablin's friendliness and Novozilov's strictness.

Captain Lieutenant Nikolay Novozilov was the *Storozhevoy's* executive officer, *starpom,* and if ever there was a no-nonsense officer it was the exec. He was a perfectionist. Everything needed to be done accurately and on time, with no excuses. There wasn't an ounce of pity in the man's body, as Gindin remembers, and he simply didn't want to hear the circumstances behind any lapse in duty. If Novozilov thought his orders weren't being carried out to the letter, he'd come down like a ton of bricks on the hapless sailor or officer. Your rank didn't matter; he was equally tough on everyone aboard.

"He was the kind of officer you never took personal problems to," Gindin recalls. "He didn't care. He was beyond that sort of thing. For him the *only* priority was the ship."

Heading down the corridor to the midshipmen's corridor this chilly Riga evening, Gindin is somewhat relieved that at least for the moment they don't have to worry about Novozilov showing up and finding fault with something his officers had done yesterday or today. Their *starpom* went home on leave to his wife and kid. His presence aboard isn't really needed for the short cruise down to the shipyard and the refit. He'll be back when they get to the base at Baltiysk and will once again put them through the wringer before their next rotation.

Or at least that's what Gindin and the others believe at this moment in time.

THE SHIPBOARD SCHEDULE

The *Storozhevoy* is a little universe all of its own, connected to Fleet Headquarters only by radio while at sea. The captain is the supreme authority, of course. He has the power of life and death over his crew. His eighteen officers are his standard-bearers, responsible for every detail 24/7. That means if an ordinary sailor makes a mistake, the first person to take the heat will be the officer in charge of his section. And the punishments, especially when Novozilov is involved, will be swift and harsh. More than one Soviet naval officer's career has been short-circuited because he didn't pay attention to how his sailors were behaving.

Two schedules are kept aboard ship. The routine daily one that starts with wake-up at six in the morning and ends with bedtime at ten in the evening. Intertwined is the duty schedule in which every sailor and officer works eight hours per twenty-four, is on call for eight hours, and is off for eight hours. That means everybody aboard adheres to both schedules at the same time, which can be grueling.

At 0600 reveille sounds and everyone in bed gets up. The ship's day has begun, and for the next thirty minutes everyone who can be spared from duty comes up on deck for exercises, no matter the weather. These are push-ups, jogging in place, stretches, and sit-ups. Afterward the men have a half hour to clean up and get dressed for duty.

Showers aboard a Soviet warship are almost as rare as democratic elections. Freshwater is very scarce, so everyone, even officers, is allowed to take a shower only every few weeks, perhaps once a month. It's just a fact of life aboard that no one questions.

After the first week at sea everyone stinks to high heaven—but it's *everyone,* so after a while no one seems to notice. But when you do get to take a shower and change into clean clothes you suddenly realize that everyone else smells really bad.

Since Lieutenant Gindin is in charge of the water makers and water-heating equipment he can be one of the more popular officers aboard.

Breakfast starts at 0700 and can last as long as forty-five or fifty minutes. It's when everyone gets to talk about the coming duty day or perhaps problems on the overnight shifts or about family and kids and letters from home. And it's the time to tell jokes—but never about a man's wife or girlfriend. It is an unwritten rule. Duty at sea is tough enough without worrying about your wife because one of your fellow officers told an off-color joke and put an idea into your head.

If Potulniy or Novozilov or even Sablin is in the officers' dining hall while they are in port, the jokes cease and everyone finishes eating as quickly as possible and gets back to work.

"We had to prove that we didn't have any extra time on our hands," Gindin says.

But at sea the atmosphere, at least in the dining hall, is more relaxed, even when the captain is there. Everyone tells jokes, because the pressure on them is enormous and a good belly laugh provides a little relief.

Even Potulniy isn't above playing a little practical joke. The *Storozhevoy* had a new dietary officer assigned to the crew. His main job was to take charge of all the food and miscellaneous supplies aboard. According to the duty roster, he was listed as an assistant to the captain. This dietary officer had never gone to any naval academy to learn a profession; he got his rank in an army college before he was sent out to the fleet, but as a captain's assistant he thought that he was a pretty big deal.

So a few days out, Potulniy sends the dietary officer to do a complete inventory of all the food and supplies, and when he is finished he bumps into Boris in a corridor.

"The inventory is finished, Comrade Lieutenant," the big shot says, a self-important smile plastered on his rat face.

But Boris has caught on right away. "I don't think so."

"What do you mean? I checked everything!"

"But not the lifeboats. They have to be checked for supplies such as chocolate and *spirt*. You know, in case we have to abandon ship we'll need those things in order to survive. But a lot of the time the sailors get into the lifeboats and steal everything."

Of course this is simply not true. Lifeboats are hermetically sealed in canisters and open automatically when they are launched into the water.

"I'll take care of it immediately, Comrade."

"But you'll need the captain's permission first," Boris reminds the young officer.

The next day at lunch in the officers' dining hall Potulniy introduces the new dietary officer to the others. "How do you like this?" the captain says. "Our new lieutenant has never seen a ship before, except in a picture, and now he wants my permission to open all our lifeboats to check the supplies. What do you think?"

The joke is on the hapless lieutenant, and the other officers have a good laugh, in part because the guy was such a self-important ass but also because the captain has just shown them that he's human after all.

At 0800 everyone not stuck at their duty stations assembles on deck to salute the raising flag. This is another time that the crew, especially the officers, is feeling a wave of patriotism. It's the same in every navy; some of the crew are happy to salute their flag, while others couldn't be bothered. And all of the patriots pretty well know who's in the other group.

The first four-hour duty shift begins at midnight, the second at 0400, and the third at 0800. So it is right after the flag ceremony when the oncoming crews assemble in the dining areas, where they meet their officers, who escort them to their duty stations to conduct the first equipment checks of their shift.

During each twenty-four-hour period one officer and a sailor-assistant are assigned the responsibility for the entire ship. It's their job to make sure that the proper officers show up at their assigned times. During the evening hours, from ten at night until six in the morning, it's the sailor's job to go up to each duty officer's cabin and remind him that his shift is coming up. During the daytime hours, it's the officer in charge who makes the announcements over the 1MC, the ship's intercom.

The officers not on duty from 0900 until noon on alternate Mondays are expected to teach political classes to the sailors in their divisions. No one likes this job except for Sablin, who often volunteers to handle it for the officers. No one turns down the *zampolit*.

On all other days, from 0900 to noon, the standby officers make sure that their areas of responsibility are clean and conduct training sessions for their sailors on the equipment and on their military duties and responsibilities.

From noon to 1300 is lunch, and afterward until 1400 is something called admiral's hour. It's when everyone aboard ship who isn't on duty gets to relax. It's about the only time in the day that anyone gets a real break, although some officers find little things for their sailors to finish up, and of course the inventive sailors make damned sure they're nowhere in sight when their officer comes looking. It is *admiral*'s hour, after all.

The 1400 period starts with a glass of juice for every sailor aboard, followed by two hours of training on emergency procedures: military actions including biological or chemical attack—the *Storozhevoy* is a warship—as well as the usual emergency procedures covering fires, man overboards, and other accidents.

From 1600 to 1800, more ship cleaning—this time not only the duty stations but every square centimeter of the ship is washed and polished. That includes the crew's *cubricks* and the officers' cabins.

From 1800 to 1900 is dinner, and from 1900 until 2030 is another free period. But this is one of the times when sailors and officers alike are expected to play catch-up with whatever they didn't have a chance to finish earlier. And there's always some of that.

A warship at sea, even in time of peace, is an extremely high-maintenance master that demands loving care and attention every minute of every day.

From 2030 until 2100 everyone aboard is served evening tea. The sailors get one slice of bread while the officers get bread, butter, and cookies.

Then until 2200 hours, or 10:00 P.M., it's time to prepare for bed, when it's lights-out, except for the officer of the day and his sailor-assistant, the on-duty officers and the sailors in their divisions, and the on-call officers who are expected to take over if the duty officers need to step away from their posts for whatever reasons.

In an emergency, like what happened in the Mediterranean Sea when the *Storozhevoy* was on the way to Cuba, everyone is on duty; no one rests. At any other given time one-third of the ship's personnel are on duty, one-third are on call, and one-third are off duty.

When Boris goes on duty just after the morning's flag ceremony, he collects his crew of seven sailors and one midshipman in the midshipmen's mess and after a few words leads them down to the machinery spaces. Among his crew are a pair of diesel specialists who watch over the engines that generate the ship's electricity, one electrician who makes sure the power distribution equipment and panels are maintained in working order, one steam specialist who makes certain that the equipment and piping to create and manage steam for heating water and the ship's compartments work, one fuel specialist who not only monitors how much fuel the ship is using and how much is left but also makes sure that the fuel pumps are up to par, and one midshipman who is in training for a job like Gindin's.

The last two of Boris's crew are the gas turbine specialists whose job is to make sure that the two marching engines and the pair of boost engines are doing what they're supposed to do. As soon as these two guys get to the engine room and before the old crew is relieved, the specialists check the books. Each of the engines has its own log in which the gas turbine specialists record the oil pressure, temperature, RPMs, air pressure, and a host of other readings, along with any problems that may have cropped up during the shift. Then they physically inspect all four engines, making sure that nothing is wrong, nothing is leaking, and all the gauges are reading what they're supposed to be reading, and then they finally sign the books. That means these two guys have accepted responsibility for the engines, under Gindin's supervision, and the old crew can go on standby for the next four hours.

Of course if it's one of the alternate Mondays the officer will have to take his crew up to their *cubrick* and teach them about Marx and Lenin and how the great Soviet experiment is a model for all mankind. It doesn't matter if the men had worked nonstop their entire shift and are filthy dirty, covered in oil and grease, and just want to get a little sleep; Marx and Lenin come first.

The worst part is when Potulniy decides that he wants to conduct a uniform inspection on deck. It's usually on these occasions when, covered in oil, Boris is rushing to his sailors' *cubricks* to make sure that they are cleaned up and their uniforms are in order and ready for inspection that he runs into a fellow officer, all spick-and-span.

"So, Boris, how is it going, then?" the officer asks sarcastically, knowing full well *exactly* how it's going. He's been there himself before and will probably be in the same spot again before long. It's just a little joke they have with each other.

"Poshel na khyi" (go fuck yourself), Boris says tiredly but good-naturedly.

During the shift, nothing at all might happen, except that his sailors will check the gauges and log the readings every hour. Especially the late-night and early-morning shifts. If nothing goes wrong with the equipment and the bridge does not ring for a change in the RPMs, Gindin and his crew might actually catch a few minutes of sleep now and then. Or maybe some of his more inventive crew might find a diversion, like stealing potatoes and cooking them. Or stealing some of the *spirt* they are supposed to use to clean equipment and hiding it in a fire extinguisher. Every now and then on their off-duty time, if Boris isn't watching, they might pause in front of the fire extinguisher for just a second. Plenty of time for a little sip. Makes a night pass a little faster.

Besides making sure that his sailors are doing their jobs, Boris has his own rounds every hour, during which he listens to each turbine using what amounts to a stethoscope to make sure nothing inside the engines is starting to go bad.

Smoking isn't allowed in the engine room, so from time to time one of the other off-duty officers will stop by to relieve Boris for a few minutes. He goes up on deck and grabs a quick smoke. From time to time he returns the favor. It's another of the military systems that are not in the regulations but seem to work just fine.

Then there is the almost continuous training. It's up to Gindin to make sure all the sailors in his section know their jobs. That means, besides maintaining the gas turbines and other equipment, he has to take each of his sailors step-by-step through every single procedure from starting the engines to shutting them down and everything in between. That also means that Boris must intimately know every single nut, bolt, lever, and knob, shaft and gear in his entire section. It's a very important responsibility that Boris has taken to heart from the day he graduated from the academy. His job is 24/7, and besides teaching his sailors he keeps himself up-to-date.

Other than Captain Potulniy, Boris Gindin probably knows the ship better than anyone else aboard.

There is perhaps a little fog beginning to form along the Daugava River, curling in wispy tendrils in and among the warships at anchor. Elsewhere in the assembled fleet sailors and officers not on duty are relaxing in their *cubricks* or cabins, maybe reading or watching television in one of the dining halls. This is the Gulf of Riga, on the same latitude as northern Newfoundland, protected from the open Baltic Sea only by the island of Saaremaa, so it is a very cold place in November. This is not Gindin's home, and there have been times since his father's death, like right now, that Boris feels a crushing sense of loneliness. He wants to get this meeting over with, he wants to get the *Storozhevoy* to the shipyard for his refit, he wants to sail back to base, and then he wants to spend some time with his mother and sister and other relatives. Then, if everything goes as he hopes it will, he will get the shoreside job that Potulniy has promised to help with, so that he can find a wife, settle down, have children, and get on with the rest of his life.

It's a happy prospect for him, yet he cannot shake the sense of doom that has been riding over his shoulder like a mid-Atlantic squall ready to pounce.

SABLIN'S PLEA

The windowless midshipmen's dining hall with fluorescent lights casting a sickly flat light is on the starboard side, just aft of the flaring bow. It's a plain, dull compartment with no pictures on the pale green walls and linoleum on the steel deck. Two long dining tables, with gray plastic covers, seat three or four in chairs along one side and, curiously, sofas with dark blue covers on the other. A small plastic table with a brown plastic bin is positioned on the left side of the room, and in the center is another small table where Sablin is standing in his uniform. Along the back wall is a tiny room that holds the movie projector.

"Comrades, take a seat, please," Sablin tells the officers as they shuffle in. Perhaps he is stepping nervously from foot to foot.

There are fourteen of them, but the tables are only meant to seat twelve, so they have to crowd together. Gindin figures it doesn't really matter, hoping they'll be out of here and back to their quarters in a few minutes, maybe a half hour.

"We ought to have a few drinks tonight," Firsov says, sitting down with his roommate. "Proshutinsky was right: You've got enough *spirt* to go around."

"We'll see when we get done with this stupid meeting," Gindin replies half under his breath. He looks over his shoulder as the last of the officers come in. "Where's the captain?"

"He'll be here," Firsov says.

Everyone is talking at once, ignoring the *zampolit*. Yesterday was a holiday and no one is in a mood to listen to what is probably going to be another patriotic speech about serving the great Soviet people.

Sablin holds up a hand. "Settle down, please. This is important."

"Pardon me, Comrade Sablin," Gindin speaks up. "Where is the captain?"

"Stop talking now, so we can get on with this meeting," Sablin says.

Gindin looks over his shoulder just as Alexander Shein, one of the ratings, closes the door on them. Their eyes meet for just a moment, but then Shein slips into the projection booth and closes that door. "What the hell—?"

"What'd you say?" Firsov asks.

"That was Shein. He's in the projection room."

Firsov glances over his shoulder at the door, a look of puzzlement on his face. "What the hell are you talking about? What's he doing here?"

"I don't know," Gindin says, but his stomach is doing a slow roll.

Every sailor aboard is assigned a duty area that he has to keep clean. Shein's duty area includes Gindin's and Firsov's cabin. He did his job without complaining, but he's also struck Gindin as being a little bit sneaky. The other sailors are watching a movie in their own dining hall, so what is Shein doing up here, closing the door and hiding in the projection room?

No one else has noticed, but gradually the other men begin to settle down, until finally the dining hall is quiet.

"To answer your question, Lieutenant, Captain Potulniy is in his quarters resting," Sablin says. He isn't smiling, like usual. "In fact, he told me that I was to conduct this meeting and he did not want to be bothered."

"Why is the door closed?"

Sablin shrugs indifferently. "So we will not be disturbed, Lieutenant." He looks at the others crammed together at the tables. "What I have to say to you tonight is very important; I want you to know that from the start."

"This is a holiday; what's the problem?" one of the other officers asks. Gindin isn't sure who it is, but the others grumble their agreement.

There is a tightening in Sablin's eyes, as if he is a little uncertain what to do next. Gindin has never seen this look of hesitancy on the *zampolit's* face before, and it adds to Boris's already tense mood.

Something wasn't right. But Sablin was a senior officer and they had to follow the chain of command. If he said there was to be a meeting of all officers, then there was no questioning such an order. But all of them thought it was a damned odd thing just then.

All of a sudden Sablin stops his fidgeting and stands a little taller, his shoulders squared, his expression set. It's as if he's made a difficult decision and he's just realized that it's the right one. He blinks as if he's coming out of a sleep, but he is not smiling, and this is the most disturbing thing of all. The Sablin standing in the middle of the room, facing the eight officers and six midshipmen, isn't the Sablin whom they have come to know. He is a completely different man, all of a sudden.

"His face did not reflect any holiday mood," Gindin relates. "There wasn't so much as a hint of a smile, or some kind of friendliness, his usual sociable self. Nothing like that. He was different. It was like seeing another side of him that we'd never seen before."

Gindin looks around the room at the other officers, and he can see that they share his misgivings.

"What I am saying to you tonight, and what I am asking you to do, is not a betrayal of the Rodina. I want to make that very clear. I'm simply making a political declaration about the bureaucracy and the corruption that has taken over our country.

"Everyone here knows exactly what I am talking about. The great principles of Marx and Lenin have been totally perverted by the Central Committee of the Communist Party."

Gindin cannot believe what he is hearing. He glances over at Firsov and then at the other officers, and he can see by their expressions that they are as confused as he is. Is this some sort of a test that Sablin is giving them? To find out how deep their loyalty to the Motherland runs?

"You know that all Russians are not treated equally. You can see that very problem here aboard ship, and everywhere you go you can see that the poor dumb *muzhiks* never have their day in court. They never have the same rights as we do."

Firsov catches Gindin's eye and he shrugs. *Eb tvoiu mat,* what the fuck is going on?

Gindin shakes his head, completely baffled. It's even possible that Sablin has lost his mind. It's happened to other sailors and officers during or just after a difficult rotation. Maybe Sablin is having troubles at home with his family. Maybe he's just found out that he has an illness. Maybe cancer.

"Each of us has to admit, to honestly confess, that we have no control whatsoever over what happens in the Kremlin or anywhere else in the Soviet Union. That means we can't do a thing to help fix the problems the Rodina is faced with. We are powerless to force our state and political institutions to make right what is wrong."

Gindin suddenly begins to get a glimmer of where Sablin is going with this speech, and his blood runs cold. There is a sharp, hard knot in the pit of his stomach that feels like a ball of molten steel.

For the first time in his life Gindin is truly frightened to the depth of his soul. Not only for himself but also for all of his fellow officers in this room, including Sablin, who most certainly has lost his mind to even hint at criticizing the Party.

It's treason!

"I have studied the problem for a long time. Our leaders over the past fifty years have done nothing more than produce a system in which the Russian people are trapped in a foul atmosphere where they are required to blindly follow orders with never a question.

"We live in a system of censorship and tyranny where everyone is afraid to make any criticisms of the Party, even though we can all plainly see that the Party has lied to us. Is lying to us!"

"Just wait a second," someone from Gindin's left shouts. Maybe it's Kuzmin, but whoever it is, he's angry.

Some of the others are grumbling, too.

Sablin holds up a hand for silence, and after a few seconds the room settles down.

"The system needs to be changed, Comrades. We are quick to make jokes, but we are just as quick to shed tears when we think of the future of the Rodina. The situation in our country has become dangerous. The Party tells us that everything is fine, yet the people can see that is a lie. The older people are afraid to speak up for fear of losing their pensions. And the young people like you know the difference between Party slogans and Party deeds."

"What are you saying, Comrade *zampolit*?" one of the officers asks.

"The system must be changed in order for us to achieve the true democracy that Lenin promised us," Sablin says, his voice clear and firm, totally without doubts. "The Party must be overthrown. It is time again for revolution."

Gindin is more than shocked, he is stunned. No one talks about these things. No one is allowed, by law, to talk about these things. Even to *think* this way is treason. Even to *listen* this way is treason. To be in the same room with a man talking this way is treason.

Still, Gindin holds out the slim hope that the *zampolit* is merely testing their loyalty to the Communist government and to the Party. He is the political officer, after all, and it is his job to find out whom to trust. But not this way.

Sadkov is half off his seat, his eyes narrowed, his jaw set, but again Sablin holds up a hand to calm them down.

"How can you even suggest such a thing?" the doctor shouts.

"You're the political officer aboard this ship! You're a Communist and a member of the Bolshevik Party."

"It's because I am a good Communist that I am raising my voice—," Sablin tries to interrupt, but Sadkov won't hear it.

"Where were you raised? How can you even talk about these things?" Sadkov shouts. He looks at the other officers for their support. "This is against our country's morals!"

Proshutinsky jumps to his feet. "Enough of this!" he shouts. "I'm getting the hell out of here."

Senior Lieutenant Vinogradov gets up. He, too, has had enough, and he's going to leave.

"Sit down!" Sablin cries. "Right now! That's an order!"

For a very long, pregnant moment, no one in the room moves a muscle. But ever so slowly Sadkov sits down, followed by Proshutinsky and Vinogradov. Sablin is a superior officer. His orders are to be obeyed. It's the same system in every military organization.

Gindin cannot comprehend what is happening. Everything he's grown up with as a good Russian, everything he has been taught in the academy, and everything he's learned aboard ship tells him that the situation he finds himself in is not possible.

Gindin wonders if Sablin is trying to defect to the West. It has happened before, though nothing was ever officially published about such treasonous acts. But everybody knows that things like that happen. And everybody knows what the punishment is. It's called Russian insurance. Nine ounces. In other words, a 9mm bullet to the back of the head.

A strange, uneasy silence descends upon the midshipmen's mess. Everyone is sitting down, looking at Sablin, and he's standing up looking at them.

"I want to sail the *Storozhevoy* to Kronshtadt," he tells us. It's about six hundred kilometers to the northeast and is at the entrance to Leningrad.

No one says a thing. None of them know *what* to say.

"When we get there we will ask the Kremlin to, first of all, treat us as a separate military base and then give us access to a television station and a radio station. I will speak directly to the Russian people and ask them to join us in the fight against injustice.

"This day of celebration for the October Revolution will be symbolic of our struggle. The people will understand. They will be with us, you'll see. It will be just like when the *Potemkin* and *Aurora* rose up in protest. The people rose up in support and the revolution began."

The irony of this situation strikes Gindin right between the eyes. In the first place, Sablin is the one officer aboard the *Storozhevoy* whose loyalty is completely beyond question. He is the Communist Party aboard ship. His is the final word in anything that has to do with politics.

And in the second place, all of them in this room are condemned men as of this moment. It won't just be Sablin preaching treason who will be punished; it will be all of those who listened.

"Now you must make a decision," Sablin says. "Each of you must search your conscience to find out what is right for you but, more important, what is right for the Rodina."

He takes the plastic container from the table on the left. The bin holds backgammon pieces, white and black. He sets a white piece and a black piece in front of each officer.

"Now you must choose," he tells them. "If you are with me, put a white piece into the bin. But if you oppose my effort to save the Motherland, then put a black piece in the bin."

He's standing in the middle of the room looking at them, challenging the officers to do the *right* thing, whatever that might be.

"I promise you that your vote will be secret, if you want it to—," he says. But all of a sudden he stops speaking. Perhaps he realizes just how stupid his promise really is. After this evening, nothing any of them will do aboard the *Storozhevoy* will be secret.

Especially not from the KGB.

THE GREAT SOVIET FAILURE

Once a word is out of your mouth
you can't swallow it.

KAK IZVESTNO (AS IS WELL KNOWN)

DOUBLESPEAK

Russians have been ruled by lousy systems for most of their history. The tsars with their absolute authority listened to no one but their own caste of nobility. After all, they had God on their side. Who was in the kulaks' corner? Indeed, what could a rabble of uneducated farmers or street sweepers or factory workers or even merchants understand about governing a country as vast as Russia? That arrogance cost the tsars their nation when in February of 1917 Nicholas II abdicated his power because he refused to take Russia out of the war with the Germans and his loyal subjects objected. Loudly.

The nobility tried to hold on when Prince Georgy Yevgenyevich and then Aleksandr Kerensky formed a provisional government, but neither of them pulled Russia out of the ruinous war, nor would they change the system that denied the peasant-farmers ownership of their own land. This was a dumb move by Moscow, because the peasants constituted 80 percent of the population.

Adding to Yevgenyevich's and Kerensky's woes were the Russian intellectuals as a class who disagreed with nearly everything. Poverty was rampant; most of the population was hungry most of the time. The generals and admirals were on the verge of a junta. And mutinies and desertions were widespread, especially among the soldiers and sailors who'd been drafted into the service. When they got back to their hometowns, they gave their weapons to the angry Socialist factory workers who were ready to move on the government.

One faction of these new revolutionaries, who called themselves the Bolsheviks, which was just another word for the most radical of the Socialists, came up with a slogan—*Land, peace, and bread*—and the concept of a system of what they called soviets that ignited the entire country into an all-out civil war.

A soviet was a council of delegates elected by factory workers or employees of other businesses. The soviets had no official status in the provisional government at that time, but theirs were the voices of the people, and Moscow did listen as best it could. Actually, it was a more up close and personal form of democracy than existed in the United States.

But once the October Revolution was over with and the government had been toppled and a constitution had been drafted, all the soviets across the country got organized and started reporting to what was called the Supreme Soviet in Moscow. It was the highest legislative body in the country, akin to the Congress in Washington. The highest executive branch of the new government was the Politburo. And the first leader of the new Soviet Union was none other than Vladimir Lenin, who was the Bolshevik leader of the Communist Party.

Lenin's first act was to withdraw from WWI, turning over most of Belarus and Ukraine to Germany.

But his second, even more important, task was to fight a civil war that threatened to unravel everything that the soviet system had accomplished and destroy the country. But at least they had the peasants, the workers, and the conscript soldiers and sailors behind them.

This is where the hard feelings against the Western powers, especially the United States, got a start.

The supporters of the tsars and the old regime formed a resistance army called the Whites to fight against the Communists, called the Reds. Had it merely remained an internal struggle it's possible that the Cold War would never have occurred. But a coalition of allies led by the United Kingdom, France, and mostly the United States, attempted to invade the new Russia to put down the Communists and restore the old royal regime to power.

It didn't work, of course, though it took the Reds until 1922 to prevail. And besides the future Cold War, it spawned a whole new way of thinking about governing a people.

Before the revolution, Lenin and his Bolsheviks argued that it would take a tight-knit and secretive organization to overthrow the government. And, they argued, because of the civil war aided by Western powers it was going to take the same sort of tight-knit, secretive organization to run the government. Lenin and his pals saw such a government as their only way out. After all, the three most powerful nations on earth were lined up against the Communists.

But Lenin went a step further by doing something no one in the West could fully understand or appreciate. To begin with, he banned all other factions or political parties. The new Soviet Union was to be a one-trick pony. Most important, he argued that the Party should consist of an elite, highly trained cadre of professional and dedicated revolutionaries who would be willing to devote their lives to the cause.

Only Party activists were put in charge of the bureaucracy, factories, hospitals, food suppliers, universities, *and the military*.

Loyalty and iron discipline were the new watchwords. It was called the *nomenklatura* system. It was the standard practice, if not the law of the land, in full force that early November 1975 in Riga.

This was supposed to be Russia's answer to democracy. The elections started at the bottom and worked up, but the orders and policy decisions started at the top and worked their way down. Before long it became tantamount to treason to question the top-down orders. And in order to protect the elite from challenge by the majority of the population, who were, after all, only kulaks, to rule meant you had to be a member of the Party. And in order to be a member of the Party you were required to take special courses, attend special political indoctrination camps and schools, pass a series of tough exams, and finally be nominated by three members of the Party who were in good standing.

It soon became an elite club. If you weren't a member of the Communist Party you were one of the little people. And little people got nothing!

Actually, it was even more complicated than that, as most things usually are. The revolution began in October 1917, and two months later the Bolsheviks created what was called the Cheka, or secret police, which several years later finally changed its name, if not its method of operations, to the KGB. The Cheka's first task was to ferret out the counterrevolutionaries and kick them out of the Party or bring them to trial. Less than one year later the secret police was charged with targeting all the old tsarists, plus any party or person opposing the revolution, including the Cossacks, who'd been around a lot longer than the Communists.

The first spymaster, Felix Dzerzhinsky, for whom a square was named in downtown Moscow, called what he was doing the Red Terror:

"We represent in ourselves organized terror. This must be said very clearly. Such terror is now very necessary in the conditions we are living through in a time of revolution."

Which was a very understandable sentiment at such a difficult time in a new government's existence. Except that after the revolution was over with and after the civil war had been waged and won, the Cheka and its descendant organizations never changed their tune. From December 1917 until this early evening aboard the *Storozhevoy* it was operations as usual.

Although technically Russia didn't become the Union of Soviet Socialist Republics until the end of 1922, when Belarus and Ukraine joined the main body of Lenin's Moscow government, by then the first serious seeds of discontent were already beginning to be sown, starting with the navy.

More than one year earlier, in March 1921, a group of sailor conscripts in Kronshtadt, the same guys who had initially supported the Bolsheviks, went on strike against the new regime. It took no less than Leon Trotsky to lead a unit of the Red Army across the frozen Baltic to put down the rebellion. The handwriting was on the wall. The people, mostly peasants, were dissatisfied with their government that was supposed to represent them. Lenin, almost always a savvy Bolshevik, instituted a new policy according to which small businesses could be privately owned, and he eased up on the restrictions against some political activities. The average citizen could then criticize the government, on occasion, and farmers could also market their own produce.

Immediately social unrest dropped off and farmers prospered.

Because peasants had more money, they could purchase manufactured goods. Factories increased production; factory workers bought more food. The Soviet Union, for a time, became the largest producer of grain on the planet, outstripping even the United States.

When Lenin died in 1924, Trotsky's Left Opposition condemned the new economic policies for inflating currency, displacing workers, and enriching the upper classes.

Soviet history then took an almost surreal turn. Trotsky and his supporters wanted to end economic freedoms. Nikolay Bukharin's faction favored the status quo. Stalin played them all, first supporting Trotsky to get rid of Bukharin. Stalin then helped the Soviet moderates who sought to jettison Trotsky.

By 1927 Stalin was Lenin's heir apparent, even though Lenin had written that he was "rude, intolerant, and capricious" and should never be given power. Stalin told the Communist Party Congress that the world's capitalists were encircling them. Soviet industry alone could ensure the Rodina's survival. They were fifty to one hundred years behind Western Europe and the United States.

Stalin created a new bureaucracy called Gosplan, the State Committee for Planning, which would guide the Soviet Union's economic development—especially its industrialization.

Stalin's bloody and brutal five-year plans dragged the Soviet Union into the twentieth century, transforming an agricultural basket case into a military-industrial giant.

Modernization came at an extremely heavy price. During the first five-year plan, miners and factory workers were forced to put in sixteen- to eighteen-hour workdays or face charges of treason. Most estimates put the death toll at more than 130,000 workers in the first years, a number that doesn't include forced-labor deaths in the gulags. In the twenty-seven years from 1927 to 1954 when Gosplan was in charge, nearly 4 million workers were sent to prisons or gulags for crimes against the revolution. Of those more than a half million were executed and another half million or so were kicked out of the country. That's not counting the estimated 22 million Russians killed during WWII, or about the same number of peasants killed, their deaths also bringing the Soviet Union into the twentieth century. All in all, nearly 50 million people were killed in the Soviet Union in its first fifty years of existence.

By some accounts those numbers are conservative, some of them by a large factor. But what all historians agree on is that a great many people died.

Under collectivism agricultural production plummeted. Widespread famine and starvation led to cannibalism, which led to a general spiritual malaise. Moscow said things were looking up, and the population tightened its collective belt. Moscow said the new Soviets lived longer and were more prosperous than any other people on earth, and the population carried their dead to the cemeteries with heads held low. Moscow said true happiness and prosperity were just around the corner, and people like Gindin's family planted gardens and hunted mushrooms in the woods so that they could eke out a bare existence.

It was called doublespeak, a term invented by George Orwell in his novel *1984* but one that most Russins understood at least on a visceral level.

For their whole lives the Soviet system had concealed the truth from its citizens—from people like Gindin and Captain Potulniy. Had it not been for Zampolit Sablin, both men might have lived out their lives ignoring the brutal, remorseless, and relentless lies they had been systematically fed.

After Sablin's revolt, however, they would never be so naive again

When Gindin and his fellow officers contemplated the white and black backgammon pieces that Sablin had placed in front of them, they were looking down the barrel of nearly sixty years of doublespeak, even though they weren't completely aware of why. But they were afraid. At this point they knew there was no going back for any of them.

THE CAPTAIN AND THE ENGINEER

Being on rotation aboard the *Storozhevoy* or just about any other warship in the Soviet navy means spending six months at sea. Usually in neutral waters such as the Mediterranean or the open Atlantic. But the real problem is that warships from just about every other interested nation are out there, too. French ships, Italian ships, Dutch ships, German ships, and of course U.S. naval vessels, the enemy.

The officers and crew aboard all these warships conduct day-to-day training just about the whole time they're out there. It means everyone is usually busy. Sometimes even too busy to really notice what's going on, because in addition to the training, the biggest job assigned to each warship is to spy on all the other warships. It's a very important and potentially very deadly game. But for each of these countries' navies what's ultimately at stake is the very safety of their own nations.

In 1975 the Soviet Union and United States are lined up against each other for domination of the entire world, against the threat of global thermonuclear war. For the first time in history two nations have, between them, the absolute ability to destroy all life as we know it on the entire planet.

The United States has allied with it the countries of NATO, among others. And the Soviet Union has as its partners the Warsaw Pact, mostly Eastern European satellite nations under the Soviet sphere of influence.

But for guys like Captain Potulniy and his officers, including Boris Gindin, the Cold War is more than just a philosophical issue. Out in the Med or the Atlantic the Cold War is a real thing, up close and personal.

It's early April 1974; the *Storozhevoy* is on rotation in the mid-Atlantic. It's stormy weather with high winds, low clouds scudding across the sky horizon to horizon, and monstrous seas. Gindin is in the mechanical spaces when Potulniy gets on the radio from the bridge.

"Boris, I need more speed," the captain orders. There is a strain in his voice. "More RPMs, Boris."

Boris follows the captain's orders, naturally, and increases the RPMs on all four power plants: the two marching engines and the two boost engines. The *Storozhevoy* shivers, as if he's a racehorse given the green light to stretch his legs, and takes off.

Twenty minutes later Potulniy is back on the comms: "Boris, more speed! Increase RPMs."

Boris does this. Whatever is happening on the bridge must be very urgent, because the gas turbines are putting out just about as much power as they are capable of producing. The gauges are nearly redlined.

Five minutes later Potulniy is back. "I need more speed."

"I cannot do that, Captain," Boris radios back. "The engines will be damaged."

"What do you mean?" Potulniy shouts. "Do as you're told!"

Boris is in a tight spot. He is between a rock and a hard place. He either disobeys a direct order or damages his engines. He radios Potulniy. "Captain, may I speak to you in private?"

After a beat, the captain is back. "Come to the bridge."

Topsides, Gindin sees that the chaotic seas are nothing short of monstrous. Close to their starboard beam is a German naval destroyer. So close that Gindin can actually see the officers on the bridge staring back at them. The German ship means to crowd the *Storozhevoy,* just to show that Germans won't take any shit from Russians. This is what Potulniy has been faced with. He needs as much speed as possible in order to outmaneuver the Germans.

"If I increase RPMs, the engines may be damaged," Boris explains.

Potulniy contemplates Boris's warning for just an instant before he nods. There is a bond between the two officers. Potulniy trusts his engineering officer, and Boris will go to the ends of the earth for his captain.

"If you want me to proceed, I'll need your orders in writing, sir," Boris tells the captain.

Potulniy nods. "Just do what you can for me, Boris. It's all I ask."

"Yes, sir," Boris says. The captain's signature is not necessary after all. Boris rushes back down to the machinery spaces, where he increases the speed of the engines by a scant few RPMs. "I can do no more than this," he radios the bridge.

"Thanks, Boris," Potulniy radios. "You are a good guy."

Later Boris learns that the encounter with the Germans was a very close call, which could have created an international incident, but because of Boris's steady and capable hand on the engines Potulniy had enough speed to outmaneuver the Germans and a disaster was narrowly averted. From that day on Poltulniy will ask only that Boris do his best and will not push his engineer any further.

The bond of trust between them has become like a hardened steel chain.

From time to time the *Storozhevoy* encounters American *avionosez,* aircraft carriers conducting their training missions. The Soviet navy is tasked with the job of watching such missions just to see how the other guys do things. Should it ever come to a shooting war, each side needs to know how the other operates.

"We Russian ships and submarines were far from our homes and our bases, right in the middle of the enemy," Gindin says. "We had to be ready at a moment's notice to strike back and defend the Rodina. We had no allies on our side in the middle of the ocean. We were on our own against the enemy, and every moment of every day we knew it."

That was in the middle of the Atlantic, but tensions much closer to home, in the Mediterranean, were just as high, sometimes higher. It's early afternoon, admiral's hour, and Boris is off duty, on the deck smoking a cigarette, when the captain's voice booms throughout the ship: "Battle stations! Man your battle stations!"

Before he can toss his cigarette overboard, before he can even move, Boris spots the periscope of a submarine just a couple hundred meters off their port side, practically within spitting distance. It's not a Russian boat.

Such a thing is impossible. The *Storozhevoy*'s sonar equipment is state-of-the-art, for the Soviet navy, and should have easily detected the presence of an enemy submarine long before he could become the serious threat he is now. After all, the *Storozhevoy* is an ASW platform. He was designed to hunt, find, and kill submarines.

Potulniy is hopping mad, and he believes that turnabout is fair play, even though warships carrying full weapons loads operating practically on top of each other create an inherently dangerous situation. One error of judgment, one slip by a helmsman, one maneuver misjudged by the enemy ship, can have dire consequences. Wars have been started in just this way. Russians have a long naval history and even longer memories, but the captain will not be denied the chance to prove that his ship and his crew are up to the task they are charged with.

Boris races belowdecks to his engines, as the *Storozhevoy* turns sharply to port while accelerating like a scalded gazelle, his active sonar systems banging away loudly enough that half of Europe can practically hear the racket.

The submarine submerges and heads away at his flank speed,

never fast enough or crafty enough to escape the *Storozhevoy*'s electronic net, all the way back to Italian waters, where he is safe.

But Potulniy knows, as does his crew, that the enemy submarine would have been theirs had a state of war existed. The fact that the sub got so close to them without detection in the first place is something not discussed with the captain or among the crew. From the moment the *Storozhevoy* was called to action he performed magnificently.

THE *ZAMPOLIT*

Nobody has made a choice, the white backgammon piece or the black. It's as if all the air has left the compartment. No one dares to breathe, let alone make a move one way or the other. Sablin stands there looking at them, a very odd, fixed expression on his face, in his eyes. He is a completely different person now from the one who hands out the materials for the political education classes that the officers have to teach every second Monday. At those times he is stern but friendly. He actually likes his job as *zampolit*, and everyone is sure that he believes with all his heart the Communist Party messages that he preaches.

Sablin comes aboard with boxes of magazines and articles put out by the Political Military Publishing companies. The routine is for him to go over the magazines page-by-page looking for the themes of each three-hour political lecture. One time it might be Lenin's ideas on collectivism applied to the Cold War. Another time might be the navy's role in defending the Rodina or the political part every man in the military has to play.

Sablin hands out the material that each officer uses to prepare extensive notes for the three-hour class he has to teach before giving the notes to Sablin for approval. Everyone hates this job, the officers as much as the sailors. But it's part of life in the Soviet navy, and during the lectures no one really pays any attention, but neither does anyone put up a fuss or crack jokes. This is deadly serious business.

Sablin might scribble a few comments in the margins and make a suggestion or two, but what he does not want to see happen is officers merely standing in front of their sailors and reading the notes.

This is the heart and soul of Communism. The Soviet people not only depend on the sailors to defend the Motherland with their lives but also expect the sailors to understand what they are fighting for and believe in it.

The Rodina believes in you; she only asks, dear Comrades, that you believe in her.

Pure Communism, and with it prosperity is just around the corner. Each five-year plan sees huge progress on all fronts, in manufacturing, in agriculture, in the glorious strides that the scientists have made in space, and in the magnificent sacrifices that the men in uniform have made and continue to make.

The ideals of Marx and Lenin are just as much alive today as they have ever been. Capitalism is the religion of greed and of the self and will fall under its own weight.

Sablin wants to believe the Party line with all his heart and soul. But like just about everybody aboard the *Storozhevoy*, and every other warship in the fleet, he knows that this is just a bunch of bullshit. All the bigwigs across the Soviet Union meet once every five to seven years in Moscow to tell the nation that progress is being made. Ministers of agriculture, transportation, buildings, defense, and culture all come to the podium and tell outright lies about increased farm yields when food is scarce, about new roads when streets even in Moscow are so filled with potholes that most cars are driving around with missing hubcaps and broken shocks, about new apartment buildings, which are crumbling even as they are being built, about improved defense, which is draining the national treasury, leaving little or nothing for the people, and about culture, which is actually the one boast that is not entirely a lie. The Bolshoi Ballet Company continues to be the best in the world, and Soviet symphony orchestras are nothing less than stunning.

"They were traitors in the pure meaning of the word," Gindin says. "All these ministers and the entire government were corrupt and totally dishonest with the people. They were enjoying the benefits of a luxurious life that we would never see or even dream of. They were telling us lies about the bright future while selling the people down the river."

It's the *zampolit*'s job to convince the officers of the *truths* of these lies and to make sure that the officers, in turn, convince the sailors. And until this early evening Sablin has done nothing short of a stellar job.

He's standing in front of the officers waiting for them to make their choice, white or black, with him or against him. But this is mutiny, and the fact that he's been such a terrific *zampolit* makes the situation all the more unbelievable. Maybe he is testing them.

MOVING ASHORE

Boris Gindin is only a couple of weeks from a much-needed leave to be with his mother and sister after his father's death. Following Boris's leave he would normally be reporting back to his ship for the next six-month rotation at sea. But that's not supposed to be the way it'll happen. Potulniy has agreed that if Boris sticks it out at the shipyard in Kaliningrad and gets the *Storozhevoy* in shape for his next rotation, the captain will write a letter of recommendation that will almost guarantee the shore job Boris wants.

Now this is an emotionally complicated situation for Gindin. On the one hand, he loves his job aboard ship, in charge of the gas turbine engines and other mechanical equipment. He has friends, he has a good crew who follow his orders without question, he has the respect of a man he considers to be one of the best captains in the Soviet navy, and despite his understanding of the propaganda coming out of Moscow, he is proud that he is making sacrifices protecting the Rodina. On the other hand, he is getting lonely and he's getting tired of it. He wants to find a girl he can marry so he can settle down and raise a family. He doesn't want to be like a lot of other young officers he knows, married and divorced already because six-month rotations at sea are almost impossibly hard on a new marriage. In his mind, he needs a shore job in order to find a wife.

In September Boris got a two-week assignment to the Zhdanov Shipbuilding Yard in Leningrad. Potulniy was ordered to send his gas turbine senior lieutenant to the yard because Gindin had been involved in the construction of the *Storozhevoy* and he had an intimate knowledge not only of the engines but also of how they should be installed in the first place.

Pushkin was Gindin's hometown, but it was close enough to Leningrad that he had a *propiska,* which is a document giving a Soviet citizen permission to live somewhere. It's often a major stumbling block to changing jobs. The employer might be willing, but unless the prospective employee has a *propiska,* taking the new job can be a moot point.

Shipyards building or repairing warships are required to have navy representatives to oversee the work, inspect the finished products, and sign off that the jobs have been done to specs. The gas turbine guy at the yard was gone, so Boris was sent to fill in.

From the day Boris arrived in Zhdanov he realized that this was a dream come true. It would be a perfect place for him to work and to continue with his career. Navy officers don't have to serve aboard ship to get paid and to get promoted. There are important jobs ashore, such as that of a ship inspector.

Not only that, but Gindin figured that if he could land a job in Zhdanov, he would no longer have to spend six months at a stretch at sea, which meant he could find a girl, get married, and raise the family he wanted. He would be a naval officer, earning good money, getting the respect of the people around him, and yet almost every night he would be able to get aboard the train to Pushkin and go home.

It couldn't get any better than that. The problem was how to do it.

Gindin scheduled an appointment with Captain First Rank Anatoli

Goroxov, the man at the shipyard who was responsible for filling all the navy specialty positions—mechanics, electrical, acoustics, rocket systems, guns, and torpedoes. Gindin was filling in as a gas turbine specialist and he wanted to know whether the position was only temporarily vacant or Goroxov needed someone permanent.

As soon as Goroxov saw Gindin's résumé and found out that he had a *propiska* for Leningrad and the area, the captain was over the moon. The *Storozhevoy*'s young gas turbine engineer was an answer to a prayer.

The only hitch was that since Goroxov had no real idea who or what Gindin was, he would need a reference. A letter from Captain Potulniy would do nicely.

Boris did his work at the yard without a hitch, and as soon as he reported back to the *Storozhevoy* he laid out his request to the captain. Potulniy was a good man. He didn't want to lose Boris, whom he had come to trust and to rely upon, but by the same token he was a fair man who did not want to stand in the way of an officer's advancement. So Potulniy said yes. He would write the letter of reference if Gindin would first go with the ship to the parade and celebration in Riga, then spend the two weeks at the Yantar Shipyard in Kaliningrad and finally help take the ship back to base at Baltiysk.

The main reason Potulniy laid those conditions on Gindin was because Captain Lieutenant Alexander Ivanov, who was commander of BCH-5, Gindin's boss, would be on leave. The job then of running the entire mechanical, electrical, and steam boiler/fuel group would fall on Gindin's shoulders.

Of course Gindin jumps at the captain's kind offer. It's a chance of a lifetime, a dream come true.

It's another gun barrel Gindin is looking down as Sablin waits for the officers to make their decisions. In the blink of an eye Gindin can not only see his career going by the wayside, he can also practically see and feel and taste the past seven years as if they were happening at this instant. Especially when the *Storozhevoy* was being built.

BUILDING THE *STOROZHEVOY*

It takes two years to build a warship that size. The *Storozhevoy*'s keel is laid down at the boatyard called Yantar Zavod 820 in Kaliningrad, which is a little less than fifty kilometers farther up the inlet from his eventual home port of Baltiysk, in 1972, and the ship is finished in early 1974.

Boris joins the building crew about five months before the ship is ready for sea. At that time they have a different *zampolit*, a pinch-faced little man who does everything strictly by the book and never cracks a smile. He'd transferred from a submarine and shortly after Boris arrives is transferred to still another ship. His replacement is Sablin, who is like a breath of fresh air by comparison.

Sablin is approachable, friendly, cracks jokes, even smiles. But he is the *zampolit*, and he believes in the Party line and does his job well, so the officers and sailors must still attend political indoctrination classes, but somehow with Sablin the mumbo jumbo isn't quite as boring. Things start to look up.

The officers and crew lived in housing outside of Kaliningrad, about twenty minutes by tram from the shipyards and thirty from downtown.

It wasn't a very large area, and it was protected by a tall fence. Guards were stationed around the clock at the front gate, and anyone wanting to get inside had to show his papers. In the middle of the compound was a three-story redbrick building that housed all two hundred of the officers and men, plus some classrooms where everyone took their political training, just like aboard ship.

The place was something like a cross between the ship and a military jail, although there was a small general store where you could buy a few things if you had the money. Canned food, candy, cookies, milk, cigarettes. The store also sold navy uniforms and insignia, so everyone was expected to look his best at all times. They had a basketball court to use in their spare time, whenever there was spare time, and a park where they could relax.

Captain Potulniy, his *zampolit,* and his *starpom,* the three senior officers, had rooms of their own. The other officers all bunked in the same room, and the rest of the crew lived in one big *cubrick.*

When a ship was built in the yard, his crew was assembled from throughout the fleet and was housed in this compound until it was time to move aboard. Then, when the next ship started construction, the new crew would take over the redbrick building until it was their time to move aboard their ship.

Gindin's typical routine during these months was morning exercise and breakfast, political training, and then down to the ship with the sailors in his section. There he would continue their training while overseeing the installation of his gas turbines, diesels, and other mechanical equipment. They ate lunch at the compound and then in the afternoon would return from the ship for more training and dinner.

Gindin was off duty the evening of every third day, which meant he could take the tram into the city and perhaps see a movie or eat at a nice restaurant. In his estimation Kaliningrad wasn't much of a city, plain and a little drab compared to his hometown of Pushkin with its trees and flowers and parks and palaces, but it was better than the compound.

The shipyard, which was also surrounded by a fence and patrolled by guards, was like a small city of long one-story buildings, called *cekhs*, in which were produced the equipment and parts that went into building a warship.

Hundreds of machinists, welders, lathe operators, and engineers worked around the clock, six days per week. The pace always seemed alive, even frantic, and very messy, with noise and smoke. The entire shipyard smelled like a combination of seawater, oil, gasoline, paint, and rancid grease, but inside each *cekh* the overriding smell almost always seemed to be that of sweat.

Building a ship was a long, hot, very hard job, done by men and women, who in those days weren't very keen on bathing regularly. Nor did Moscow care. Ships needed to be produced as fast as humanly possible to defend against the enemies of the Soviet Union.

Inventory depots of spare parts that had been manufactured elsewhere were contained in two- and three-story buildings scattered throughout the shipyard. And there were two buildings, both of them three stories tall, that housed the medical staff, a complete dispensary, and a hospital. Building ships at the pace Moscow wanted them built was not only a difficult business; it was also a risky business.

Railroad sidings crisscrossed the entire yard where not only warships were being constructed but also civilian ships such as tankers and transport ships of every kind were built or repaired. Six long piers stretched out to deep water at Yantar Zavod, and each could accommodate two or three ships at the same time.

The shipyard was a busy place.

"I was very excited to be doing my job," Gindin recalls. "To me it was one of the most prestigious jobs an officer could have. I was part of a great experience. I was part of not only building the *Storozhevoy* from the keel up; I was on the first crew that would take him to sea.

"We were giving birth to our ship. We had a feeling of pride, excitement, contentment, and a sense of accomplishment."

Even after the mutiny and its consequences, Gindin will consider these months at Yantar Zavod the most satisfying, gratifying times of his life. A period, in fact, that he would live over again without a moment's hesitation. Powerful stuff for a kid in his early twenties. A Russian Jew from Pushkin.

Finally it's time for the officers and sailors to move from the compound to the ship. They'll be living aboard, even as work is still being done, but now just about everyone is happy and in good spirits. They are the crew who are building this ship, and they are the crew who are the first to sleep and eat and work in the compartments, and they are the crew who will take him to sea for his trials, and they are the crew who will sail on his first rotation.

Painting still needs to be finished, and trim work needs to be completed, though on Soviet warships there is very little of that sort of nonutilitarian nonsense. Adjustments need to be made on every single system aboard; that includes all the electrical wiring and equipment, all the weapons systems, all the electronics, all the plumbing and fuel tanks and piping, and the four main gas turbine engines as well as the small diesel engines that provide electrical power. The cabins and galleys and mess halls and *cubricks* and the bridge all need finishing. When that's done, the ship is sailed to his base at Baltisk where the missiles and mines and ammunition for the guns need to be loaded aboard so that during sea trials all the weapons systems can be tested.

It's this mix of civilian shipbuilders and navy crew aboard at the same time, working around the clock to finish the ship and take him to sea, that creates some moments of frustration but other moments of sometimes black humor.

Nikolai Lisenko, who is the civilian manager for all the painting jobs on the *Storozhevoy*, needs Boris's signature certifying that work done in the machinery spaces has been finished to strict military specifications.

Fifteen huge fuel tanks hold 175,000 gallons of diesel oil low in the hull, divided port and starboard. They supply the fuel for the four big gas turbines and for the diesel auxiliary engines. Gas turbines and diesel engines do not run if the fuel is dirty. That means that the *insides* of the big tanks need to be painted thoroughly. No spot can be missed, and that includes dozens of small connectors, valves, and piping through which the fuel is distributed.

Lisenko comes to Boris to report that the tanks and piping have been painted. He wants the lieutenant's signature on the compliance certificate.

It's what Boris has been waiting for, because he watched the entire process. Lisenko hired women to climb through the access hatches and do the painting. But the women Boris saw doing the work were big, heavy boned, even fat. There is no way that they could have done a good job. They don't have the agility.

"I'm sorry, but I can't sign the certificate," Boris says.

Lisenko's face falls. He wants to argue, but Boris is firm.

"There is one condition, however," Boris tells the supervisor.

"What is it, Lieutenant?"

"I need paint."

Lisenko is to deliver to the ship three barrels of fresh paint and a very large bag of new, clean brushes. Boris will have his own sailors finish the job.

Within the hour the paint and brushes are delivered and Boris signs the certificate. How Lisenko will explain the missing supplies is his own business, but Boris is certain that his engines will get clean fuel.

About two weeks later Lisenko is back for another signature. His crew has finished painting the bulkheads and decks in the machinery spaces. Boris is doing some paperwork in his cabin when Lisenko shows up. The man is in his forties, short, stocky, always moving fast, his eyes shifting. He tries to smile, but it never looks sincere. His blue coveralls don't fit, his hair is always a mess, and he's usually spattered with paint.

"How are you, Boris?" he says. He has a small, round face and beady eyes. He's clutching some papers in his hand. "We're finished painting your spaces. Is everything okay? I'd like you to sign—"

Boris cuts him off. "You must be kidding? Do you see my cabin?"

"I'm not sure I understand you," Lisenko says. He's looking around Boris's cabin, trying to figure out what he's missing. But so far as he can see, the paintwork looks pretty good.

"Well, let me explain something to you, Nikolai. I'll be going out to sea on a six-month rotation. But you already know this."

Lisenko nods. "*Da*, I'm aware."

"I don't know how it'll be possible for me to relax in here on my off-duty hours. I have no place to put my shoes, for instance. Not even a drawer. And my bed is damned uncomfortable. It would be so much better if I had a nice sofa with a good mattress. It would make my life defending the Rodina so much easier to bear."

Lisenko's smile is suddenly genuine. "I don't think that will be a problem, Boris," he says. "Could you please leave your cabin and come back in . . . let's say two hours?"

Boris grabs the papers that he's been working on and heads up to the officers' dining hall. When he returns to his cabin two hours later, a drawer has been installed for his shoes and sitting against the wall is a very comfortable-looking sofa.

Lisenko hands the compliance papers to Boris, who signs them, and leaves. It's another of the systems in the Soviet navy that work.

A few days later Potulniy happens to walk past Boris's cabin and knocks on the door. Potulniy wants to discuss the progress that has been made aligning the main gas turbine engines. He notices the changes immediately.

"Very nice, Boris," he says.

"Thank you, sir," Boris replies, wondering what'll happen next. What he has done is not strictly by the book, and the captain has a reputation for following Soviet naval regulations pretty closely.

"You seem very cozy in here. Not bad for a senior lieutenant. I guess if I were to ask you how you got this sofa in your cabin it would sound silly, so I won't ask."

"Yes, sir," Boris says. He's not even going to try to explain.

"It looks like only you and I among all the officers got sofas." Potulniy smiles.

He knows that Boris has been putting in some very long hours getting the work done belowdecks, and he's guessed that Boris has made some good connections with the contractors, which means the jobs that Boris oversaw have been done right. Potulniy decides to cut his senior lieutenant some slack.

The captain smiles again. "Good work."

WARSHIP

It's five months now that Boris has been aboard ship. He is an engineer by education at the academy, but perhaps even more important, he is an engineer by birth. He loved and respected his father, who was an engineer. Some things run deep in a man's blood. Especially a Russian man's. Which translates to mean that Senior Lieutenant Gindin knows the machinery and machinery spaces aboard this ship better than anyone else aboard, except perhaps for Potulniy, the precise captain. In fact, that's one of the reasons both men have a building respect for each other.

Make no mistake, this is *the captain's* ship, no matter how Gindin already feels about him. So when it it's time to send the *Storozhevoy* down the ways, launch him into the water, it is Potulniy's wife, Nadezhda, who is given the honor of breaking the bottle of champagne against the bow.

The entire crew is gathered on the dock, along with the shipyard workers and managers, plus a lot of navy dignitaries. It's a crisp late-fall day, with a sharp blue sky and fast-moving white clouds. A fairly good breeze is kicking up small whitecaps in the harbor, and everyone is in high spirits. The *Storozhevoy* not only looks like a deadly Soviet warship of the line, but also is beautiful, with graceful lines and a design that U.S. Navy analysts would later call "neat, workmanlike, and elegant." He bristles with weapons systems, rocket launchers, torpedo tubes, deadly-looking guns, rotating radar antennas, and dozens of systems that many of the visitors can only guess and marvel at.

"It was the true moment of the *Storozhevoy*'s birth," Gindin recalls. "We felt like parents about to see their first kid taking its first steps. I was new, but still I sensed that I was a part of what would be a significant event in my life. I was very proud of *my* ship and *my* crew, that we were going to be serving in this state-of-the-art vessel."

The port side of the ship rises sharply above the crowds. Nadezhda climbs four steps up to a wooden platform that puts her within swinging distance of the sharply flaring bow, her husband at her elbow to make sure she doesn't trip and fall, and some admiral and his aide next to them.

Potulniy hands his wife the bottle of champagne that is suspended by a thin rope from a truss above the platform. She is to swing the bottle in an arc so that it will break against the hull. "God bless this ship and all who sail on him," someone in the crowd is bound to mutter as the bottle breaks.

Nadezhda raises the bottle over her head and swings it as hard as she can toward the *Storozhevoy*'s bow. The bottle makes its short arc, slams against the thick steel plating of the bow, and bounces off.

All those gathered for the ceremony on the dock heave a collective sigh. Such missteps are not unknown at ship launchings, but Gindin feels goose bumps on his skin.

"I can't explain," he remembers. "But something inside of me tightened up. My gut clenched and I felt a terrible uneasiness. It sounds silly, I suppose, but I had the feeling that maybe the *Storozhevoy* was a cursed ship."

Not all men who go to sea are superstitious, but most of them are, and sitting in the midshipmen's dining hall, facing Sablin, Gindin is remembering that launching day on the dock at Yantar Zavod 820 with a certain amount of dread. Maybe he was right after all.

But that day in Kaliningrad there is no time for that kind of a sentiment. Nadezhda Potulniy swings the bottle again and this time it breaks, to everyone's relief. Once the *Storozhevoy* is in the water the work gets more intense.

In the first place, the remainder of the crew come to live aboard, which means that in addition to testing, aligning, and adjusting the myriad of systems, the officers—including Gindin—must teach their sailors everything, which includes showing them where and what the equipment is, how it works, and what they need to do to service it. He has to prepare the written instructions for all of those tasks as well, explain where each man's post is, what his responsibilities are, and what his duties are under every circumstance imaginable.

In addition to getting the ship ready for sea, getting settled in, getting to know one another, the officers must teach their three-hour political indoctrination classes every second Monday, come rain or shine, come commissioning or war.

Four months later they sail the fifty kilometers west-southwest to their base at Baltiysk, where Potulniy assembles his crew on the dock for a brief ceremony with the commander of the Division of Big Antisubmarine Ships, *Bolshykh protivolodochnykhn korablejj*, Bpk Captain Second Rank Gennadi Zhuravlev. They're all wearing their holiday uniforms because the *Storozhevoy* is being formally accepted into the division and readied for the shakedown process that will finally get him prepared for his first rotation. The testing and training become intense. The sooner the ship is certified, the sooner he can put out to sea to help defend the Motherland.

The *Storozhevoy* spends much of his time tied up at the dock while his systems and his crew are shaken out, but he also puts out to sea in the Baltic, sometimes for just a few hours, sometimes for a few days, no matter the weather. Every single system, down to the last nut and bolt, the last soldered connection, the last paper chart and pair of binoculars, the last set of parallel rulers, must be aboard and must be just right.

Then, finally, the blessed day the crew has been working for arrives. The *Storozhevoy* is given his final sign-off. His sailing orders. He is ready to put out to sea on his first six-month rotation.

The Storozhevoy *is a warship.*

ENGINEER

When Gindin looks back on his twelve years of service in the Soviet navy it is with a certain amount of nostalgia and pride, even though his career ended badly and even though at its best his career was hard. There was almost continuous training, dealing with recalcitrant sailors, working long hours, no social life, putting up with the political indoctrination. Not very glamorous. In fact, at times Gindin had to wonder what was so good about the life of a Soviet navy officer.

"I always liked mechanics," Gindin says. "It runs in my blood. I was never afraid to roll up my shirtsleeves and do the dirty jobs. I could work for hours and never notice where the time went. I enjoyed working with my hands. It wasn't often you'd see people who were happy with their lives. But I was."

Gindin has a growing love affair with the *Storozhevoy* from the moment he first lays eyes on him at the shipyard. Each time Gindin steps off the ship and walks away, he has to stop on the dock so that he can turn around and look at the *Storozhevoy*. Gindin knows everything there is to know about the ship, which makes him love him all the more.

To a true sailor a ship is more than just a collection of nuts and bolts, engines and pumps, wires and gauges, hatches and portholes, ladders and companionways. He is a living, breathing being that, very much like a high-class society woman, needs constant attention. That is perhaps why in most navies a ship is referred to as a *she*.

The *Storozhevoy* is in the Atlantic on the way home from his first rotation. In addition to the two marching gas turbines and the two boost engines, there are five much smaller diesel engines aboard that provide electrical power. After nearly six months at sea one of the diesels has broken down, and Gindin has used all the spare parts he's managed to hoard. The diesel will not run properly, so he shuts it down so that it won't damage itself beyond repair. If that happens the engine will have to be scrapped and Gindin will have a lot of explaining to do.

He gives his crew strict orders that under no circumstances will they start diesel number three. But there are two problems. The first is that according to regulations these engines have a five-thousand-hour life span before they should be rebuilt or replaced. That's about one six-month rotation, plus a little safety margin. As with all things Moscow dictates, if a piece of machinery doesn't live up to its expectations, the factory where it is built will not be found at fault, but the men who've been given the thing will be held accountable. The fact that this engine quit before its scheduled time is Gindin's fault.

His solution is simple. His men will continue to log the engine's hours in the book as if it were running. That way when they get back to base at Baltiysk diesel number three will have performed up to expectations and can be rebuilt or replaced. This is another system in the Soviet navy that works, despite regulations.

The second problem is Gindin's sailors. These are the same young boys who steal potatoes so they can have midnight snacks because they're hungry. The same guys who carry heavy wrenches back and forth so that they can get out of work. The very same kids who won't get out of bed in the morning because they claim their fathers are alcoholics. They're country bumpkins, *muzhiks,* and *prostofiljas,* but they are as curious and inventive when the need arises as they are usually bored. Just about every minute of every hour of every day and night of their lives is scheduled for them. They have to do something or they'll go crazy. It's called *ispytyvat' sud'bu,* or, testing fate, pushing the envelope, just to see what happens.

It's early afternoon of a lovely day. Gindin has gone up to his cabin to get a technical book when Igor Sheskin, one of his sailors, comes rushing up the companionway, all out of breath and red faced, screaming something about diesel number three.

Gindin jumps off his chair. "What are you talking about?" he demands.

"We can't stop it!" Sheskin shouts. "It's gone crazy!" He's a blond kid with broad shoulders, one of Gindin's best men. Sheskin is one of those born mechanics, a guy who knows how to use his hands.

There's no time to ask questions. Gindin slams past the sailor and races headlong down the passageway and the stairs to the motor room. When he gets there, diesel number three is working like it's been invaded by an evil spirit. It's shaking nearly off its motor mounts, making crazy noises, belching smoke, and the RPMs are steadily increasing. The engine means to tear itself to pieces, and when it blows it will be like a bomb sending a spray of hot oil and jagged metal pieces in all directions. The motor room will be destroyed, and every wide-eyed sailor in the compartment will be cut to shreds. But none of these boys, not even Sheskin, know what to do.

Gindin has no time to think about the consequences. He rushes up to the engine and hits the EMERGENCY STOP button, with absolutely no effect. Diesel number three has a malevolent mind of its own.

He tries closing down the fuel distribution line, but that has no effect, either. Apparently the engine is siphoning fuel from one of the other distribution lines.

Finally Gindin yanks the handle that controls the air intake line, and almost immediately diesel number three begins to sputter and die, its RPMs slowly coming down and stopping.

The relative silence in the compartment is nearly deafening. Gindin is sure that his sailors can hear his heart slamming against his rib cage as he tries to catch his breath. He wants to tear into these guys. He'd given very specific orders that diesel number three was not to be started for any reason. For just *this* reason. If the engine had blown apart there would have been a lot of casualties down here, and all of them would have been on his shoulders.

At that moment he feels like slamming his fist in someone's face. But Gindin is an officer and a gentleman.

Gindin has his sailors line up at attention and demands to know who started diesel number three and why. No one speaks up.

Gindin asks again, and still not one of his sailors speaks up.

Gindin has to go down the line, looking each sailor in the eye as he asks the same questions: "Did you start the engine, and if you did, why?"

Finally Andrey Bazhanov looks down and nods. "I did it," he says.

Gindin holds himself in check. "I gave orders not to start diesel number three. Why did you disobey?"

"I knew something was wrong with the engine. I just wanted to see how it would work if it was started."

Gindin reads the sailor the riot act. Bazhanov was young, he was bored, and he wanted to do something, anything, to make his day a little more interesting. They're all warned that if something like this ever happens again, the guilty sailor will be court-martialed. Probably sent to prison!

Everyone learned a lesson that day. Gindin's sailors learned that they were to obey orders at all times, and Gindin learned that he has to keep his ear to the ground and his eyes open so that he will know what is going on with his crew and his ship.

Another link has been forged in a chain that binds them together. Gindin does not report the incident to the captain. This hiccup in BCH-5 will stay there, and the sailors appreciate it.

The little incident will come back to pay big benefits at the very end of that same rotation when the *Storozhevoy* returns to his base at

Baltiysk. According to the engine logs, all five diesels have completed their scheduled life spans. They are to be replaced in the fitting-out process. This job, however, has to be done *before* Gindin or any of his sailors can go on leave. They've been on rotation for six months; everyone just wants to get off the ship, no matter how much they may love him, and go home.

Gindin reports to the assistant division commander who is in charge of all mechanical equipment. Replacing the five diesels should take one month, maybe a week or two more. It's how long other crews have needed to get the job done.

"So, Senior Lieutenant, you may begin scheduling your crew's leaves in thirty to forty-five days," the guy says with a smile. "Good luck."

Back aboard, Gindin calls a meeting with the six sailors responsible for the diesels to tell them that they can go on leave only after the diesels have been replaced. The sooner the job is finished, the sooner they can go home.

Everyone is eager to get started. This is a very well-motivated bunch of young men.

In order to remove a diesel engine from the ship, all of its supporting systems need to be disconnected, which includes the fuel lines, oil lines, air lines, and electrical cables. Gindin organizes a series of wooden crates in which the parts from each support system, for each diesel, will be labeled and stored after they have been thoroughly cleaned and checked.

Once that job is started, Gindin marches over to the building where the replacement diesels are stored and holds out a bag containing three bottles of *spirt,* the nearly universal Soviet naval scrip, in front of the depot manager.

"I want my five diesel engines delivered without delay," Gindin says. "Is this possible?" Usually it takes three to four weeks for a delivery.

The manager grabs the bag and nods enthusiastically. "Lieutenant, if you give me twenty-four hours' notice, you will have your diesels."

Seven days later, the old diesels have been completely disconnected, and Gindin calls the depot manager, who is as good as his word. The next day his crew shows up with a lifting crane to remove the old engines and deliver the new ones.

Seven days after that, all the supporting systems have been reconnected and the five new diesels have been run up and checked out.

Gindin reports back to the assistant division commander that the work is done, but the guy doesn't believe it.

"That's impossible," he sputters.

"Please, sir," Gindin says, smiling. "Stop by yourself and check our work."

Already Gindin has the reputation at Baltiysk as the young senior lieutenant who is almost always walking around with a grin on his face. The assistant division commander doesn't have to put up with this kind of shit. "In the first place, Lieutenant, it takes twice that long just to get new diesels delivered, let alone installed."

The grin on Gindin's face widens. He can't help himself. This is fun. "I insist, sir. Come see for yourself."

The assistant division commander does just that, and he can't believe his eyes. The five diesels have been installed, and they are running perfectly. Without another word he signs leave papers for Gindin and his sailors and storms off the ship and back to his office, wondering where the hell he went wrong.

BALTIYSK

The loyalty of Gindin's crew is the barrel of still another gun that Gindin is looking down facing Zampolit Sablin in the midshipmen's dining hall. The *Storozhevoy* may be his master, but his crew is the ship's servant and Gindin needs to take care of both in any way he can.

But the situation is more complex than that. It's not the ship, officers, and crew as separate entities that must work and live together. They're three legs of a triangle, *ship-officers-crew*, that function together as a single entity. It's another of the relationships that most civilians can't appreciate at the gut level but that anyone who has ever served aboard a warship understands immediately.

At this moment on an early November evening aboard the *Storozhevoy,* faced with such a monumentally impossible decision, Gindin can perhaps be forgiven if he allows his mind to drift a little. He's barely treading water in a monstrous ocean. In the troughs all he can see is black water in which he will surely drown. But at the tops of the waves he catches tantalizing glimpses of the base at Baltiysk, near enough to the home of the Baltic Fleet at Kaliningrad to be a safe haven.

The fleet, which consists of nearly forty major surface warships, more than three hundred small combat vessels, 150-plus auxiliaries, two dozen submarines, 250 navy aircraft, and the one naval infantry brigade that Admiral Gorshkov promised each unit, is a formidable power. And yet the town of Baltiysk, where the bulk of the fleet put in after each rotation, is not much more than a village that opens to the Gulf of Gdansk and the Baltic.

Gindin recalls that the base was always busy with ships coming and going. While they were in port they were tied alongside four long docks and were connected to the shore by not only the bow and stern and spring lines but also lines and hoses that supplied electricity, potable water, and fuel.

The base always stank of oil and foul bilge water drained overboard. But everyone felt a sense of invincibility here. At sea you were sometimes surrounded by the enemy—American aircraft carriers, Italian submarines, the bastard German destroyer that had tried to crowd them—but at Baltiysk you were home free. Safe.

The main street of the base is tree lined in the summer, pleasant with buffets and little shops where sailors can buy milk and cookies and cigarettes and other homely little things.

And there is soccer competition. Eight ships in the *Storozhevoy*'s Bpk division have formed a league. They play on a field near the docks, with benches on the sidelines for the fans. Gindin and Firsov are among the men representing their ship, and whenever they play, Potulniy and Sablin and most of the other officers not on duty or away from the ship come down to the field to give their noisy support.

Soccer is the national sport of the navy, if not of all the Soviet Union. The competition is fierce, as such things are among young military men, and in the end tournaments are held to see which ship will get the Bpk division award.

Those are the very best of times that Gindin remembers now. The *Storozhevoy*'s team is playing a very tight match when one of the midshipmen sprains his ankle. The game is stopped until the injured man can be helped off the field and brought back to the ship and a replacement player put in.

That evening Zampolit Sablin visits the midshipman's quarters to make sure he's not in too much pain and to ask if he needs anything. It's almost surreal at this moment thinking about the incident. But Gindin can't help himself; he's fallen into another trough.

Across the street is the security guard at the main gate. Once you clear that point you are free to go into the town, which is right there on the other side of the fence. But it's tiny, only three restaurants, two movie theaters, and a few stores spread out here and there. Plus the *gaubvachta,* the military prison, there to remind every man, officer and sailor alike, that the Soviet navy takes its regulations very seriously.

During the winter the chimneys constantly belch wood smoke, which fills the sharp, crisp air. The townspeople mostly stay indoors, so when it's cold the streets are all but deserted. It feels like life has been halted in mid-step, waiting for the spring to return.

In the summer, however, the streets are filled with wives pushing baby carriages or taking the children to the park to play. Sometimes off-duty officers will go to the park, too, where they will mingle with the children and the locals.

Gindin remembers a town beach that everyone could use, civilians as well as naval personnel. But the only way to get to it was through the base, so everyone had to be cleared at the gate and driven down to the water.

Other than that there was almost nothing for the wives to do while their husbands were away at sea for six months at a stretch. It was only one of many reasons that the divorce rate among young officers was so high.

Nevertheless, thinking about Baltiysk gives Gindin a little warm feeling. The base is safe, the workload there is 10 percent of what it is at sea, and it's where the Rossia, his favorite restaurant, is located. Food aboard a Soviet warship, even aboard the *Storozhevoy* and even for an officer, is not very good compared to the meals they can get ashore.

When the ship is at base and Gindin is not on leave, he and the other officers and crew are given a part of one day in four when they can go through the gate into town. The wives of some of the officers live in Baltiysk, and others take the train to the base whenever the *Storozhevoy* is in port. But for Gindin, who is single, the Rossia is the first place he heads for.

The restaurant is cozy and the lighting is dim and romantic, things that speak to a Russian's soul. The Rossia is a place where a guy like Gindin can dream about a wife he's yet to meet. Besides that, the food is fantastic and there's always entertainment, someone playing a guitar and singing sad Russian folk songs.

Gindin is a regular customer, he tips very well, and he is obviously single. Every waitress in the always-crowded house loves him. There are always lines of people outside waiting to get in. Any spot inside will be fine. But when Gindin shows up, the waitresses scramble to get him a special place right in front of the singers. Even if every table is filled, one of the waitresses will race to the back room, grab one of the spares, and hustle it out to the floor for the lieutenant.

The crowds are usually split eighty-twenty between navy people and civilians. But everyone in Baltiysk serves the navy in one way or another, either in uniform or as a subcontractor or as a waitress in the Rossia. So every night the main topic of conversation in the packed restaurant is the navy. The faster the vodka flows, the faster the stories blossom, and the faster the guys grab any available girls and get up on the dance floor. As the noise level rises, so does the fun.

The Rossia is the place to be in Baltiysk. It has an atmosphere of relaxation and excitement. A secret place only a few hundred meters away from the ship that is light-years away from military duty, discipline, and responsibilities.

"Hey, Boris," one of the waitresses calls when Gindin finally gets into the restaurant. She is carrying a table across the room, and he threads his way across the packed floor to where she sets it up.

She's a pretty girl, with long blond hair, blue eyes, and a million-watt smile. She can afford to be extra nice; Boris would make a great catch. She brings him vodka, then herring and fried potatoes, pickles, stew, crusty bread, a quintessentially Russian supper, and he is in seventh heaven.

He has friends in the restaurant, and they have to wonder why he is getting such good service when they may have to wait for a drink or something to eat. But Boris is a regular, he's an officer, he's single, and he tips 30 percent.

That night in particular sticks out in Boris's mind at this moment in the midshipmen's dining hall, because of the warmth he felt. He was at peace with himself and the world. There were no difficult decisions to be made. No white or black backgammon piece to choose.

The waitress watches him that night, and at one point she comes over and lets him know that she gets off work at one in the morning. She's interested. She would definitely like to spend some time with him. But it can't happen. He has to be back aboard ship by midnight.

"Maybe another night," Boris tells her.

She lowers her eyes in disappointment. "Sure, Boris," she replies. She looks up and smiles. "May I get you another vodka?"

"Please," he says.

After she leaves, he spots some friends, who join him for a few hours of fun. They've brought a girl, Olya, and everyone dances with her and sings and drinks and has something to eat. It's not the most perfect night of his life to that point, but it sticks out in his mind right this moment, facing Zampolit Sablin and an absolutely insanely impossible choice.

SENIOR LIEUTENANT

Gindin's thoughts are tumbling over one another now so fast it's getting difficult to concentrate on any one thing, except for some crazy reason he fixates on how his fellow officers and sailors see him. It's as if he's looking at himself through the wrong end of a telescope. He's way down at the end of the long tunnel, but he can't make any sense of the details.

He's always had what he feels is a good relationship with Captain Potulniy and just about everyone else aboard the ship. That includes the cook. But at this moment one incident sticks out in Gindin's mind. He's spent two days and nights fixing one of the diesel generators. He's had little or no time to sleep, nothing substantial to eat, and he's dead on his feet and hungry enough to eat a bear when he finally gets back to his cabin.

It's late, well after the dinner hour, when he calls the officers' galley and asks if the cook could send something up to his cabin.

"I'm sorry, Lieutenant, but dinner is done. All the food has been put away, all the dishes have been washed, and the galley will not be open again until morning."

"Okay," Boris says. "I understand." He goes to bed hungry that night. It's not the end of the world, but a little something to eat would have been nice.

As it happens, the very next day the cook rushes to Gindin's cabin. There's absolutely no water—hot or cold—with which to wash the dishes. "We have to carry all the dishes and all the pots and pans back to the crew's galley, where they've got water," the cook complains bitterly. "It's damned hard work, Lieutenant."

Boris is combing his hair in the mirror and doesn't even glance over at the cook. "I guess it must be *very* hard work. But I'm sorry; there's nothing I can do about it."

The cook knows better. It's not that Gindin *can't* do anything about the water problem—he's the engineer after all—it's that he *won't* do anything about it.

After that Gindin never has a problem with the galley. If he has to work overtime and misses a meal, the cook personally delivers something good to eat to the senior lieutenant's cabin, and in turn the galley is never without all the hot and cold running water it needs. Gindin doesn't think he's ever abused the system, but sitting now in the midshipmen's dining hall he can't be sure.

And yesterday, after the parade, when the entire ship was in a festive mood, Gindin made the rounds of all the machinery spaces to check everything, including the bilge pumps that ensured the *Storozhevoy* would not sink at his mooring if he were to take on water.

Gindin was in a mixed mood all that day, happy about the parade, proud to be a Soviet naval officer, sad about his father's death, looking forward to his new job at Zhdanov, and impatient to get on with his life.

It's possible, he thinks now, that he might have been impatient with his sailors, too. It was a holiday after all, yet he spent nearly two hours going over every single detail. Nothing missed his scrutiny, not a grease fitting that wasn't cleaned properly, not an engine gauge reading that was off by one tiny decimal point, not a finger smudge in one of the logbooks. Everything had to be exactly correct.

Maybe at the end of a six-month rotation, when all they could think about was getting off the ship and going home to see their families, they felt he was being too tough on them. Maybe they resented his orders. Maybe Fomenko, who couldn't get out of his bunk because his father was an alcoholic, was hatching some revenge plot.

Afterward Gindin went to lunch with some of the other officers. They talked, he remembers that much now, but he cannot seem to focus. He can't get a grip in his head. For the life of him he cannot remember one single scrap of conversation at yesterday's lunch. Not one word of it.

He does remember returning to his cabin to lie down, but Sergey Bogonets knocks on the door. He wants to talk because he's lonely. They all are. It's a holiday and they're missing their families. Sergey talks about his wife and son. She flew down to Baltiysk, but they could only stay a couple of days before they had to fly home. Their leaving put Sergey into a depression and he just wanted a little human contact.

They went out on deck to smoke a cigarette. It was getting dark and cold by then. Only a few people were still out and about to admire the ships. Now that the lights were coming on throughout the town and aboard the fleet, the evening was getting pretty. Even festive.

Gindin does remember thinking that the people of Riga were at home now, behind the brightly lit windows with their families, getting set to celebrate the holiday: "We envied all those lucky strangers."

He and Bogonets stayed on deck for a long time before they parted. Gindin went back down to the engine room, this time not to inspect but to talk to his sailors. They seemed to be in just as odd a mood as he was, lonely, missing their families, feeling a little strained.

So they start to talk about their lives before they were drafted into the navy. One of them is a big, tall guy from the suburbs near Dnepropetrovsk in south-central Ukraine. He came from a family of farmers and he and his four brothers had to help with the chores. They had chickens, rabbits, and pigs but no refrigerator. In the spring they would slaughter a pig, cut it into small chops and roasts, pack it in salt, and store it in the root cellar, where it would stay cool. One pig would provide enough meat to feed the entire family all winter. When they wanted to have pork for dinner, a cut would be brought from the root cellar the night before and soaked in freshwater to get rid of the salt.

"It was always salty, just the same," the sailor lamented. But he would have exchanged the *Storozhevoy* for just one bite of his mother's cooking, salty or not.

THE BIG LIE

The Soviet Union has lied to Gindin as well as it has to Sablin. The only difference is Gindin knows that he personally can't do a thing about it, while Sablin believes that he can do something to change the system. Not only that, he feels that it's his *sacred duty* as a good Communist to do something.

It's these similar but divergent views that create the problem.

In the academy and then aboard every ship and at every base Gindin has been assigned to he's had to give political classes to the sailors who report to him. It's nothing new. It's a fact of life for every officer in the Soviet military. And like the vast majority of officers, Gindin does what he's told, but he doesn't have to like those orders, nor does he have to comply beyond the strict letter of the law. He's given his lectures, every second Monday, and at this moment, sitting in the midshipmen's dining hall, for the life of him he could not give even a simple report of any political lecture he's ever given. Not even the one from last week in which Sablin had taken such an interest.

Gindin had jotted down his lecture notes from some *Pravda* article and had brought them up to Sablin's cabin for the *zampolit*'s approval.

"This is exciting, Boris; don't you think so?" Sablin had enthused. "We'll be sailing to Riga to help celebrate the great revolution. What a perfect time this is."

For another boring political lecture? Gindin has to wonder. But the *zampolit* is lighting up like a May 9th fireworks display to celebrate the end of WWII.

"Anyway, this stuff doesn't matter," Sablin says, glancing at Gindin's notes. "The only truth is what we make."

"Sir?"

"You'll see," Sablin says, almost slyly, but he's smiling.

They are now facing each other in this completely insane situation, and the same look of holy zeal is in Sablin's eyes.

Political officers are born, not made. In Sablin's case he was brought up as a navy brat, on navy bases, knowing little or nothing of the world of civilians beyond the main gates. From the moment he could walk and talk a number of stern principles were drilled into him: Duty, discipline, and patriotism. The military way. Loyalty to the Soviet system. The pure ideals of the Communist man. Child of the revolution. Never lie. Despise hypocrisy. Hate injustice.

When he was only sixteen, Sablin applied to the Frunze Military Academy and was accepted. He was a model student and in his first year was elected to run the *Kommunisticheksi Soyuz Molodioshi*, Komsomol, the Communist youth organization on campus. He became the *conscience of the class*.

His classmates said they all believed in the ideals of Communism and Socialism. They were educated to believe. But Sablin not only believed with all his heart; he also wanted to put the ideals into action.

All the ideals.

That meant the democracy Lenin promised after the revolution. That meant all men were to be treated as equals. That meant everyone produced to the best of their abilities and everyone received what they needed. There was to be no poverty. No hunger. No homelessness. No injury or illness that wasn't addressed. Universal work and education.

But Sablin was not a stupid young man. He looked around and he saw that the bureaucracy since Lenin was filled with hypocrisy and that everyone was supposed to close their eyes to it all.

They swore oaths to Lenin and to Communism, but it was nothing but a pack of lies from Stalin to Brezhnev.

When Sablin was still in school he wrote an angry letter to Premier Khrushchev. "Social inequalities," Sablin argued, "are bastardizing the ideals of the Soviet state. Something must be done before it is too late."

Moscow was not amused. A letter of reprimand was sent to Frunze, and Sablin's graduation was put on hold, maybe permanently. The wisdom of the time was that the young man's career was over before it had really begun.

But Sablin was a starry-eyed idealist, the class conscience. Despite the setback, he finished his studies and graduated with honors. Not long afterward Khrushchev was kicked out and Brezhnev took his place, with the goal of making the Soviet navy the best seagoing force on earth.

Within five years Sablin emerged from the ashes of his reprimand like a phoenix to be offered command of a destroyer. He was of a good military family, he was a Frunze graduate, he was a loyal, if overzealous, Communist who sometimes took the Party line to extremes, and he obviously was fearless.

But Sablin turned it down, opting instead to go to the Lenin Political Academy, where he could study doctrine so that he could truly understand Communism. Instead of commanding a ship in battle, he wanted to command a ship's crew in grasping the ideals of Socialism.

It's possible that even then, at the age of thirty, Sablin was already planning to make his mark by challenging Moscow.

But if he expected to find the answers at the academy he would be disappointed, because those kinds of explanations did not exist. He dived headfirst into Lenin and Marx and Engels in the original books and articles. He was trying to understand the October Revolution at the intellectual level. But like a Catholic priest who begins to doubt his faith and the reasons for his celibacy, Sablin was already starting to have trouble swallowing the doctrine. Wherever he looked he saw corruption, inequality, and the unearned privileges of the *nomenklatura*.

They fought the revolution to stop all that, to stop the class system, to give the working class the true power, but all that had gone by the wayside. A few old men in the Kremlin, not the people, were in charge.

When he tried to dig even deeper—after all, the revolution was perfection; it was simply his understanding that was faulty—he discovered that a lot of material was off-limits. For instance: Leon Trotsky had been one of the revolutionaries alongside Lenin, but his books and articles were not available. Not even to academy students, who were supposed to be the crème de la crème of Communist youth. The guys who were supposed to go out into the service and, like pastors, guide their flocks. It was as if seminary students were not allowed to speak about the Devil.

Despite the censorship, despite the disappointments, Sablin graduated and went out into the fleet a dedicated Communist who wholeheartedly believed in the philosophy, if not in the bureaucracy.

In a capitalist world the ordinary workers had to accept the fact that there would be rich people and there would be poor people. It was a natural outcome of such a system, and like it or not, the proletariat had to live with the consequences. But in Socialism there weren't supposed to be such inequalities. Communism was designed to be the purest form of civilization. In theory.

In practice even the most casual observer could see that reality in the Soviet Union didn't come anywhere close to the ideal.

The men who ran the nation from Moscow would never voluntarily give up their power. There would be no elections. The new revolution had to come from within. This time a *zampolit* would have to provide the spark.

Sablin's favorite theme in his political lectures was revolution. Especially the October Revolution and the mutiny aboard the *Potemkin*.

In fact, it's the *zampolit's* position that revolution is a fine navy tradition that shouldn't be discontinued.

"Before you make your choice, there is something more I have to tell you," Sablin says.

He has the absolute attention of every officer and midshipman in the dining hall.

"I and the officers and men with me will take the *Storozhevoy's* mooring lines in and leave in the morning for Kronshtadt." It's in the Gulf of Finland just twenty kilometers from Leningrad. "I will declare that this ship is a military base all by itself, and I will demand that Moscow give us access to radio and television so that I can personally speak to the people of the Soviet Union."

This is even worse than treason. It's outright insanity. Sablin means to get them all killed.

"How can you even suggest such a thing to us?" Sadakov shouted angrily. "You're our political officer. You're a good Communist. You're supposed to set an example."

We didn't jump up and get out of there, Gindin remembers. None of us stormed to the front of the room to take our *zampolit,* who obviously was a criminal, into custody. "All of us officers were trained in military academies where we were taught to follow orders no matter what. Sablin outranked us, and it was mandatory to obey him. It was our legal and moral duty."

The Russians say that all the brave men are in prison. You're the boss, and I'm the dummy.

Someone gets up, walks to the table, and drops one of the backgammon pieces into the basket. Gindin can't remember who was the first, nor could he see which piece the officer chose, but they are voting now.

The silence in the dining hall is thick. It's like they are attending a funeral. Their own.

Gindin gets to his feet and walks up to the table. He stops for a second to look Sablin in the eye. The *zampolit* is fairly glowing with excitement. This is real history in the making. There will be movies and books and maybe even songs about this mutiny. It'll be just like the *Potemkin.*

Gindin slowly holds his hand out. As he turns it over he opens his fist and a black backgammon piece falls into the basket. But it's in slow motion. It's as if the laws of gravity have been erased at that instant. Time is all but standing still.

The black backgammon piece turns end over end, falling, it seems, forever from an impossible height.

Gindin looks up again into Sablin's eyes. The *zampolit*'s excitement fades like the smile from the lips of a jilted lover.

"Boris," he says sadly.

In Moscow the Kremlin is all but deserted. Brezhnev and most of the Party's leadership are at home, enjoying the day after the holiday, with perhaps a vodka or two, maybe some sweet Russian champagne. It is a time for families. They think that they'll be back at their desks in the morning. But they'll be back a lot sooner than that, and for a reason not one of them can possibly imagine at this moment.

THE MUTINY OF FFG *STOROZHEVOY*

**When the sheath is broken
you cannot hide the sword.**

KAK IZVESTNO

POTULNIY'S ARREST

Leadership aboard a Soviet warship, aboard any warship, is from the top down. Obviously. But what's not quite so obvious is that if the captain of a warship is suddenly removed like Bligh aboard the *Bounty*, the absolute authority devolves to the next in command, or whoever deposed the captain.

The big rub is that the other officers and crew have served under the captain and not the first officer or, in the case of the mutiny aboard the *Storozhevoy*, the *zampolit*.

Captains are to be obeyed instantly and without question. It has been a law in every navy the world over for the entire history of men at sea. And for good reason. It is only the captain who has been trained to command his ship. It is only the captain who has earned the trust and respect of his men by taking them to sea and bringing them home alive. It is only the captain who has the absolute authority of life and death over every man aboard. The *starpom* is only in training for the job, and the *zampolit* is nothing more than the Party hack.

Everyone knows the system and the law, but there's probably never been a warship on which at least one of the crew has not thought about mutiny. Captains have to make dozens, if not hundreds, of decisions every single day their ship is at sea. If a captain is under stress, such as during a storm or time of war, his orders come even faster and must be instantly obeyed for the safety of the ship and his crew.

No one can agree with every order, nor can every order please everyone or even be understandable, say, to a kid fresh off the farm and out of boot camp.

Over time these kinds of misunderstandings and resentments can lead to a full-blown mutiny. Some little incident provides the spark, rage boils over, and a part of the crew takes over the ship. Like with the *Potemkin* sixty years earlier. People get killed. The survivors go to prison.

Another separate class of mutinies exists in which one of the men aboard ship, and it's usually an officer, wants to make a statement, sometimes about a tyrannical captain, as in the case aboard the British sailing vessel *Bounty,* or sometimes, like this moment at a mooring in the Daugava River, a *zampolit* wants to make a statement about the rotten government he serves under.

Something dreadful has happened that Gindin, who has just dropped his black backgammon piece into the basket in the midshipmen's dining hall, has no way of knowing. Only three men at this moment share that knowledge, Potulniy, Sablin, and Seaman Shein, the sailor in the projection closet. But everyone else is about to feel the consequences, which carry the very real likelihood that all of them will die.

Earlier that afternoon, when one-third of the crew had been given liberty to go ashore, Sablin had retired alone to his cabin to write a letter outlining exactly what he planned to do this evening. He was going to explain his purpose to the key officers and crew, who would take over the ship and first thing in the morning leave with the rest of the fleet. But instead of heading to the shipyard for his two-week refit, the *Storozhevoy* was going to lay off Leningrad, where Sablin would broadcast his statement to the Soviet people.

It was the same message he'd written to his wife, Nina, and had posted from Baltiysk four days ago just before they'd sailed up here. He carefully folded this letter and sealed it in a plain white envelope on which he wrote: *Cptn. Potulniy.*

Next, he called Seaman Shein to his cabin. Sablin had taken the young mechanic into his confidence before they'd left Baltiysk a couple days ago, promising that if the sailor could convince some of his friends to help with the mutiny Sablin would guarantee their demobilization when it was all over.

It meant that if Shein and his friends helped the *zampolit* they would get orders allowing them to leave the navy and return home. It was a no-brainer, except that Sablin didn't have the authority. But the kids didn't know that.

Shein's only real worry is that Sablin might be planning to defect to the West with the ship. The seaman has learned to have a lot of respect for the *zampolit,* but he asks point-blank if Sablin is a foreign spy.

Sablin has to laugh. He claps the young man on the shoulder. "If I were a spy I would simply blow up the ship; I wouldn't bother with a mutiny," he says. "Nor would I bother to send a message to the people."

Shein has listened to the tape-recorded message, which made little or no sense to him. He is just a kid from Togliatti, a small town on the remote Chinese border, who got into some trouble and was forced to join the navy or go to jail. What does he know about political statements? All he knows is that if he and the others help out, the *zampolit* will get them out of the navy.

"If this goes wrong, we'll all be shot," Shein argues. He's frightened, and it shows. "The KGB doesn't screw around."

"No one's going to get shot; trust me," Sablin promises. "Anyway, if something like that happened it would only be the officers, not the enlisted men."

"I don't want to end up in a gulag, freezing my ass off, eating rats."

"It won't be like that, either," Sablin says. "Are you with me?"

Shein nods a little uncertainly, still not 100 percent sure of anything, except that he would like to get out of the navy and return home.

"Good man," Sablin says, beaming. He hands Shein the envelope addressed to the captain and instructs the seaman to go to the ship's library and pick out a few books that Captain Potulniy might like to read.

Again Shein nods uncertainly, even less sure what's going on. What does getting some books for the captain have to do with a mutiny?

"I want you to take the books and the letter down to sonar parts compartment two," Sablin orders. It's far forward and at just about the lowest point in the ship, except for the bilges, and at this hour of the evening, at a mooring, the compartment will be unmanned. "Then I want you to disconnect the phone and take it out of there."

"Yes, sir," Shein says. He's really confused, but suddenly Sablin makes everything frighteningly clear.

"As soon as you have the compartment ready, let me know. It's where we'll keep the captain after I arrest him."

Shein steps back a pace, the enormity of what they are about to do striking him in the gut. Arrest Captain Potulniy? The captain is not a bad man. In fact, Shein has never exchanged so much as one word with him. And it's not the captain who's at fault for what Sablin preaches is a failure of trust by Moscow.

Sablin pulls a Makarov 9mm pistol out of a drawer. "Take this, and when you're finished belowdecks go directly to the midshipmen's dining hall, and I'll meet you." He grins. "Right now Comrade Mauser is empty, but I'll give you the magazine in plenty of time."

"I don't want to shoot anybody," Shein complains.

"Not to worry, Alexander, you won't have to shoot anybody," Sablin says, getting to his feet. "I promise you. Now hurry and get the compartment ready for our guest; we don't have much time left."

Shein turns and leaves, but before he does Sablin can read the confusion and worry in the boy's eyes. To this point Shein had been led to believe that Captain Potulniy was going along with the plot. There was going to be a mutiny, but in name only, because the captain himself would be a part of the conspiracy. It is a small white lie, in Sablin's mind, but a necessary lie to ensure that everything goes well.

If Potulniy gets so much as a whiff of the plot before he is secured in the compartment below, he will sound the alarm and fight back. At that point all of Sablin's carefully laid plans will be reduced to nothing more than an exercise in futility.

A dangerous exercise in futility, because officers who attempt mutiny and fail at it get their nine ounces. A 9mm bullet to the back of the head.

The next fifteen minutes while Sablin waits for Shein to report back that the sonar compartment is ready are difficult for Sablin, who paces his compartment. This part of the plot wouldn't have been so critical if Potulniy had gone ashore this afternoon for a few hours of liberty. Sablin had planned on going with the captain and somehow ditching him in Riga.

How Sablin had planned accomplishing that part will probably never be known, but he was, if nothing else, a romantic, and ditching the captain ashore sounded swashbuckling.

But Potulniy refused. He had too much work to do aboard before they sailed for the shipyards tomorrow. Which was too bad, because Sablin had a real respect for the captain, and everybody knew it.

Shein appears back at Sablin's cabin. "It's done," he says, a little breathlessly. His face is pale and his brow sweaty.

"Good," Sablin says. "Now get yourself to the midshipmen's dining hall and wait for me."

"What about the bullets?"

"As soon as I'm finished with the captain," Sablin says. "Now go!"

When Shein disappears down the corridor, Sablin takes a moment to compose himself before he rushes to the captain's cabin and without knocking throws the door open.

Potulniy, in shirtsleeves, is sitting at his desk doing some paperwork, and he looks up in surprise. "What is it, Valery?"

"Captain we have a CP!" Sablin shouts. It is a *Chrez'vychainoy Polozhenie,* a situation.

"What has happened?" Potulniy demands, getting to his feet.

"Some men are drinking belowdecks, in the supply compartment," Sablin reports. "Captain, I think they mean to do some damage unless they're stopped."

"We'll see about that," Potulniy snaps. "Come with me."

He rushes forward and down ladder after ladder, deep into the forward bowels of the ship, his *zampolit* right on his heels.

Reaching the sonar compartment, Potulniy looks over his shoulder. "Here?"

"Yes, Captain, just inside," Sablin says.

The captain pulls open the hatch and climbs down into the compartment. The moment his head clears the level of the deck, Sablin slams the hatch shut and dogs it down.

"Valery, what are you doing?" Potulniy shouts. At this point he has no comprehension of what is happening.

"Saving the Soviet Union," Sablin calls back, and even to his ears the statement seems grandiose.

"What are you talking about? Let me out of here. That's an order!"

"I can't do that, Captain, not until later. For now, most of the officers and I are taking control of the ship."

"Mutiny?" Poltuniy screams. "You bastards. You'll all hang."

"What I'm doing is just as much for your benefit as for the Rodina's. Can't you see?"

"I thought you were my friend."

"I am. Believe me, Anatoly, I am your best friend."

"Then why are you doing this? Have you gone insane?"

"We're going to broadcast on radio and television directly to the people."

"Broadcast what?"

"A call for revolution. A return to the true meanings of Marx and Lenin. We're tired of the lies, tired of the stagnation, tired of having no say in our future. Can't you see—?"

Potulniy slams something that sounds like a piece of metal against the hatch. "You bastard! You miserable fucking traitor! Let me out now!"

Sablin steps back, his heart pounding nearly out of his chest, until he finally catches his breath. He makes certain that the hatch is truly locked, then turns and heads back up to the midshipmen's dining hall, for the next part of the mutiny to unfold.

MUTINY

The act of mutiny is punishable by death in just about every navy in the world. Even failing to report a suspicion that someone else aboard ship is about to commit mutiny can be punishable by death. National governments take this crime *very* seriously.

Technically, mutiny is a crime of nothing more than disobeying a legal order. If the captain says, "Scrub the decks," and the sailors refuse, they may be court-martialed for mutiny. The reason the crewmen disobey the order doesn't matter; all that matters is that the order was a lawful one.

That means the captain of a ship has been placed in charge of the vessel and his crew. *Every* order the captain issues is, by definition, a legal one, unless of course it goes against all common sense or is clearly against the Geneva Convention. But even then the issue is almost impossible to prove, because the benefit of the doubt always lies with the captain. According to the British Royal Navy's Articles of War (1757), which most nations, including the Soviet Union, adopted:

ARTICLE 19: If any person in or belonging to the fleet shall make or endeavor to make any mutinous assembly upon any pretence whatsoever, every person offending herein, and being convicted thereof by the sentence of the court martial, shall suffer death: and if any person in or belonging to the fleet shall utter any words of sedition or mutiny, he shall suffer death, or such other punishment as a court martial shall deem him to deserve: and if any officer, mariner or soldier on or belonging to the fleet, shall behave himself with contempt to his superior officer, being in the execution of his office, he shall be punished according to the nature of his offence by the judgment of a court martial.

ARTICLE 20: If any person in the fleet shall conceal any traitorous or mutinous practice or design, being convicted thereof by the sentence of a court martial, he shall suffer death, or any other punishment as a court martial shall think fit; and if any person, in or belonging to the fleet, shall conceal any traitorous or mutinous words spoken by any, to the prejudice of his majesty or government, or any words, practice, or design, tending to the hindrance of the service, and shall not forthwith reveal the same to the commanding officer, or being present at any mutiny or sedition, shall not use his utmost endeavours to suppress the same, he shall be punished as a court martial shall think he deserves.

Probably the most famous of all mutinies was that of HMS *Bounty* in the spring of 1789, when First Officer Fletcher Christian and twenty-six sailors of the forty-four crewmen arrested Captain William Bligh and the eighteen remaining crew and set them adrift in a twenty-three-foot launch in the middle of the Pacific Ocean. That story and its aftermath have been the stuff of books, articles, novels, and, in the last seventy years or so, movies.

In at least one aspect the incident aboard the *Bounty* was similar to that of the *Storozhevoy*—how the officer who mutinied felt about his captain. Aboard the *Bounty*, Christian and Bligh were close personal friends, and aboard *Storozhevoy* Sablin and Potulniy had gotten along from day one. They had a mutual respect for each other. That's one of the reasons the captain so blindly followed Sablin's lead down into the bowels of the warship, where he could so easily be locked up.

When the *Bounty* sailed from Spithead, England, two days before Christmas 1787, she carried Captain Bligh, who was the only commissioned officer aboard, and a crew of forty-five men. Most crewmen aboard British men-of-war at that time were pressed into service. Very few of the ordinary sailors were volunteers. In fact, the author Samuel Johnson complained often and bitterly about the practice, writing that "no man will be a sailor who had contrivance enough to get himself into jail, for being in a ship is like being in jail with the chance of being drowned . . . and a man in jail has more room, better food, and commonly better company."

But it was different aboard the *Bounty* because every man in the crew had volunteered for the cruise. So there wasn't supposed to be any trouble. At least that's what Bligh and Christian thought at the beginning.

Bligh was a short, stout man with thick black hair, pale blue eyes, and a milky, almost albino complexion. But he knew what he was doing. He'd gone to sea at the age of sixteen as an ordinary seaman, but less than a year after he'd signed on he was given his warrant as a midshipman because he was bright, energetic, and earnest. He loved being in the navy, and he put every bit of his heart and soul into being the best officer he could be.

By the time Bligh had turned twenty-three his reputation was such that Captain James Cook tapped him to be the navigator for the famous South Pacific explorations of the fabled Tahiti and beyond. When the expedition was all over, Cook couldn't write enough good things in the ship's log about Bligh, and in fact the nautical charts that the young navigator drew from that expedition were so good, so precise, that many of them were still in use more than two centuries later.

Near the end of the expedition, Cook was killed by natives in the Hawaiian Islands, and it was Bligh who brought Cook's ship, HMS *Resolution,* back to England, which was a pretty good bit of navigating for a man not yet twenty-five.

War broke out with France, and Bligh did a good job in the fleet, earning a promotion to lieutenant, got married to Elizabeth Bethman, was appointed master of HMS *Cambridge,* and got to know and become friends with Fletcher Christian, who taught him how to use the sextant and who, he wrote in his diary, treated him like a "brother."

Then disaster struck in the form of peace. England cut its navy in half and Bligh, like just about every officer, had his pay cut in half. But his wife was rich and she had connections, so Bligh was given command of a merchant ship, the *Britannia,* which sailed to the West Indies and back on a regular schedule. Fletcher Christian also served aboard, and their friendship grew and solidified.

In 1787 Bligh was given command of the *Bounty,* technically HMAV (Her Majesty's Armed Vessel) *Bounty,* for which he had to take another pay cut. Navy men were paid less than merchant marine officers. But he saw it as a chance for promotion. The deal was that if he made it back from the South Pacific in one piece he would be promoted to captain. And that was a big prize.

A lot of things were happening in the world at about that time. In Europe the French Revolution was getting off the ground, in America the Constitution was being voted on, and in England George III was being battered by the prestigious Royal Society to do something—anything—that would promote England scientifically or economically. The war with the colonies had been lost; it was time to get past it. England needed to save some serious face in the world arena. And Bligh, who needed to do the same for his own career, was just the man for the job.

The situation wasn't all that dissimilar to Potulniy's. He came from a naval background, and already as a sixteen-year-old he had been accepted to attend the Frunze Military Academy. He did his apprenticeship aboard a number of warships, and when the *Storozhevoy's* keel was laid he was tapped to be the ship's first commander.

That was a big opportunity for Potulniy to prove himself. A lot of things were happening in the world in 1974. The Cold War between the Soviet Union and the United States was at its height, the United States had beaten Russia to the moon, and already the seeds of the people's discontent with Moscow were like brush fires, easy to spot but difficult to extinguish.

And there were a lot of similarities between Christian and Sablin. Both men had been born to well-to-do families; both knew what they wanted to do very early on—Christian went to sea at sixteen, and Sablin applied for and was accepted to the Frunze Military Academy at the same age. Both were about the same height and build, both had dark hair and complexions, and both men were described by friends as being mild, open, humane, generous, and sometimes a little conceited.

Bligh and his crew were to sail the *Bounty* down to Tahiti in the South Pacific via Cape Horn at the southern tip of the Americas to take on as many breadfruit plants as they could carry and bring them to the West Indies. The plantation owners wanted something cheap to feed their slaves, and breadfruit, which grew in Polynesia but not in the West Indies, was just the thing. This trip was just as much political as it was humanitarian. The plantation owners were a rich and therefore a powerful political faction, and the king wanted to appease them.

The *Bounty* had started her life as a coal ship named *Bethia*. And despite the bad luck associated with changing a ship's name, as soon as the collier had been converted into a warship she got a new name. In effect Bligh and his crew were the first to sail the *Bounty*, as Potulniy and his crew were the first to sail the *Storozhevoy*.

At 215 tons, the *Bounty* was ninety feet on deck and was armed with four four-pounders and ten swivel guns. Because space had been made to carry the breadfruit plants, there wasn't a lot of room aboard for the young crew, who ranged in age from fourteen to thirty-nine.

Like with Potulniy and his crew there was a certain distance between Bligh and his sailors. It was a gap that was filled by Sablin aboard the *Storozhevoy* and by Christian aboard the *Bounty*. The ordinary crewmen liked and respected those officers, who both had sympathetic ears.

Bligh had learned early in his career that ships are run by men and that men needed to be well cared for if they were to do their jobs well. To combat scurvy, a disease resulting from deficiency of vitamin C that was very common in those days, Bligh made sure that sauerkraut was served at every meal. And he also knew that exercise was vitally important, so he brought aboard a blind fiddler named Michael Byrne to play music to which the men could dance. No one liked it, but the crew *was* kept fit. Just like the Russian farm boys aboard the *Storozhevoy* exercising every day up on deck, it was one of those systems in the military that worked.

The *Bounty*'s crew bitched about the food and they bitched about the exercise, but Bligh just stamped around on deck and swore at them. He wasn't going to give any consideration to their complaints. He was the captain and that was the end of it. If they wanted to grumble, they could bitch to Christian for all Bligh cared.

But Bligh, like Potulniy, wasn't a bad man, even though he was mostly aloof from his crew. For instance, he split the ship's company into three watches, instead of the normal two, which was unusual for that day. It made duty much easier. The men could get some rest between watches. And after trying to get around Cape Horn for nearly thirty days, being pushed back into the Atlantic by storm after storm, he thanked his crew for a valiant effort, then turned tail and headed for the Pacific by the longer, but easier, route across the Atlantic and around the southern tip of Africa.

The *Bounty* arrived in Tahiti in the late fall of 1788 and had to remain at anchor for nearly six months until it was the proper season to harvest the immature breadfruit plants. This was Bligh's big mistake. Six months with no sea duty, at an island filled with good-looking and very willing Polynesian women, for whom white men were a novelty, corrupted the crew. Compared to England, and especially compared to life aboard ship, Tahiti was a paradise. Many of the men had girlfriends, and in six months a lot of the relationships were just as strong as any new marriage. When it was time to leave, a lot of the men didn't want to go. A few of them even deserted, hiding up in the hills, where they hoped to wait it out until the *Bounty* sailed away.

But Bligh would have none of that. He took a party and searched the island, finally rounding up the deserters after three weeks of tromping through the mountains and jungles. But he was a humane man. Instead of flogging them and then hanging them from the yardarms, as was the practice, he just had them flogged.

The *Bounty* finally weighed anchor in the spring of 1789, loaded to the gills with breadfruit plants and a very unhappy crew, miserable that they were being made to leave paradise. Bligh stormed around the deck, swearing and bitching, especially at Christian, all day long, every day, and yet each night Christian was invited to dine with the suddenly civilized captain.

Like Potulniy, who never suspected that Sablin would turn against him, Bligh never had the slightest suspicion that Christian would lead a mutiny. Such an act was utterly unthinkable.

A couple of weeks out from Tahiti, Christian decided to build a raft, jump ship, and somehow try to make it back to Tahiti, where he'd had a warm relationship with the chief's daughter. He confided in one of the midshipmen, who warned that there were sharks in the water.

"Anyway, if you want to do something like that, why not do away with the old man and take the ship?" the midshipman may have said. "Most of the crew would be with you, sir."

Christian ran the idea past a few of the crewmen, who agreed. That early morning of April 28, 1789, Christian broke into the arms chest, distributed the weapons to his supporters, and arrested Bligh.

The captain, still in his nightshirt, was brought up on deck, and the assembled crew was asked who wanted to get off the ship with Bligh. Thirty of them raised their hands, and Bligh pleaded that he had a wife and four children and asked for some kind of mercy.

"It's too late for that," Christian told the captain. "You have forced us through hell these past weeks, and now there's no turning back."

Some of the men who wanted to go with Bligh were forced to stay behind, because there was no room for them aboard the captain's gig. So Bligh and eighteen of his crew were set adrift with enough food and water for only five days.

Sablin knew the story, of course, and the next parts must have given him some pause. Captain Bligh made it back to civilization after a forty-eight-day voyage in which he had to ration the food and battle storms, losing only one man when they tried to come ashore for provisions on an island filled with cannibals.

For that tremendous feat of seamanship Bligh was court-martialed, acquitted, promoted to captain, and given command of HMS *Providence*, plus an escort vessel, *Assistant*, and was sent back to Tahiti for more breadfruit. This time without trouble.

Bligh, on the one hand, wrote a couple of successful books about the *Bounty* mutiny and then was involved in two other mutinies, including one while he was governor of New South Wales in Australia in 1805. Bligh died in 1817, with the rank of Vice-Admiral of the Blue, a well-decorated hero.

The mutineer Christian, on the other hand, wasn't so lucky. He conned the *Bounty* back to Tahiti, where they picked up the Tahitian women and a few Tahitian men, and eventually they made their way to the remote island of Pitcairn, where he burned the ship to the waterline to prevent anyone from escaping and reporting their whereabouts.

The Polynesian men and the white crew were unhappy almost from the start. And within less than three years five of the original *Bounty* crew, including Fletcher Christian, and all the Polynesian men, were murdered.

Then, one by one, the Tahitian women killed all but two of the original mutineers, leaving only John Adams and Ned Young. Young died of natural causes in 1800.

The officers and midshipmen looking down the barrel of the gun in the midshipmen's dining hall could not even guess at what prospects Sablin was facing, except that all of them knew that an invisible line had been crossed that would change all of their lives forever.

No matter what choice any of them made.

Even the U.S. Uniform Code of Military Justice is specific on this point:

> . . . [a member of the crew] who fails to do his or her utmost to prevent and suppress a mutiny or sedition being committed in his or her presence, or fails to take all reasonable means to inform his or her superior commissioned officer or commanding officer of a mutiny or sedition which he or she knows or has reason to believe is taking place is guilty of a failure to suppress or report a mutiny or sedition. [Violations of this article can be punishable by death.]

THE OFFICERS DIVIDED

Gindin has made his choice and is waiting for the other officers to make theirs—white or black. Some of them seem to have calmed down a little. Maybe they think that this is some sort of a joke after all, or maybe it's simply that they are whistling as they pass the grave-yard, gallows humor. Among the others only Lieutenant Sergey Kuzmin, the sonar systems officer from BCH-3, acts like he's taking Sablin's insane proposal seriously. Kuzmin had a bad marriage that will end in a divorce, but it hasn't soured him on women, and he and Gindin often talked about the day they would settle down with a wife.

Kuzmin is the same height as Sablin, only his hair is blond and he has a tiny mustache. He walks up to the table and faces their *zampolit* eye to eye and drops a black game piece into the basket. Sablin doesn't have the same reaction he had with Gindin; maybe it's because he expected Kuzmin to vote against the mutiny or thought that because Gindin was a Jew and hated the system there was more hope.

Kuzmin comes back to his seat, and one by one all the officers cast their votes. Besides Gindin and Kuzmin, those voting against mutiny include Captain Lieutenant Nikolay Proshutinsky, who is commander of BCH-3, Senior Lieutenants Smirnov and Vinogradov, and Warrant Officers Gritsa, Khokhlov, and Zhitenev.

Which leaves Lieutenant Dudnik going along with the mutiny and midshipmen Viktor Borodai, Gomenchuk, and Kalinichev also each dropping a white backgammon piece into the basket.

Everyone has voted now, except for Gindin's roommate and best friend, Firsov, who slowly gets to his feet and approaches the table where Sablin is standing. Vladimir is clutching a backgammon piece in his right hand so tightly his knuckles have turned white. No one is making any noise now, not because they are concerned about Firsov's vote but because all of them are finally beginning to realize the enormity of what is happening. Gindin just wants his friend to drop the black piece into the basket and find out what happens next.

Firsov reaches over the basket and drops the game piece. But his body is blocking Gindin from seeing the color—white or black. When Firsov turns around to face the room it is impossible to tell from his expression how he voted, but Gindin is worried because Vladimir is not returning to his seat. He stands at Sablin's left as if he wants to say something, as if he wants to explain to Gindin what he's just done.

"This vote shows who is with us and who is against us," Sablin says. He doesn't seem as sure of himself as he did just two minutes ago. In fact, he seems resigned, which as far as Gindin is concerned is another bad sign. "I am giving you one last chance to change your minds. This is the most important decision of your lives."

"It's the most important decision of your life, Captain," Gindin says from where he's gone back to his seat at one of the tables. "You'll kill us all if you go though with a mutiny. You should know this."

"I'm doing this not to kill you, but to save your lives!" Sablin cries passionately. "You must be able to see this. Our government must be thrown out before it's too late for all of us. We need another revolution, the time is now, and this ship will be the spark that begins it."

Gindin is at a loss for words, finally. Maybe this is a test after all.

At length Sablin nods. He understands the situation, probably better than anyone else in the room, although his idealism will probably be his undoing. "I will ask those officers who voted against me not to stand in our way."

No one moves a muscle; no one says a word.

He nods again. "Very well. I would like everyone who voted against us to leave the room."

Still no one makes a move. "We were afraid of our own shadows," Gindin recalls. And he wanted to find out how Firsov had voted.

Finally someone stands up, Gindin can't remember who, but then he is on his feet with the others, and they shuffle out from behind the tables and timidly approach the door they came through. "We didn't know where we were supposed to go," Gindin says. "Certainly not to our duty stations. Maybe back to our quarters, or perhaps up on deck where we could have a smoke and talk about what was happening." Sablin said they would not be leaving Riga until morning, so there was still time to do something. What that might be no one had a clue, but at least they had overnight to figure something out.

But Firsov is not joining the officers leaving the midshipmen's dining hall. His backgammon piece was white. He has voted to go with Sablin. Firsov has voted to mutiny.

"I could not believe my eyes," Gindin says of that moment. "It felt as if a speeding train had just run through my head." Thoughts and emotions tumble end over end in his gut. A dozen questions he hasn't even been able to form yet are seething to the surface from some cauldron deep within his Russian soul. He feels confused, betrayed, deceived, more frightened than he's ever been to this point in his life. Why had Vladimir chosen to side with Sablin? It made no sense. Was Vladimir completely out of his mind? Was he flustered? "Maybe he was trying to save his own life," Gindin muses.

A couple of the officers who'd voted to go along with the mutiny get to their feet and stand beside Sablin as if the *zampolit*'s rank or power might protect them.

Gindin wants to ask again what has happened to the captain, but the vastness of the chasm that has opened before him and the shock of Firsov's betrayal strike him speechless for those few moments.

One of the officers opens the door. Metal chains have been stretched across the corridor to the left and the right, blocking them from returning to their duty stations or from going up on deck. The only path for them is through an open door directly across the hall and down a companionway to the next deck below. It occurs to Gindin, and probably the others, that they are being herded like sheep. Or, more darkly, like lambs to the slaughter.

Gindin's fear spikes, yet he doesn't call out in alarm. Nor does anyone speak, because a stocky enlisted man holding a large Makarov is standing in the corridor just beyond the chain to the left. He is scowling, and he looks as if he means business. Sablin has promised the enlisted men the moon. He is the one officer they can trust. They will do anything for him, even kill the other officers if it comes to that. Gindin and the others read something of that from the young man's expression.

The first officers through the door into the corridor pull up short when they are confronted by the sailor with the gun and try to turn back, creating a logjam.

Gindin spins around, but Shein has stepped out of the projector closet and he, too, is holding a big Makarov pistol in his meaty hand, and he, too, looks as if he means business. There will be no turning back. They have no other choice than to cross the hall and take the companionway stairs down to the lower deck, though what awaits them below is anyone's guess, but Gindin is truly afraid for his life now. Not only from the authorities when word of the mutiny gets out but also from his *zampolit* and his armed crewmen.

Gindin makes a last, mute appeal to his roommate, but Firsov looks away. He cannot meet Gindin eye to eye. Vladimir is embarrassed, and Gindin believes that is a positive sign.

He turns back again to follow the other officers out of the mid-shipmen's dining hall, and he feels a faint glimmer of hope that Firsov will come to his senses at some point and stop this madness from going any further.

It's up to Firsov now.

Across the corridor they climb down the steep, vertical stairs about three and half meters to where another enlisted man with a pistol is waiting for them at an open door into one of the sonar parts compart-ments.

The situation is bizarre. No one says a word at first; no one is ob-jecting; no one is giving orders. The officers climb down the stairs and one by one soundlessly enter the compartment.

When everyone is inside, the sailor looks in at them with utter con-tempt in his eyes. "Sit down," he tells them. "Keep your mouths shut and no one will get hurt."

Suddenly the situation is filled with high melodrama, like the Amer-ican cowboy movies that the theaters sometimes show.

The sailor slams the door and dogs the latches, locking them in.

One of the officers bangs an open palm against the bulkhead. "Hey!" he shouts at the top of his lungs. "We're in here; let us out!"

"Shut your mouth!" the sailor just outside the door shouts back. "No noise!"

"In one instant everything had been turned upside down," Gindin says. "We were in the position of taking orders from an enlisted man with a gun. We had to obey his instructions. There was nothing else for us to do."

THE GATHERING STORM

Sablin's wife, Nina, has gotten the letter about the mutiny that her husband posted four days earlier at Baltiysk, but she's not told anyone in authority about it. So far as Moscow is concerned, nothing has happened yet, nor is anything about to happen. It's just another day after a holiday in the Soviet Union. Tomorrow morning everyone will get back to work.

Yesterday, when Seaman Shein was ashore on liberty after the parade he sent letters to his sister and best friend back home telling them what he was about to do. His biggest worry was that Sablin was actually a spy and intended to defect to the West. Probably to Sweden. In that case they would be doomed. There would be no way out of it for any of them. Shein wanted to explain that he believed the *zampolit* was a man of his word, who merely wanted to send a message to the Russian people about their rotten government. In return for helping him, all the sailors were promised an early out from the navy. No one wanted to be a traitor. All of them loved the Soviet Union; so Shein maintained. But all of them wanted to get out of the military and go home. Was that so terrible?

And no one was really afraid of the KGB's retaliation after this thing was finished, if they didn't think about it too hard. Sablin was the *zampolit;* his word was practically the same as a promise from the Communist Party itself.

In the West the workers have to accept the fact that there will be rich people and that there will be poor people, Sablin tells Shein and the other enlisted men. It's a fact of life that cannot be denied. But in a socialist system all that is supposed to be different. There cannot be rich people and poor people. We're all alike! We must all be equal!

Communism is the highest form of civilization.

"So, what has gone wrong in Mother Russia?" Sablin asks rhetorically. "There is a clear contradiction between the words and the deeds in the Soviet Union. Everyone knows this in his heart of hearts. It is up to us to talk openly about the issues. Force Moscow to listen to the hearts and minds of our people."

"What is the use of all this stupid window dressing?" Shein asks Sablin at one point. Shein's comment is typical of the cynicism throughout the country. "When we go to war, who are we supposed to defend with all this fancy talk?"

None of Sablin's enlisted crew think much about the consequences of their support of the *zampolit.* They're going home soon, and that's all that counts.

Even most of the midshipmen seemed sanguine. The crew thought highly of Captain Third Rank Sablin, according to Viktor Borodai. But the captain had warned Sablin more than once about getting too close to the enlisted crew. A warning that he never heeded.

For Seaman Shein it started one evening when Sablin called him into the dining room where the political lectures were given. The enlisted man had no idea what the *zampolit* wanted with him, but orders were orders.

"I have a question for you, Sasha," Sablin says.

Shein nods uncertainly. He's never been talked to like this by an officer. He doesn't know what to say or how to act. This is new territory for a kid from Togliatti.

"How would you like to work for the KGB?"

It's like a hot poker has been stuck up his ass. He's disappointed and pissed off. After everything the *zampolit* has taught them about honor and equality and the true meaning of Communism, now he's recruiting his crew to be spies, informers for the KGB.

Shein turns on his heel and starts toward the door. He may get in trouble for walking out on an officer, but he doesn't have to stand there taking that kind of shit.

"Wait, Sasha!" Sablin cries. "You have to calm down! I was just making a little test. I don't want you to be angry with me."

Shein turns back. He's confused. What's he supposed to do? What in heaven's name can Sablin want with him?

"I want you to sit down now," Sablin says, his voice lower. "I want to talk to you. This is serious stuff."

Sablin had an agenda from the start, and nothing in heaven or on earth would stop him. He meant to take his message to the people.

"Moscow has betrayed the October Revolution, so it's time now for another revolution. All it will take is a bold stroke and positive leadership and the workers will rise up again. They will be with us, Sasha. I need you to be with me!"

That was three days ago, and this evening the first seeds of Sablin's revolution are beginning to sprout.

Once the officers and midshipmen who had voted with the black pieces are safely locked up below, Sablin sends Shein down to the forward port compartment to stand guard over Potulniy in case the captain figures out a way to escape.

Next Sablin gets on the 1MC and calls a muster of all the crew on the quarterdeck for ten minutes after eight. This will be the moment of truth. A few officers and a handful of midshipmen cannot operate the *Storozhevoy* without the help of most of the crew. If he has the enlisted men behind him, Sablin knows that he has a real shot at doing this thing, actually disconnecting from the mooring in the morning and getting under way up to Leningrad, where he can broadcast his message of the new revolution directly to the people.

Most of the crew has already returned from liberty ashore. Those in the dining room watching the movie and those in their quarters or already up on deck having a smoke are the first to pull on their winter coats and form up on the aft deck. The others, either on duty or, like Shein, armed and guarding someone, have already been recruited by Sablin. They are his core supporters.

Now it is up to him to convince the bulk of the crew that what he is asking of them is not only necessary but also right and just and that they will have a real chance of succeeding.

The evening is turning surreal in more than one way. A fairly thick fog has formed so that the shore is mostly lost, but the quarterdeck is bathed in a strong white light from the spreaders, and straight overhead the stars are visible, as is a full moon. It's as if the *Storozhevoy* and his crew have been transported to a distant universe and for all practical purposes are utterly alone.

Sablin hesitates at a midship hatch before going out on deck and heading aft to confront the crew. He is wearing his black winter coat, with officer's shoulder boards, and a standard-issue Makarov pistol in a belt holster. His heart was racing earlier in the midshipmen's dining hall when he was talking to the officers, but he's calmed down now. In any event, the die has been cast and there's no way of reversing the clock.

He's about to step outside when he becomes aware that something is going on belowdecks. He can plainly hear that someone is shouting. It sounds like Potulniy.

Sablin turns and races downstairs as fast as his feet will carry him.

"Sablin is a traitor!" Potulniy shouts. His voice is faint, coming all the way forward near the bow of the ship, but the message is clear nevertheless. There's trouble.

Coming around a corner, Sablin yanks the pistol out and plays with the safety catch. He's not much of a shot, but he does know how to fire the weapon.

He pulls up short. Shein is standing at the end of the short corridor in front of the hatch to the sonar compartment where the captain is being held prisoner. The seaman has a dazed, frightened look on his broad peasant's face. He looks like a deer suddenly caught in the headlights of an onrushing truck.

"Sablin is a traitor!" Potulniy shouts again.

Standing in front of Shein are three of the warrant officers who voted with white backgammon pieces: Gomenchuk, Kalinichev, and Borodai.

"What's going on?" Sablin demands. "The crew has assembled up on deck. They're waiting for me!"

"I tried to stop them, but they wouldn't listen," Shein stammers.

"Stop who?" Sablin shouts.

"Valery, is that you?" Potulniy cries. "Let me out of here. Don't be a fool." It's more than obvious that the captain is hopping mad, and the warrant officers are clearly distressed. They didn't count on this complication.

"A couple of sailors down here heard the captain and they tried to be heroes and rescue him," Borodai explains. "We stopped them."

But there is no one else in the corridor. "Where are they?" Sablin wants to know. He's getting shaky again. "Have you locked them away?"

Borodai shakes his head. "There was no reason for it. They won't cause any trouble now."

"They'll tell the rest of the crew!"

"Comrade *zampolit,* isn't that exactly what you intend to do on deck?" Borodai asks politely. "By now just about everybody aboard knows that something is going on. So maybe you should get up there and explain the situation."

Sablin's heart is racing. He is torn with indecision, even though he knows what has to be done. "Shoot the next man who tries to release the captain," he gives the order to Shein. "Do you understand me?"

Shein nods that he understands.

Sablin gives the warrant officers a bleak look, then turns on his heel and, holstering his pistol, races back up to the assembled crew on the quarterdeck.

On deck, in the shadows just around the corner from where the men are assembled, Sablin stops a moment to compose himself. The message he's going to tell these boys is the same one he told the officers an hour ago. Only this time he'll use easier words, simpler sentences, more clear-cut concepts, and above all a flair for the dramatic and an appeal to their patriotism.

There's probably not a boy among them, not even among the cynics, the self-proclaimed tough guys, who doesn't get misty when the idea of defending the Rodina is presented to them. These boys have the black Russian soil beneath their fingernails and the sad Russian songs in their souls; they will jump at the chance to come to the Motherland's rescue against all enemies—Americans or Moscow bureaucrats.

When Sablin steps out into the light, someone calls the crew to attention, and they snap to.

When Sablin takes his position at the head of the formation he does not guess that word of the mutiny has already spread like wildfire among the crew. Shein and the few other enlisted men Sablin has taken into his confidence have convinced the others that once this necessary business is over they can all go home.

Zampolit Sablin has given his solemn promise.

He hesitates for a moment, mustering the correct words. This is a singular moment in time. He actually feels the long history of the Russian navy stretching back four hundred years. He is becoming an important part of that history.

"We cannot go on like this any longer," he begins. "You have been lied to. We all have been lied to, even the officers. The Rodina is on the verge of defeat. But the real enemy is not across the ocean, he is right here in the Motherland, and we must do something before it is too late for us all."

Not one of the 150 enlisted men assembled says a word. No one moves a muscle. It's obvious that they are surprised by what their *zampolit* is saying to them, even if they don't yet fully understand what they are being told. But like Sablin they understand that this is a moment in time that none of them will ever forget.

"I offer no criticism of the Communist Party or of the October Revolution. Those are pure. But there are men in Moscow who are bringing the Rodina to her knees like a common whore. Your mothers and sisters have been told so many lies that they may have to go begging on the streets. They may have to get down on their hands and knees just to feed their families! To feed you fine boys!"

There is a stirring now among the assembly. Sablin is painting a dramatic, if dreary, picture of what will happen unless they do something about the sickness and corruption that has gripped Moscow.

"The people of Russia—your fathers and your brothers—have no rights! They're starving while a few old men in the Kremlin drink champagne and eat caviar and blinis.

"Brezhnev and his pals are making fools of you. It is finally up to us, the men in the military, to protect our Motherland from the real enemy, and we must let the people know what we are doing.

"Russia must finally become the democracy that Lenin promised us, or else we will remain a backward country, a poor country with no opportunities."

The first of the rumbling dissent begins, and Sablin's heart picks up a pace. He has them now!

"We need new leaders to run the country! Leaders whom the people will elect! Honest men who are patriots, willing to do as *we* tell them, not as they tell us!"

Sablin is overcome by his own words.

"The Party leaders in Moscow are getting rich off the labors of your fathers and brothers, and the heroic sacrifices of your mothers and sisters. It must end now!"

The murmuring is getting louder. These sailors, most of them twenty or younger, are being moved by the *zampolit*'s impassioned words.

"I want you to follow me to Kronshtadt, where we will go on television and take this message directly to the people," Sablin tells the crew.

"I have spoken with honest officers in many military units all across the country who agree with me. They have promised to rise up to support us, if we will only lead the way."

This is a lie; the only person he's told about his plans who isn't aboard the ship at this moment is his wife. But the crew believes him.

"We'll be lined up and shot!" someone shouts. It's the same fear that Shein had expressed.

"No one will be shot," Sablin assures them. "I'm an officer, and I'm giving you men a direct order. No one in the Soviet navy has ever been shot for obeying a direct order."

"What if we don't agree?" someone else shouts. "What if we just return to our *cubricks?* You can't have a fucking mutiny without us." The speaker is anonymous in the darkness and in the ranks, so he's braver than those in the front row.

"That doesn't matter," Sablin says. "Because I've already told Moscow what we will do. If we don't get out of here in the morning, the KGB will come aboard and arrest us all. You included. So make up your minds right now."

No one says a thing.

"I want to know who is with me!" Sablin cries.

He strides directly to the first man in the formation and looks him directly in the eyes. "Are you with me?"

"Yes, Captain Third Rank!" the young man shouts without hesitation.

Sablin steps to the next man. "And you?"

"I agree," the crewman responds immediately.

The polling of votes goes very quickly. In the end, not one of the crew is against the mutiny.

"You will not regret your decision," Sablin tells them from the head of the formation. "Officers in all the fleets are standing by for word from us to join the revolt."

CAPTIVE

Gindin and the five other officers and three midshipmen who voted against Sablin are locked in a compartment near the bottom of the *Storozhevoy* that is used as a maintenance depot for the ship's main sonar stations. For the next couple of hours they are left to their own devices; in fact, they can hear no sounds of any struggle topsides, no shouting, no gunshots. Nor does anyone come to talk to them or threaten them. But that business is inevitable, and they all know it.

"This is a mutiny," one of the officers says. "And we're a part of it, whether we like it or not."

"What are you talking about?" Vinogradov asks. "We're not part of anything. We voted against Sablin!"

"Yes, but we did nothing to stop him."

"Didn't you see the guns? What did you want to happen, that we be shot down like stupid heroes?"

"Well, we'll probably get our nine ounces in the end," Vinogradov says. "Doesn't matter whose gun it comes from, one of Sablin's cronies from the crew or one of Brehznev's pretty boys from the KGB." He pokes a finger toward Gindin. "What do you think, Boris? Will we get out of this one alive? Or maybe this is a test. Just some sick joke that our *zampolit* has played on us?"

Gindin shakes his head. "This is no joke, and I think we have to find a way to get out of here before Sablin carries it too far."

"He can't get the ship out of here and sail to Kronshtadt without us," Sergey Kuzmin says.

Some of the others are swearing, and a few of them are banging their fists on the metal bulkheads and the door. But they stop suddenly and look across at Sergey. Maybe he has a point and the situation isn't as desperate as they first thought. If Sablin couldn't get out of here in the morning when the rest of the fleet was leaving, someone would come over to investigate, and the jig would be up.

"I'm not so sure," Gindin says. He is remembering the odd conversation he had with Sablin a couple of days ago. The *zampolit* came down to the engineering spaces and asked all sorts of questions about the engines and their control panels.

"*Complicated machinery down here, Boris,*" Sablin said. "*It must be difficult to teach these boys how to do their jobs.*"

"*Not so tough,*" Gindin replies. He's proud of his crew. They are good sailors, for the most part, and he's taught them well.

"*They couldn't be left on their own, if there was an emergency,*" Sablin said. He is looking at gauges on the control panel. "*Say if you were delayed for some reason, they wouldn't know what to do. They'd be lost.*"

"*If it was a big enough emergency and our lives depended on getting under way, they could manage until I could get down here,*" Gindin said.

Now, locked in the compartment, he realizes just how shortsighted he'd been.

"What are you talking about?" Vinogradov demands.

Gindin looks at his fellow officers. All of them have stopped their shouting and banging, and they're all staring at him like he was a man from Mars. "If he has the enlisted crew with him, plus Vladimir and the other officers, he could do it."

"What, start the engines and sail out of here?" Kuzmin demands.

Gindin has talked with some of the other officers who found Sablin's behavior over the past few weeks just as odd as he has. The *zampolit* has been asking a lot of questions.

"I think so," Gindin says.

"Who'll navigate for him?" Vinogradov wants to know.

Gindin shakes his head. "He could head down the river, and once out in the open Baltic he just has to follow his nose."

"So he follows his nose, Boris," Vinogradov asks. "But to where?"

"Sweden," Kuzmin breaks the sudden, dark silence.

"My God," one of the other officers says softly. "The bastard's insane. He means to defect. We're all dead."

"Not unless we can get out of here first," Gindin says. "Sablin told us he wasn't leaving until morning."

"But there's only nine of us," Kuzmin points out. "If he convinced even half the crew to go along with him, there's nothing we could do about it. There's just too many of them. They wouldn't even need guns."

"If we can get out of here we'll find the captain; he'll know what to do," Gindin says.

"If they haven't killed him," someone counters. "Or if he's thrown in with the mutiny, and is just lying low."

Some of the others start to object, but Vinogradov holds up a hand to silence them. "Shut up and listen to me. The captain would never go along with a crazy scheme like this, no matter how convincing Sablin is."

No one says a thing,

"Has anyone seen him this afternoon?"

Still no one says a word. The compartment is absolutely still. They all understand that their lives hang in the balance of a great number of factors, most of which are totally out of their control.

"Maybe Sablin shot him and hid his body somewhere," Vinogradov suggests.

"That's not possible," Gindin says.

"How do you know, Boris? How can you be sure? Are you willing to bet your life, all of our lives, on Sablin's kindness? If he's killed the captain, what's to prevent him from killing us all?"

"I don't know anything for sure," Gindin admits. "Except that unless we get out of here we'll never know."

"If we try to escape, what will our chances be?" one of the officers asks.

"I don't know that, either," Gindin says. "But I know for sure that unless we try our chances will be zero."

The sonar supply compartment is actually two small rooms, equipped with only one work bench, a small closet that contains the power supplies, repeaters, targeting computers, and other electronic equipment that supports the sonar stations, and drawers that contain some non-classified schematics, a set of spare parts and a few screwdrivers, socket sets, and other small maintenance tools and testing gear.

At this point there is no phone in the compartment, nor is there any way in which to signal someone else aboard the ship, other than by banging on the light blue steel bulkheads.

The second, somewhat smaller compartment contains only more built-in drawers that hold more tools and test equipment and some technical manuals, which are supposed to be kept three decks up in the library.

Gindin steps through the open doorway into this compartment and almost immediately spots a water pump bolted to the deck in one corner. Pumps like these are located throughout the ship to move potable water from the tanks below to the various compartments where it's needed. The designers placed the pumps wherever they saw fit in order to minimize the lengths of pipe runs. It is one of those Soviet economy measures that aren't very elegant and don't look good but work.

Some errant thought enters Gindin's mind from way back. It's a lecture or a discussion at the academy about sabotage, what to look for, how to spot it, and how to prevent it. "This was a new territory for me," Gindin says. "My job was always to make sure that all the mechanical systems aboard the *Storozhevoy* worked the way they were designed to work. Thinking about how to prevent Sablin from getting away from Riga by maybe sabotaging the ship was alien to me. And frightening."

DISAPPOINTMENT

The mood among the crew is high with enthusiasm, but Sablin carries a tight knot in his gut. So many things can still go wrong with his plan that he can't help but stop for a moment to reflect on just what it is that he has set in motion this evening. Two hundred officers and men are depending on him to get them through this ordeal. The burden is on his shoulders.

Sablin may be an idealist, but he's far from being a stupid man. He knows that he will have one shot, and only one shot, at surviving this business. If he can convince the Russian people themselves to rise up in revolt, the Kremlin will be all but powerless to stop what he believes will be a groundswell—just like the revolt that toppled the tsarist government in October 1917.

He has worked out a plan for that.

Almost as soon as he had formulated his idea for the mutiny, Sablin began working on a speech that he would broadcast to the Russian people. He has recorded it, and once the *Storozhevoy* is in position near Leningrad and he has been given access to Russian radio and television, he means to broadcast his plea directly to the people.

"... *our announcement is not a betrayal of the Motherland, but a purely political, progressive declaration, and the traitors to the Motherland are those who would seek to stop us.*

"*My comrades want me to pass on to you our assurance that if our nation is attacked, we are fully prepared to defend it. Right now we have another goal: to take up the voice of truth ...*"

But first he has to get away from Riga and the rest of the fleet, and to do that he has to make sure that the ship is secure. For that they will need weapons.

The warshots for all the *Storozhevoy*'s combat systems—the rockets, depth charges, and ammunition for the deck guns—have already been off-loaded before he heads to his refurbishing berth. This is routine. But the ship has two armories of light weapons, mostly pistols and AK-47 assault rifles.

Sablin got a set of keys for one of the armories from their *starpom* Nikolay Novozilov, before the exec went home on leave. Now Sablin takes a few of the enlisted crewmen with him, and they retrieve all the weapons and ammunition they can carry.

Then he begins issuing the orders crucial for their survival until they can slip their mooring and get out into the open Baltic. First he posts two armed crewmen on the bridge to make sure that not only the ship's controls are theirs but also that no one can sneak up and use the radio to call for help.

Next he sends several crewmen belowdecks to help Shein make sure no one tries again to release the captain. Sablin sends others to the sonar compartment where Gindin and the others who voted with the black backgammon pieces are under arrest and one young man with a rifle to guard his cabin.

At this point Sablin has every right to be paranoid, but he wants to prevent someone trying to find the recording of his speech and destroy it.

Finally, he sends men from each division to watch over their own equipment. Among them are several from Gindin's gas turbine division who have as much enthusiasm for the project as everyone else.

"No matter what happens, you must keep in control of the engine room," Sablin tells the kids who are by this time jumping all over the place.

They want to tell their stories about how rotten things are at home and how once they get back everything will be better.

"Of course life will get better once we have elected some proper leaders," Sablin assures them. "But for now no one gets to the engines unless I give the order."

"Yes, sir," they chorus.

"Once everything is secure down there, I want you to get the engines ready to start on an instant's notice. Can you do this?"

One of them nods. "Yes, of course. Our lieutenant is a good man; he taught us—" The kid stops in mid-sentence, a little embarrassed by the betrayal of an officer he actually admires.

"I understand," Sablin says. "None of them will come to any harm. Anyway, this is just as good for them as it is for us."

The embarrassment passes. They're eager to begin.

"As soon as you're ready, call me, or send a runner," Sablin tells them. "Now go, and be careful."

Sablin watches them with real affection as they scurry belowdecks to carry out his orders. He is alone for just that moment, and perhaps he listens to the sounds of the *Storozhevoy*. His ship now. An instrument, like the *Potemkin*, for a nation-changing revolution.

It's chilly up on deck, in the open, and the fog has thickened. He might think that he is alone at this point in time. Not one person aboard this ship has any real idea what he is trying to do for them, for the Rodina. Nor, he supposes, will they understand what has happened even after it is all over with and the revolution has come and gone. Only afterward, when their lives have become materially better, might they stop from time to time to think of what part they played this evening.

When that happens they will feel proud. Sablin is utterly convinced of it, and he is filled with a holy zeal.

He takes a quick turn around the decks to make sure that everything is in order, then ducks through a mid-ship hatch and heads forward to his cabin. He sincerely hopes that when the time is right Potulniy will hear him out with an open mind. He wants to apologize to the captain for the rough treatment. Sablin has to keep reminding himself that under the circumstances there was no other way. Potulniy either had to be placed under arrest or had to be killed, and Sablin will make sure the captain understands just how humanely he was treated.

A crewman, whose name Sablin can't remember, is standing guard in the corridor. He snaps to attention as Sablin comes around the corner. It's obvious that the crewman is almost as frightened as he is excited. He's had a little time to think about the situation that he and the others have gotten themselves into with their captain locked up and their *zampolit* in charge.

"How's it going, Seaman?" Sablin asks kindly. "No trouble here?"

"No, sir."

"That's good. Very good. Just keep a sharp eye."

"Yes, sir," the boy says. He might seem a little less tense now. After all, Sablin is their political officer. Who would know better than such a man?

Sablin enters his cabin and goes directly to his wall safe, where he's locked the reel of tape on which he recorded his speech. But before he can retrieve it, he has another idea. He looks at his wristwatch. It is coming up on nine; the men from the midshipmen's dining hall who voted with the black backgammon pieces have been locked belowdecks for nearly two hours. Maybe some of them have had a change of heart.

He sincerely hopes so. It would be better if he had all of the officers behind him.

"Stay here," he tells the seaman at his door, and he heads down the corridor and below to the compartment.

The two armed sailors guarding the hatch stiffen to attention when Sablin comes around the corner.

"How's it going?" he asks. "Are they giving you any trouble?"

"They were raising some hell to start with," one of the kids reports. "But they finally shut their traps."

"We made sure of it, sir," the other sailor says.

"Open up."

"Sir?"

"Open the hatch; I want to talk to them," Sablin says. Discipline is already starting to get a little ragged. The sailors are taking time responding to clear orders. He expected it, but not so soon. Once they get under way in the morning he hopes moving into action will calm them down.

One of the sailors opens the hatch, and Sablin steps up, though he does not go inside. The nine men are looking at him. Some of them are leaning against the work bench; others are seated on the floor or on the two chairs. Gindin is standing in the doorway to the other section of the compartment.

"Is everything okay in here?" Sablin asks. The question sounds ridiculous even in his ears.

No one says a thing.

"It's twenty-one hundred hours. Would you like some tea?"

Vinogradov steps forward. "Stick it up your ass!"

Sablin rears back. "I don't mean to offer you any harm, or—"

"Get out of here before we tear you apart!" one of the other officers shouts.

"Traitor!"

"Bastard!"

Sablin looks to Gindin. He'd sincerely hoped at least Boris would have changed his mind by now. A man such as Boris should understand the real score, even if the others didn't. But Gindin's expression is stony.

"You'll get us all killed," Kuzmin says. "You'd better get out of here."

Sablin steps back and slams the door.

RAGE

The hatch is dogged with an audible clang.

"You dumb bastards!" Gindin shouts. He can't help himself, but he is overcome with a sudden rage. It doesn't matter that he's outranked by Captain Lieutenant Proshutinsky, and Senior Lieutenants Smirnov and Vinogradov; what they've just done is nothing short of insane.

"That's enough, mister," Proshutinsky warns.

"Do you understand what's just happened, sir?"

"You're being insubordinate."

Gindin turns to the others. "Don't you get it?" he demands. He thinks that he's going insane. Or maybe the others are crazy.

"What are you talking about, Boris?" Kuzmin asks. "Sablin is a traitor. What, are we supposed to treat him like a tsar? He's going to get us killed."

"Exactly," Gindin agrees. "Unless we can somehow get out of here and stop him."

"That's the point—," Kuzmin starts to say, but then he realizes what

Gindin is trying to tell them. Kuzmin averts his eyes. "Shit," he says. "*Pizdec.*"

The other officers aren't sure.

"We had a chance when Captain Sablin had the hatch open," Gindin explains. "We could have rushed him and the guards. We might have been able to get out of here and grab their weapons."

The officers are silent for a long time, each with his own dark thoughts. Gindin is thinking about his own vote. If he had voted with the white backgammon piece, pretending to go along with Sablin, he would be free right now, with the possibility of doing something to stop the insanity.

Maybe that was Firsov's thinking.

Right now all Gindin and the others have is hope.

REVOLT

If he cares to admit it to himself, Sablin is shaken by the reaction to his offer of a little humanity. It was just some tea, after all, not some political statement. On the way back to his cabin he can't help but think about the letter he sent to his wife, Nina. In it he'd outlined his plan and his reasons for going through with the mutiny, but he never expected the kind of anger he got from his own officers.

He believes that given the chance Gindin and the others might have actually done him bodily harm. He shakes his head. The Kremlin would not be amused when they found out what was going on. But his own officers?

If he couldn't explain the necessity for what he was doing to Gindin and the others, how could he explain it to the Russian people? He was starting to get seriously worried.

When he reaches his cabin the young sailor standing guard can't help but notice that something is wrong.

"How's it going?" The kid uses Sablin's own words back at him.

Sablin looks up and manages a slight smile. "No problems," he says. "It's going to be a quiet night. We'll get under way first thing in the morning with the rest of the fleet."

"Yes, sir."

Inside, Sablin once again walks over to his safe, but he just stands there. An almost overwhelming lethargy may have overcome him, as he realizes perhaps for the first time the enormity of the thing that he has set in motion. All of his life he has been a good Communist. Despite his student letter to Khrushchev, which very nearly derailed his career, he has been the textbook-perfect *zampolit*. Almost like a Baptist minister, he has tended to his flock, guiding them through the minefields of understanding, appreciating, and believing in the system they were born into.

Now he's not so sure.

He has reached down to twist the dial for the first number in the combination when he is distracted by a commotion in the corridor. He looks up as someone pounds on the door.

"Captain Sablin!" they are shouting.

In three steps Sablin is across the cabin and he flings open his door. The sailor who has been standing guard has been joined by another sailor, Seaman Aleksei Sakhnevich, who is red faced and all out of breath.

Sablin's heart is in his throat. "What's happened?"

"It's Lieutenant Stepanov and some others in his cabin! They're talking about freeing the captain and coming to arrest you!"

It's as if Sablin has stuck his finger in a light socket. "How do you know this?" he demands.

"They're in the lieutenant's cabin and the door is half-open! I heard them talking when I walked past!"

"Are you sure?"

"They've got guns."

"Stay here," Sablin tells the sailor guarding his cabin. "You, come with me," he tells Sakhnevich, and they race down the corridor.

Lieutenant Stepanov was one of the officers who hadn't reported for the meeting in the midshipmen's dining hall. He was on duty, and Sablin had planned on talking with him and the few others, all of them warrant officers, who'd also been aboard ship but absent later this evening. What could a handful of officers do to interfere with the rest of the ship?

At the lieutenant's cabin, Sablin pulls out his Makarov pistol, kicks open the door, and bursts inside, Sakhnevich holding back in the corridor.

It's Lieutenant Stepanov and Warrant Officers Kovalchenkov and Saitov, and they all have pistols. They look up in alarm as their *zampolit,* brandishing a gun, comes through the doorway.

"What's the meaning of this meeting?" Sablin cries, and his words sound stupid even in his own ears.

Stepanov steps back, raises his pistol, and thumbs the safety catch to the off position. "You're a traitor!" he shouts.

"I'm trying to help!" Sablin pleads. "Most of the officers and all the sailors are with me! We have to do this!" He is pointing his pistol in the general direction of Stepanov and the others, but he's neglected to switch the safety off. His weapon is not ready to fire.

"It doesn't matter, because this mutiny will soon be over," one of the warrant officers blurts out.

"What are you talking about? We're getting out of here in the morning, and I'm going a make a broadcast to the people. It'll be up to them to decide who is right."

"This ship is going nowhere under your command!" one of the others shouts. He, too, has raised his pistol and is pointing it directly at Sablin's chest. His face is white, but whether it's from rage or fear even he doesn't know for sure.

The four men are facing each other, like gunfighters at the OK Corral. All it will take is for one man to make a mistake and blood will be shed in this tiny compartment.

"I order you to put down your weapons," Sablin tells them in a measured voice. He is catching his second wind. Whatever fate is in store for him, he feels the first test is now.

"No," Lieutenant Stepanov replies coolly. "We're all going to wait here until help arrives. Then you will be arrested and the captain will be set free." He shakes his head. "Thank God you weren't dumb enough to kill him!"

"There is no help coming—"

"Yes, there is!" Kovalchenkov shouts. "Lieutenant Firsov is leaving the ship—"

"Shut up, you stupid fool!" Stepanov cries.

Sablin is rocked back on his heels. All of his planning, everything he has worked for, is disappearing before his eyes.

He turns to see if Sakhnevich is still there, but the corridor is empty. Sablin's heart sinks even lower.

"Grab him!" Stepanov shouts, and suddenly Sablin is rushed, hands are plucking at his sleeves, someone is trying to take the pistol out of his hand, and he is shoved up against the bulkhead, his head banging against the steel plating.

Sablin manages to break free for an instant and he raises his pistol, meaning to fire a warning shot overhead, but Seaman Sakhnevich is suddenly crowding into the cabin with three other young sailors.

Stepanov and the warrant officers are armed, but not one shot is fired as the sailors roughly pull and shove them away and manage to drag their *zampolit* out into the corridor and slam the door.

One of the sailors produces a key and locks the door from the outside. There'll be no escape for the three officers now. The *Storozhevoy* is a sturdy Russian warship; there'll be no shooting their way out for the three officers.

Sablin's heart, which has been pounding practically out of his chest, is beginning to slow down as he catches his breath.

Firsov.

The name crystallizes in Sablin's mind.

There'd been absolutely no doubt which way Firsov had voted. The young senior lieutenant of the electrical division had dropped a white backgammon piece into the basket. He was *for* the mutiny. He had grasped perfectly what Sablin was trying to do.

Gindin was a disappointment, but Firsov was solidly behind the plan.

Sablin focuses on Sakhnevich. "Good work, Aleksei," he says. "Thank you. But we have to find Lieutenant Firsov, before he gets off the ship."

"Maybe he's already gone," Sakhnevich says.

"If that's the case I need to know it immediately. The entire operation depends on it."

Sakhnevich and the other sailors are rooted to their spots. They're not quite sure what to do. They realize that this situation has the potential to change everything. Their lives could literally be hanging in the balance.

"Now," Sablin urges. "Before it's too late. Find him!"

DESERTER

Crouched in the chilly darkness at the massive anchor hawsehole near the bow, Senior Lieutenant Vladimir Firsov is at odds with himself, as he has been ever since he'd first begun to suspect what Sablin was up to. That was weeks ago when Sablin began asking questions about how the electrical systems aboard the ship were supposed to work, that and the *zampolit*'s not-so-subtle comments about what a mess the bureaucrats in Moscow had made of Lenin's fine ideas.

Firsov has acted as head of the ship's Communist Party Club. That meant that he ran meetings once a month for the dozen or so men aboard who were already members of the Party or had been nominated for membership. This is a big deal in the Soviet Union and an even bigger deal in the military. Being a member of the Party opens all sorts of doors, and with them come privileges.

Because Firsov is a Communist Party cell commander, the *zampolit* has treated him especially well. Firsov is one of the chosen few, with a fine future ahead of him.

But hunched down and shivering now he isn't so sure of anything except for the look on his friend Boris Gindin's face in the midshipmen's dining hall. Boris was disappointed, and that hurt more than anything Firsov can ever recall. He has a great deal of respect for his roommate. Firsov hopes someday to explain what he did this evening and why.

Gindin never thought about Firsov's Party membership until much later, but by then it was too late to bring it up. "I thought that at first Vladimir might have shared Sablin's ideas, but later, after he'd had time to calm down and think things through, he might have had a change of heart, so he jumped ship to call for help.

"Maybe he realized just how dangerous a situation Sablin had gotten us into and decided to warn somebody what was happening before it was too late."

Or maybe Firsov was even smarter than that.

"Maybe it was Vladimir's strategy to try to save us all," Gindin recalls. "Maybe he volunteered to go over to Sablin's side to penetrate into the *zampolit*'s circle in order to find a way out of the mess."

It's not known for sure what Firsov's actual motivations were on that evening or exactly what he was thinking at that moment near the bow of the ship.

Someone shouts something from aft, toward the starboard side of the superstructure, and Firsov turns toward the noise. He heard his name! Somehow they know! Sablin has set men to look for him!

Someone else shouts something.

Firsov rises up just tall enough to look over the side of the bulwarks. An Alpha submarine, low in the water, dark, menacing, is at the same mooring as the *Storozhevoy*. He can make out a dim red glow from the open hatch at the top of the sail. The sub's captain will know what to do.

Firsov looks over his shoulder to make sure that there's no one to see him, and he wiggles through the hawsehole, the filthy seventy-centimeter mooring line getting his uniform dirty, and scrambles down to the bow deck of the sub.

THE ALARM

Sablin is hanging over the rail at the bow of the *Storozhevoy* trying to peer through the fog at something going on in the water below, just to the starboard side of the submarine sitting low in the water, his decks just a meter or so above the surface of the water.

It is a few minutes before 2300, and by now the entire ship has been thoroughly searched from stem to stern and from top to bottom. The sailors and officers have checked every single compartment, crawl space, and locker where a man could possibly hide.

Senior Lieutenant Firsov is not aboard. Kovalchenkov and the others locked in Stepanov's cabin below were right. Firsov has somehow gotten off the ship and is sending for help. Right now Sablin thinks he knows how it was done.

There is something going on below. He can make out a dim red light coming from the open hatch at the top of the sail. The *Storozhevoy*'s mooring line goes almost straight down. A man such as Firsov could have easily have crawled through the hawsehole, shimmied down the mooring line, and made it to the deck of the sub.

But would the submarine's commander or anyone else aboard believe such a wild story about the *zampolit* arresting Potulniy and taking over the ship?

A brief flash of white light from below illuminates someone scrambling down into a small launch tied up to the side of the sub. It's like a pulse of a strobe in Sablin's eyes, an image of a slightly built man in a navy uniform getting into that little boat.

Moments later the small boat's engine comes to life, and the launch heads away from the submarine.

Sablin rears back. He can hear the speech he means to broadcast as if the recording were playing right now through the ship's 1MC.

"*. . . we are demanding that our ship be recognized as a free and independent territory. We are demanding daily broadcasts on radio and television for thirty minutes. Our goal will be to oppose the current regime . . .*"

Words and bits and pieces of his speech buzz inside his head like insects around a night-light.

"*We are neither traitors to the Motherland nor are we adventurers who seek recognition for our deeds.*"

He looks over the rail again, but the launch is long gone, lost in the fog on its way ashore.

To report the situation aboard the *Storozhevoy*!

To call for help!

To stop them!

"*. . . the people find themselves trapped in a stagnant atmosphere of blind obedience to authority . . .*

"*. . . it's political tyranny and censorship . . . Our people have already suffered much . . . we have laughed a million times, but our laughter is mixed with tears at the thought of the Motherland's future.*"

He turns and looks up at the superstructure, the windows of the bridge. No light is showing, but he has posted guards up there. All he needed was a few more hours before morning reveille, when the entire fleet was scheduled to drop their moorings and head to sea. The

Storozhevoy would have slipped away with the others, entirely unnoticed.

He has to figure that once Firsov gets ashore he will alert the Riga naval duty officer and the harbormaster. If the *Storozhevoy* is caught here, still tied to the mooring, there will be no way out.

The only chance for them is to get the ten or fifteen kilometers downriver to the Gulf of Riga, then past Saaremma Island and out into the open Baltic, where at least they'll have room to maneuver.

That's exactly what has to be done! And done right now!

Now that Sablin has a plan to deal with this unexpected emergency it's as if a liter of adrenaline has been dumped into his system. He crosses the foredeck as fast as his feet will carry him, slams open the hatch, and takes the stairs two at a time up to the bridge.

The armed guards he has posted hear him pounding up the stairs, and they raise their Kalashnikov rifles in alarm. With the way things have been going around here tonight, there's no telling what might be coming their way. They're plenty scared now that they've had a few hours to think about things. But they're also fatalists, as many Russians, especially small-town country boys, are.

Russians have three principles, so the old proverb goes. *Perhaps, somehow, and never mind.* It's hard to make a decision.

But it's their *zampolit,* and they lower their weapons in relief.

"Has anyone tried to come up here?" Sablin demands.

"No, sir," one of the sailors replies.

Sablin is furiously weighing his chances now. If they sail out of here and make it to the open sea, he's all but certain the Soviet navy won't fire on one of its own ships. If they can get that far before the river is blockaded, they'll have a real chance of pulling this thing off. But if they stay, if he goes below and releases the officers he's put under lock and key, the captain will arrest him and turn him over to the KGB. They might even arrest everyone who supported the mutiny and keep the *Storozhevoy* right here in the middle of the river for everyone in Riga to see until a replacement crew could be rounded up and brought down.

There's no choice, not really. He's started this business, and he will see it through. Once he gets his message to the Soviet people, the Kremlin won't be able to touch them.

"Go below and round up the bridge crew," Sablin orders the two sailors. "Get them up here on the double; we're leaving tonight!"

The young crewmen might be confused, but they have their orders and finally they know what to do. They don't have to think about anything else except doing what they're told to do. They turn crisply and race down the stairs, as Sablin snatches the ship's intercom phone off the overhead and calls the engine room.

It buzzes once, then again, then a third time. "Come on," Sablin mutters impatiently. "Pick it up!"

Outside the bridge windows the fog is so thick that he can see only a few meters beyond the *Storozhevoy*'s sweeping bows and nothing much of the city except for the halos of some lights.

Someone answers the call. "Engine room, aye."

"This is Captain Third Rank Sablin; do you recognize my voice?" Sablin demands.

"Yes, sir," the young man answers after a brief hesitation.

"Start the engines! All four of them!"

No one responds.

"This is an order! Start all four engines now! I need full power as quickly as possible! Call me on the bridge when everything is ready!"

Sablin slams the phone back on its bracket and looks around the bridge at all the electronic equipment, switches and dials, the wheel, the engine telegraph, radar, controls for the weapons systems. He's not an engineering officer, nor is he a bridge officer or navigating officer or communications officer or weapons officer. He is the *zampolit*. If the crew will not follow his orders, the *Storozhevoy* will stay here tonight.

"*. . . I don't think there is any argument that these days the servants of the state have already become the masters of the state . . .*"

Sablin can hear the words of his speech as if he were broadcasting the recording at this very moment.

Someone comes up the stairs in a rush, and Sablin turns out of his daydream as three sailors appear in the doorway with the two guards. He recognizes them, but he can't recall their names at that moment, though he knows that they are part of the normal bridge complement.

"We must leave now," he tells them. "Take your posts."

"What about the engines?" one of the sailors asks.

At that moment the ship's phone buzzes. Sablin yanks it from its bracket. "Bridge!"

"The engines are ready for full power," one of the engine room crew reports.

"Very well; stand by to answer bells," Sablin gives the same order he's heard Potulniy give before. He hangs up and turns to his bridge crew. "The engines are ready. We have to get out of here now."

"Where?" the helmsman asks.

The other two are hurriedly powering up the electronic equipment, including the vital navigation radar they'll need to get under way.

"Downriver, out to the gulf."

"Yes, sir," the young crewman replies. "But first we'll need someone on the bow to take in our mooring line and untie it."

Sablin figures that will take too much time. Someone from one of the other ships is bound to notice something funny going on, and the alarm will be sounded. He makes another decision and turns to the guards.

"Find an ax, get out to the bow, and cut our mooring line. Be sharp about it."

"Yes, sir," the two men chorus, and they disappear again down the stairs.

BETRAYAL

The first thought that comes to Gindin's mind when he feels the vibration in the deck, which means the engines have started, is disbelief. This cannot be happening. The engines were never supposed to be started without a gas turbine officer physically present. Those were standing orders that everyone understood. Besides, a thousand things could go wrong that ordinary enlisted men wouldn't know how to deal with.

The second thought that comes to Gindin's mind is betrayal. He's given his men the best of everything within his power as a Soviet navy senior lieutenant. He's covered for them with the captain. He's given them extra privileges. He's seen to it that they could take their leaves ahead of just about everyone else aboard ship. Sometimes he's been tough on them but never unfair. Never that.

Now they have betrayed him, by taking up arms with the *zampolit* and starting the engines.

Everyone else in the sonar compartment has felt and heard that the engines have started, and they all shoot Gindin dirty looks, as if he is to blame for this latest development.

He wants to tell them that he was just doing his duty, teaching his men their jobs. But he holds his tongue, sick to death at what this means. Sablin will try to get out of here tonight. Something has gone wrong, and very likely they all are facing a death sentence.

Captain Lieutenant Proshutinsky gives Gindin a baleful look. "Boris, perhaps you have trained your men too well."

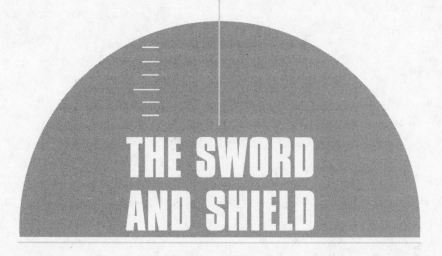

THE SWORD AND SHIELD

All the brave men are in prison.

KAK IZVESTNO

THE KGB

Our society is infected. The Party apparatus of the government and the highest most successful levels of the intelligentsia are profoundly indifferent to violations of human rights, the interest of progress, the security and future of mankind.

ANDREY SAKHAROV'S LETTER TO PREMIER BREZHNEV

It is very important to defend those who suffer because of their nonviolent struggle for an open society, for justice for other people whose rights are violated. It is our duty and yours to fight for them. I think that a lot depends on this struggle—trust between the peoples, confidence in lofty promises, and, in the final analysis, international security.

ANDREY SAKHAROV'S LETTER TO PRESIDENT JIMMY CARTER

It is necessary to defend the victims of political repression, within a country and internationally, using diplomatic means

and energetic public pressure, including boycotts. It is also
necessary to support the demand for amnesty for all prisoners of
conscience, all those who have spoken out for openness and
justice without using violence. The abolition of the death penalty
and the unconditional banning of torture and the use of
psychiatry for political purposes are also necessary.

ANDREY SAKHAROV

By the late forties Sakharov was working with Igor Kurchatov on the design of the Soviet Union's first atomic bomb, made possible in part because of the KGB's spying on the Manhattan Project in the United States. By 1950 the young scientist and hero of the people had moved to the development of the hydrogen bomb, which was successfully tested in 1953—several months before he had even earned his doctorate, which was given to him at the same time he was awarded the first of his three Hero of Socialist Labor medals.

Two years later he developed the first hydrogen bomb in the megaton range using his own design, which in 1961 led to the test of a fifty-megaton hydrogen bomb—the largest man-made explosion ever.

About that same time he developed an old Russian idea for what's called the *tokamak*, which is a way to control plasma in a nuclear fusion reactor, still in use around the world today.

He was elected to the Soviet Academy of Sciences, came up with the idea of induced gravity as an alternative to quantum mechanical gravity, and was awarded another Hero of Socialist Labor medal.

All this by the time he was forty years old.

But then Russia's most famous and brilliant scientist came up against the KGB, and it was no contest.

Around the late fifties, Sakharov began to worry about the moral implications of his work on nuclear weapons designs. After all, he reasoned, big hydrogen bombs were only useful for one thing—destroying major cities such as New York or Washington, Moscow or Leningrad, in one blow. There were no peaceful uses for the hellish devices.

By the early sixties he came out publicly against nuclear proliferation, by 1963 he had become a major player in the Partial Test Ban Treaty signed in Moscow, and by 1965 he pulled completely out of nuclear weapons research and turned his energies to the study of cosmology—how the universe came into being and how it worked.

None of this endeared him to the leaders in the Kremlin. Even as he was being awarded his third Hero of Socialist Labor medal, talks at the highest levels centered on the question of what to do with Sakharov.

Two things happened then to seal his fate. The first came in 1967 when the idea of an antiballistic missile defense system started to become a big issue in Soviet–U.S. relations. In a secret letter to the Kremlin in July, he wrote that the Americans had to be taken at their word that they would never launch a pre-emptive nuclear attack on the Soviet Union, so a fabulously expensive, nation-bankrupting antiballistic missile defense was not necessary.

Otherwise, he argued, an arms race for this new technology would almost certainly increase the possibility of all-out nuclear war.

He asked for permission to publish his views in newspapers, but of course the Kremlin refused. In fact, they ignored him. But the decorated hero of the nation was not about to give up, and neither was the KGB.

In May he wrote an essay, *Reflections on Progress, Peaceful Coexistence, and Intellectual Freedom,* in which he argued that an antiballistic missile defense system would pose a major threat to increase the chances of nuclear war. It was first circulated in the Soviet Union as a *samizdat* publication, which amounted to mimeographed copies passed hand to hand in the underground. Even worse than that, however, a copy reached the outside world and was published for everyone to read.

The KGB had enough, and it struck back, immediately canceling his security clearances and banning him from all military-related research.

Unbowed, Sakharov founded the Moscow Human Rights Committee, and the KGB began tailing his friends, opening his mail, and monitoring his phone calls.

He married Yelena Bonner, who was another human rights activist, and the KGB began spreading vicious rumors about him, trying to drag down his moral character in the public eye.

In 1975 he was awarded the Nobel Prize for Peace, but the KGB revoked his external passport, and his wife had to go to Stockholm to read his acceptance speech.

By 1980, the KGB struck back even harder. Sakharov couldn't be shot or even jailed; he was simply too important a figure in Russia as well as in the rest of the world. They did the next best thing by exiling him to the closed city of Gorki, now called Nizhniy Novgorod, out in the boondocks three hundred miles east of Moscow. While he was there, the KGB continually harassed him, following him, listening to his phone calls, reading his mail, and even breaking into his apartment and stealing manuscripts he'd written. Sakharov wrote:

> The Deputy Procurator of Gorky explained the terms of the regimen decreed for me: Overt surveillance, prohibition against leaving the city limits, prohibition against meeting with foreigners and criminal elements, prohibition against correspondence and telephone conversations with foreigners including scientific and purely personal communications, even with my children and grandchildren.

It wasn't until 1986, with Gorbachev's policies of perestroika and glasnost, that Sakharov was finally allowed to return to Moscow for the last three years of his life.

That was still in the distant future for the officers and crew aboard the *Storozhevoy* getting ready to get under way this crisp early November evening. But if the Soviet Union's most influential and famous citizen couldn't stand up to the KGB, how could Sablin and his mutineers expect to do any better?

Just about every modern nation has its variety of secret service, but none of those organizations, not the CIA, not Britain's MI6, not even the Nazi's Gestapo, ever came even close to the all-encompassing power of the Soviet Union's Committee for State Security, the *Komitet Gosudarstvennoy Besopasnosti.*

The KGB was into just about everything, with roughly the same powers and responsibilities as the U.S. Central Intelligence Agency, the Federal Bureau of Investigation's Counterintelligence Division, the Federal Protective Service, the Secret Service, and the Border Patrol and Coast Guard.

Besides spying on other countries, conducting sabotage and assassinations, the KGB regulated all thought, behavior, and speech in the Soviet Union. It controlled the arts, religion, education, the sciences, the news media, the police, and, in some ways most important, the military. Every unit and ship, including the *Storozhevoy,* had its KGB snitch embedded. On this evening Captain Lieutenant Aleksey Bykov, the KGB representative aboard the *Storozhevoy,* was gone. He'd been transferred to another ship, and his replacement wasn't due aboard until after the refit at the shipyard.

The KGB kept track of the ethnic minorities across all of Russia and her republics, it stopped its citizens from skipping over the border to freedom, it kept a constant surveillance of troublemakers, such as Sakharov, and it made sure that every man, woman, and child in the country worked for the Rodina and for nothing else. No person, no thought, no ideal, was more important than the Motherland.

The KGB conducted its own arrests, its own interrogations, very often involving brutal torture: electric prods to the genitals, bamboo shoots under the fingernails, toenails ripped out with pliers, skin flayed off in long strips, hot branding irons under the armpits and in the groin, dentist drills without anesthetic, cold water hoses up the anus, not to mention various forms of psychological torture, including the use of a wide variety of drugs, including hallucinogens.

And the KGB conducted its own trials, usually in secret, the outcomes of which were never in doubt. After all, if the KGB had reason to believe you were guilty of a crime against the Soviet people, you must be guilty.

Lenin himself wrote that the "scientific concept of dictatorship means nothing more or less than unlimited power resting directly on force . . . not limited by anything . . . nor restrained by any laws or any absolute rules."

Nothing had changed between the October Revolution of 1917 and the cold November night of 1975, except that the KGB, which had been christened the Cheka under its first chief, the sadist Felix Dzerzhinsky, was more efficient and scientifically brutal than ever.

One of the primary missions of the KGB was the suppression of dissidents and dissent, what was officially termed *unorthodox beliefs,* which included keeping things quiet. KGB chief Yuri Andropov, who would later become president of the Soviet Union, made it his prime mission to make sure every Soviet citizen toed the Party line: ". . . every example of dissent is a threat to the Soviet State . . . and must be challenged and . . . all the resources of the KGB must be mobilized to achieve this goal."

Andropov even set up a separate organization within the KGB— the Fifth Directorate—to look out for and put down dissent anywhere and everywhere, including inside the military. The KGB was serious, and it was into this buzz saw that Sablin was leading the officers and crew of the *Storozhevoy.*

Among the more successful methods of dealing with dissidents and so-called threats against the Rodina was the Serbsky Institute of Forensic Psychiatry in Moscow. Behind tall stone walls and iron gates, guarded by armed KGB troops, a KGB colonel and doctor of psychiatry, Daniil Lunts, was in charge of what was called Diagnostic Department I, where Soviet citizens who had been arrested for *political noncomformity* were locked up for treatment. By definition, enemies of the Rodina were insane and therefore had either to be executed before their insanity could infect the entire nation or be treated with drugs, psychoanalysis, or, in the most extreme cases, prefrontal lobotomies.

Sometimes more conventional treatments seemed to work best. In 1969 Army Major General Peter Grigorenko publicly called for the withdrawal of Soviet troops from Czechoslovakia. He had been awarded the Order of Lenin, the Order of the Red Star, the Order of the Patriotic War, and two Orders of the Red Banner, his nation's highest honors, yet he was arrested for unorthodox beliefs.

Colonel Lunts determined that the general was suffering from paranoid schizophrenia and immediately transferred him to the mental hospital/prison at Chernyakhovsk for immobilization treatments. The patient was tightly wrapped in wet canvas, head-to-toe. As the canvas dried it began to shrink. Slowly. The pain was said to be excruciating. Most patients, when asked, promised that they were cured and no further treatments would be necessary.

The KGB was very good at what it did.

Nobody was safe, not famous scientists, not decorated war heroes, and certainly not Catholic priests. In 1971 the KGB accused a Lithuanian priest, Father Juozas Zdebskis, of teaching the catechism to children in his parish. In the eyes of the state this was a crime of political noncomformity, because no idea or ideal higher than the religion of the Motherland could be taught.

The priest's trial was supposed to be a secret, but the word got out and more than five hundred people, most of them carrying flowers, showed up to hear the testimony of several children who told the court that Father Zdebskis taught them that they should never steal or break windows.

KGB thugs scattered the crowd, breaking ribs and arms and bloodying some noses. But enough people were there to see a battered priest being led out of the courthouse to serve a one-year sentence at what was called a corrective labor camp.

"Whatever children need to know will be taught in school, not in church," the judge ordered.

Catholics and Jews could live quite openly in the Soviet Union, as long as they didn't preach any of their mumbo jumbo or teach children or try to get out of the country. Valeri Panov, a Jew who was one of the top dancers with the Kirov Ballet in Leningrad, announced one day in 1972 that he wanted to emigrate to Israel. Less than three weeks later he was denounced as a traitor to the Rodina and kicked out of the ballet company, and his wife, a prima ballerina at the Kirov, was demoted and her salary cut.

But that wasn't the end of it. A couple of months later he was arrested on the street and thrown in jail for two weeks for spitting in public. Less than one week after he was released he was again arrested for spitting and spent another two weeks in a jail for political criminals.

Some dancers in the West tried to send him money, but the KGB put a stop to that, so Panov was out of work and out of money, for which he was subject to arrest again because he was unemployed. Obviously the hapless man was guilty of *hooliganism*. There was absolutely no way out for him once he had come to the attention of the KGB.

Anyone who got in the way of the KGB was in trouble. It didn't matter who. It didn't even matter if you weren't a Soviet citizen.

Three years before Sablin took over the *Storozhevoy,* the KGB went after a Danish boat fishing for salmon just forty miles off Sweden's coast, not even close to Soviet territorial waters, and, coincidentally, 350 miles from Riga.

She was the *Windy Luck,* her skipper Arne Larsen. Early in the afternoon one of the crewmen spotted a small, open motorboat coming up behind them from the east. Larsen came out on deck as the motorboat came alongside.

"*Sind Sie Kommunists?*" the man in the boat shouted in German. Are you Communists?

He was the only person on the boat, and he appeared to be frightened out of his skull and half-delirious with exposure and probably hunger and thirst.

"No, we are a Danish fishing vessel!" Larsen called back. "Where do you come from? What are you doing out here?"

"I'm from Lithuania," the man explained. "I am defecting to Sweden, but I'm out of food and water and very nearly out of gas, and I'm cold and very tired. Can you help me?"

"Yes, of course!" Larsen shouted down to the man. He motioned for his crew to bring the man aboard and take the motorboat in tow.

"God bless you!" the defector cried. "Are we far from Sweden?"

"Only a few hours," Larsen assured him.

"I've been making my plans for a long time," the Lithuanian explained. "I thought I had enough gas and food and water to make the crossing. But I ran into a headwind, and the seas were too big, so I was slowed down." He shook his head. "I would not have made it without you."

The crew pulled in their nets as Larsen brought the bow of the *Windy Luck* around to the west on a direct bearing for the Swedish coast and increased power to cruising speed.

Within a half hour a fast-moving ship appeared from astern on the horizon. Larsen added a little more power, but it soon became apparent that the ship chasing them could not be outrun and that he was a warship. As he got closer Larsen identified the ship as a Russian Shershen fast-attack hydrofoil boat, and what's worse, it was flying a green ensign with the hammer and sickle, which meant it was a KGB coast guard boat.

But these were international waters, so the Russians had no jurisdiction. Larsen did not reduce speed or alter his course, but he ordered the Lithuanian defector to go below and hide in one of the cabins.

Within a half hour the KGB boat pulled alongside the *Windy Luck* and an officer came out on deck and raised a megaphone. "Heave to!" the officer shouted in Russian.

Larsen ignored the command.

The officer said something to another officer at the open door to the bridge, and within seconds several sailors scrambled out on deck manning a pair of 30mm guns.

Suddenly the KGB patrol boat veered directly into the *Windy Luck*'s stern, just brushing her with a glancing blow.

"Heave to; we mean to board you," the Russian officer ordered, this time in English. "If you do not comply we will open fire."

Larsen threw up his hands. There was nothing he could do. He cut power, and as soon as his boat had slowed down, four Soviet officers armed with pistols scrambled aboard.

"We will search the ship," one of them told Larsen.

"These are international waters!" Larsen shouted. "You have no rights!"

The officer smirked and nodded toward the KGB warship. "We give the orders here."

Within five minutes the Lithuanian defector was found and brought up on deck. *"Auf Wiedersehen,"* he said as he was hustled aboard the KGB ship.

The KGB took the man's motorboat in tow and within a half hour they were gone over the horizon. Poor bastard, Larsen thought. But at least that's the end of it for us.

But that wasn't to be the end of it, because the KGB has not only a long arm; it also has a very long memory.

Three weeks later another Danish fishing vessel, this one the *Thomas Moeller,* fishing for salmon well within Swedish waters, was rammed by a Soviet warship and nearly sunk. After the collision, the Soviets plowed through the fishing nets and then took off, not bothering to see if there were any injuries or to offer any help.

The incident was a clear warning to all Danish fishermen that trying to help Soviet defectors could be a very risky business.

If Sablin knows these stories and countless others of a similar nature, which he very well may have, he is not deterred as the mooring lines are cut and the engines are engaged.

The *Storozhevoy* shudders as if he is a racehorse that has thrown off his reins, heading toward a future that no one can predict, except that the KGB will undoubtedly play a major role in how it all turns out.

Sablin looks out the bridge windows, the fog still so thick that he can't see much of anything beyond the bows. But there are enough buoys marking the safe passage downriver that making it out to the open sea won't be impossible.

But only if their luck holds.

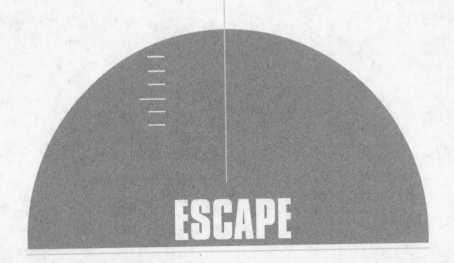

ESCAPE

The strongest of all warriors are these two—
time and patience.

LEO TOLSTOY
WAR AND PEACE

SABLIN

The problem Sablin faces is that if this business of his fails, he and his crew will either be destroyed at sea or fall into the hands of the KGB. The only hope is to get out into the open sea and send his tape by radio over the public broadcast bands to anybody who will listen. At that point their fate will rest in the hands of the people.

He signals for all ahead slow, and almost immediately the two marching engines spool up and the *Storozhevoy* begins to move.

Seaman Oleg Maksimenko is standing by at the navigation radar to help them pick their way downriver in the fog. But first they have to get out of the tight spot they are in, wedged between the Alpha submarine and a frigate, plus all the other warships and tenders at anchor or on moorings downriver. The tide is running out now, giving them a 6-knot boost in speed in return for taking away some of their maneuverability.

Petty Officer First Class Viktor Soloviev is steering the ship, and although he's the best helmsman aboard, he is extremely nervous. All of them are a hairbreadth away from disaster, and he more than anyone else aboard knows it. A collision with another boat under these conditions is almost certain.

"We must go slower, Captain," Soloviev tells Sablin. "I can't see a bloody thing."

"Steady," Sablin orders. "Are we clear?" he asks Maksimenko at the radar.

"I can't tell yet!" the seaman shouts. He is nervous as hell. This job normally would be done by a petty officer or even a warrant officer, not a rating. Maksimenko wants to be home planting potatoes in the garden, not taking responsibility for an entire ship like this. He looks up and Sablin is saying something. Maksimenko figures the only way he'll ever get home to the garden is to do what he's told.

"Can we turn?" Sablin shouts.

Maksimenko tries to make some sense of what he is seeing on the radar screen, but everything is confusing. "*Da!*" he calls out. "We may turn now."

Sablin is also caught up in the moment, and he doesn't stop to think that perhaps the sailor is merely telling him what he wants to hear. "Turn hard to port now," he gives the order to Soloviev, who puts the wheel hard over.

The *Storozhevoy*'s bows come around smartly and there is a collision. They have hit something! Not such a hard blow that they will have to stop here or even sink in the river, but they have hit something.

The ship seems to shudder, then shrug off the hit, and immediately begins to accelerate into the left turn, which will put their bows facing downriver.

Sablin cannot live with the possibility that by his actions he not only has damaged a Soviet navy ship but also might have hurt someone. He tears open the hatch on the starboard side and rushes out onto the wing and looks over the side. They are rapidly leaving their mooring barrel and the Alpha submarine rocking in their wake. They evidently struck a glancing blow to the blue-striped barrel, but so far as Sablin can tell no damage has been done, and it's not even likely that the crew aboard the submarine has taken notice of the small wake. He takes a deep breath of the cold night air, as if it's his last.

He steps back inside, relief washing over him at least for the moment. But they have a long way to go before they're out of trouble. "Tell me when we're lined up with the channel," he orders Maksimenko. The buoys marking the path downriver will show up clearly on the radar screen.

"I'm sorry, Captain," the sailor stammers. The collision was his fault and he is afraid of the consequences for himself.

"Don't worry about it, Oleg. Just tell me when we are lined up with the channel. This is very important."

"*Da*," Maksimenko responds, and he turns back to his radar set as the *Storozhevoy*'s bows continue to swing around to the north.

The bridge door is open to the corridor that leads aft and down. Even this far up Sablin can hear the commotion below. Each time the *Storozhevoy* got under way there was a great deal of activity as the crew jumped to their stations and carried out their duties. But this sounds different to Sablin. Not as ordered. More chaotic. It's disquieting, and certainly not how he imagined their departure on what he thinks is a grand and noble endeavor.

"We're coming into the channel now, sir!" Maksimenko calls out.

"Very well," Sablin says. "Ease your helm, Viktor." It's the same kind of command Sablin has heard Potulniy give countless times before, only the captain never used an ordinary sailor's first name.

Soloviev straightens the helm, and the *Storozhevoy* slips into the groove that will guide them the fifteen kilometers or so to the mouth of the river. From there they will have to get around the islands of Saaremaa and Hiiumaa before they will be well out into the gulf and where Sablin figures he will be able to breathe a real sigh of relief.

Firsov's jumping ship bothers Sablin more than he cares to admit at this moment; he's just too busy to think about it. But it's there, like a nagging toothache that will not go away. Conning a ship the size of the *Storozhevoy* in the open sea is a piece of cake. Simply set a course and speed, dial in the autopilot, and keep a sharp radar and visual lookout. But driving a ship down a narrow river, at night, in the fog, with a heavy current running, while all around are moored vessels and God only knows what other hazards on and below the surface, is something else entirely. This sort of an endeavor takes not only the cooperation of the entire bridge and engine room crew but also a knowledgeable, experienced man in command, whose entire mind is on the job at hand.

It's something Sablin is not, and he is acutely aware of his lacking.

"We're lined up with the fairway, sir!" Maksimenko calls out. He's lined up the buoys on the radar screen.

"Are you certain?" Sablin demands.

"Yes, sir!"

Sablin reaches over to the engine telegraph and signals for all ahead full. It takes several moments for the gas turbine crew to respond, and he is just about to pick up the phone to call down there when the answering bells sound. The *Storozhevoy*'s engines spool up and their speed quickly rises.

In calm seas the two main engines can drive the ship to around 24 knots, but with the current propelling them downriver their actual speed over the bottom rises to 30 knots.

"We're going way too fast, Captain," Soloviev warns.

There is no other choice. They have to get out of here as soon as humanly possible. "Steady as you go, Viktor," Sablin orders. "Keep us in the channel!" he calls to Maksimenko.

Sablin feels like a maniac on a carnival ride that has run amok. There is no way to get off.

Soloviev is muttering something under his breath. He is peering out the big forward windows trying to spot the lit buoys before they run over them or, worse yet, drift out of the channel. If he drives the *Storozhevoy* aground at this speed, not only will the ship sustain crippling damage, but it's also a safe bet that there will be casualties among the crew. Possibly even deaths.

Maksimenko suddenly looks up from the hooded radar screen as if he's just stuck his finger in an electric socket. "*Eb tvoiu mat,*" he swears, and he reaches up for a handhold to brace himself.

Sablin's blood runs cold. "What is it?" he demands.

"A ship!" the sailor stammers weakly.

Soloviev spots the looming shape of a big ship directly in their path at the same time as Sablin and, before the order can be given, hauls the wheel hard over to the right.

The *Storozhevoy* heels sharply to starboard, probably well past twenty degrees, which is extreme even for a warship, and Sablin is only just in time to grab a handhold to stop from being propelled across the bridge and dashed against the bulkhead.

From below they can hear the sounds of equipment and loose gear flying all over the place, crashing into stanchions and walls with tremendous noises. Men are shouting in anger.

If they were under battle stations orders they would have taken preparations for such violent evasive maneuvers, but they'd been given no warning.

Sablin manages to regain his balance as the *Storozhevoy* looks to clear the very large ship now sliding rapidly off to port. He is a tanker leaving the dock and just coming into the fairway to head out to sea.

If Soloviev had not been paying attention they would have slammed their bows directly into the side of the ship. It would have been a disaster. The tanker would probably have exploded, and there almost certainly would have been the bodies of a lot of incinerated sailors floating in the river, but there would have been civilian casualties ashore as well.

"Bring us back into the channel," Sablin orders softly. He's suddenly not very sure of his voice. His mouth is dry.

Soloviev doesn't say a word as he brings the *Storozhevoy* back on course.

Away from the lights of downtown Riga, it seems as if the fog has cleared a little. In any event, they are able to pick out the buoys marking the fairway by eye.

Sablin had planned to shut down the ship's radar once they had cleared the river and were out into the gulf. He was enough of a naval officer to understand at least rudimentary battle tactics. If their radar sets were banging away, whoever the fleet sent out after them would be able to home in on them. Besides, Maksimenko was too nervous to do a very good job.

"Shut down the radar, Oleg," Sablin ordered.

"Sir?"

"Turn the radar set off. We don't want anyone picking up our signals."

Maksimenko shuts off the power as Sablin picks up the intercom handset and keys the push-to-talk switch.

"This is your *zampolit* speaking." His voice is broadcast to every compartment aboard ship. "All hands—*boevaya trevoga*—man your battle stations. All hands, man your battle stations."

"But, sir, we have no rockets or ammunition," Soloviev points out.

"It's all right," Sablin says calmly, the first major crisis behind them. "They need something to keep them busy."

FIRSOV

Standing on the quay watching the *Storozhevoy* disappear into the fog, Firsov figures that if he had not waited so long to abandon ship and sound the alarm, none of this would be happening.

The petty officer who brought Firsov ashore from the submarine is still there on the launch watching the same thing. He and the two sailors on the crew cannot believe what they are witnessing. First the *Storozhevoy* crashed into a mooring bouy, and then he very nearly collided with a gasoline tanker leaving the dock.

The petty officer looks up at Firsov. "*Pizdec*, whoever is in command of your ship is a crazy man. He's going to get your crewmates killed if he keeps up like that."

"He's probably already done so," Firsov replies. He wants to tell the petty officer that if the skipper of the submarine, Captain Second Rank Leonid Svetlovski, hadn't been so slow on the uptake, this could have been prevented.

As soon as Firsov had made it to the deck of the submarine, he ran aft to the sail, where he shouted up to the pair of sailors on the bridge on watch trying to keep warm.

At first they wouldn't look down. But they must have heard him. He was making enough racket to wake the dead.

"*Bljad,* pull your heads out of your asses up there!" he shouted even louder. He glanced back up at the *Storozhevoy's* bows looming overhead, fearful that someone might realize that he'd jumped ship and spot him down here. God only knows what order Sablin might give.

Finally one of the sailors looked over the coaming and spotted an officer, his uniform filthy from climbing down the mooring line. On the one hand the sailor had a responsibility for the security of his ship, while on the other he had to show respect to an officer. Right then the sailor was caught between a rock and a hard place, which is fairly common in the Soviet navy.

"Sir, do you need some assistance?" the sailor calls down. It's the only thing he can think to say.

"Is your captain aboard?" Firsov asks.

"Yes, sir."

"With compliments, tell him that Senior Lieutenant Vladimir Firsov from the *Storozhevoy* is on deck and would like to have a word with him. Tell him it's urgent."

"Yes, sir," the sailor replies, and he disappears, presumably to use the submarine's interphone to call the captain.

Still no one has come to the *Storozhevoy's* bow, but Firsov suspects that can't last much longer.

The sailor is back in a couple of moments. "The captain asks that you come below!" he calls. "Just through the hatch, sir."

A hatch opens at the base of the sail, and a warrant officer beckons from inside.

Now it begins, Firsov tells himself, not at all sure how this will turn out. But the one thing he's feared the most turns out to be justified. When he tells his story to the sub's skipper, Captain Second Rank Svetlovski, he's met with stunned disbelief.

"A mutiny of the officers is impossible," Svetlovski fumes. "Such things no longer happen aboard Soviet warships. Where is your KGB officer?"

"He's been reassigned, sir. The mutiny was ordered by our *zampolit*. He's arrested Captain Potulniy and a few of the officers who tried to stop him."

"What, are you crazy? I know your captain. He would never allow such a thing to happen."

The next two things Svetlovski does are completely predictable given the circumstances and given the general mood in the Soviet navy. First he steps a little closer so that he can smell Firsov's breath. Accurate or not, it's been said that half of all Soviet military forces are drunk half of the time. But Firsov has not had a drink all night, though he wishes he had some of Boris's *spirt*.

The second thing the submarine captain does is pass the buck. "I cannot do anything without authorization, Senior Lieutenant," he tells Firsov. "I'm sending you ashore. You can tell your fantastic story to the duty officer, and it will be up to him. Though if he doesn't have you shot I'll be surprised, because God help us all if you're telling the truth."

It takes more than a half hour for the launch to be summoned and bring Firsov ashore and several precious minutes longer to convince the security guards on the quay to call the duty officer.

Nobody believes Firsov's story. Nobody wants to believe him.

Yet the *Storozhevoy* dropped her moorings, nearly collided with the submarine next to her, almost ran down a tanker, and has sailed downriver into the fog.

The security guard comes back from his post. "The duty officer is on his way, sir."

"Thank you," Firsov replies politely, though he feels anything but polite at this moment.

The security guard and the crew aboard the launch are looking at him as if he were insane or as if he were a bug under a microscope. None of them has any real idea what he's been talking about, but to a man they understand that very big trouble is afoot, and they are thanking their lucky stars that they are not involved.

Another half hour passes before Petty Officer Nikolai Aksenov finally shows up in a *gazik*, which is the same sort of general-purpose military vehicle as the American jeep. He gives Firsov's filthy uniform a hard stare, then takes in the security guard and the launch and its crew before he offers a salute.

"Senior Lieutenant, I understand that there may be some trouble," the duty officer says.

Firsov snaps a sketchy salute in return. "There has been a mutiny aboard the *Storozhevoy*."

"How do you know this, sir?"

"He's my ship. I just came from there!" Firsov shouts. He wants to punch the stupid kid in the mouth. "He just dropped his moorings and headed downriver."

"What, at this hour? No ships are scheduled to leave until morning."

"It's true," the petty officer aboard the launch says. "We just saw him leave in a big hurry. And he damned near ran down a tanker."

"I know about the tanker's schedule," the petty officer says. He looks downriver, as if he's trying to spot the departing ship with his own eyes. Of course nothing is to be seen except for the fog and the indistinct hulking shapes of the fleet still at anchor in the middle of the river.

"Well?" Firsov demands.

"I'm sorry, sir, but what do you want me to do?" Aksenov asks. This situation is way beyond him, except that, like the others, he understands there is the potential for a great deal of trouble. He wants to cover his own ass. It's the sensible thing to do.

"I want you to call the harbormaster and alert him to the situation before it's too late."

Aksenov steps back a pace.

"If they make it out to the gulf there's no telling where they'll end up!" Firsov shouts.

"I'm sorry, sir, but the harbormaster has given strict instructions that he is not to be disturbed this evening."

"*Bljad,* call somebody!"

Aksenov stares out across the river in the direction the *Storozhevoy* has gone, hoping against hope that either this is a nightmare or the ship would come back. But he's not asleep in his bunk, dreaming all of this, nor can he see anything moving in the fog.

"Brigade Seventy-eight," he mutters. It's the navy detachment here at Riga that is responsible for all military security, especially security for whatever warships happen to be in port. It's the next step up in the chain of command, and Firsov realizes that he should have thought of that himself. But time is racing by.

"Well, make the call. Now!"

The duty officer hesitates for just a moment longer, hoping that somehow the situation will resolve itself without him. But that's not going to happen and he knows it.

"Yes, sir," he says, and he walks to the guard post to make the first call alerting the Soviet navy that a mutiny has occurred aboard one of its ships.

POTULNIY

Locked in the forward sonar parts compartment all evening, Potulniy has had time to think about the consequences, for not only Sablin and the crew, but also himself. After the mutiny aboard the *Bounty*, after Captain Bligh was set adrift with some of the crew, after he'd made the impossible voyage in a small open boat halfway across the Pacific, saving the lives of all but one of his men—after all of that—Bligh still faced a court-martial.

Bligh had survived and he was made to answer the same kinds of questions that Potulniy knew he would face if he survived.

"What actions did you take, or what actions did you fail to take, over the course of the previous twelve months, that would have driven your crew to rise up against you?"

"How is it that you failed to become aware of the conditions that led to the mutiny?"

"When the mutineer Captain Third Rank Sablin came to your quarters that evening, claiming that there was a CP belowdecks, why did you decide to personally handle the situation instead of sending a subordinate, therefore needlessly placing your person in jeopardy?"

"It is clearly documented that you were close to your *zampolit;* why is it we should not believe that you at least played a passive role in the mutiny?"

"Why is it that you did not have the support of the majority of your officers?"

"Why is it that you failed to keep a record of potential troublemakers?"

"Why did you allow your KGB representative to leave the ship before you had secured his replacement?"

"Can you honestly tell this commission that you were and are fit to lead men into a battle to defend the Motherland?"

"Can you honestly swear to this commission that you were and are a good Communist?"

"Why didn't you give your life in defense of your ship?"

"Why didn't you make more of an effort to escape and regain control of your ship? Or was it that you did not care about the outcome?"

The biggest blow after Sablin tricked Potulniy into entering the compartment and allowing himself to be locked in was the realization that it wasn't just his *zampolit* who was guilty of mutiny. A substantial number, if not all, of his officers must have gone along with the insane scheme. Otherwise someone would have come down here to let him out.

There'd been a commotion out in the corridor earlier. He'd recognized Sablin's voice and he tried to talk some sense into the man. But it hadn't worked, and now they were under way.

They'd hit something, but as best Potulniy could judge it was just a glancing blow. No water is rushing into his ship from some gash in the bows, but the engines had spooled up way too fast for navigation in the confines of the river. If they hit something at this speed they could very well sink the ship, and he would die down here locked in a compartment with no way to get out.

Like most sailors, Potulniy has a particular aversion to drowning at sea. Getting blown up in some great sea battle or even dying in a train wreck while on leave would be infinitely better than drowning.

There isn't much in the compartment, except for a section of hefty steel pipe about twenty millimeters in diameter and one meter in length. Two hatches open from this tiny chamber, one out to the corridor and one up to the compartment directly above.

Using the pipe as a pry bar, Potulniy manages to undog the upper hatch and climb up the ladder. This compartment is normally used to stow spare equipment for the electronic gear. But all those parts have been used, and the compartment is empty until they put in for a refit and load a new set.

But there is another hatch to the corridor, and Potulniy sets to work on this latching mechanism. It's a wheel about the diameter of a big dinner plate. Turning it left causes the locking bars to withdraw from the receivers, allowing the hatch to be opened. But the wheel can be dogged down from the outside, making it impossible to turn.

After a minute or two with the pipe, the locking mechanism comes free, and Potulniy is able to turn the wheel.

The locking bars are withdrawn, but the hatch will not open. Something is blocking it, possibly a shoring beam.

At that point a nearly overwhelming sense of hopelessness and indignation and even rage threatens to overcome Potulniy. He attacks the door like a madman, smashing the heavy steel pipe against the locking mechanism. The racket makes it nearly impossible to think.

Between blows Potulniy hears someone shouting just outside in the corridor and he stops in mid-swing.

"Captain, you must stop!"

It is Seaman Shein. Potulniy recognizes the kid's voice from the incident earlier this evening. "Let me out of here!" Potulniy shouts. "That is a direct order from your commander!"

"Sir, I can't do that."

Potulniy tosses the pipe aside and puts his shoulder into the hatch.

Once, twice, a third time, and he is rewarded with the noise of the wood beam falling away and the door budging open a few centimeters.

"Captain, no!" Shein cries. "I have a gun; but I don't want to shoot you!"

Someone else is out in the corridor with Shein. Potulniy can hear them scrambling around. "Do you understand what you are doing?" he shouts. "You will face a firing squad."

"No, Captain!" one of the other crewmen shouts, but Potulniy doesn't recognize his voice.

Potulniy puts his shoulder against the door again, but this time nothing budges. They have replaced the shoring timber. There is no way he's going to get out of there, and he knows it.

GINDIN

The mood among Gindin's companions locked in the sonar compartment changed the moment the engines were started and changed again
when the *Storozhevoy* actually got under way.

"Until that point the rest of them were dismissive of the entire incident," Gindin says. "Nothing terrible was going to happen. In a few hours
they would be released and everything would get back to normal."

Sablin and Shein and some of the others would be placed under
arrest, and Captain Potulniy would come down on them like a ton of
bricks for not doing something to stop Sablin. Heads would definitely
roll.

But now that they were actually under way, to God only knew
where, everything had changed. Now they were in the middle of a full-
blown mutiny. And the punishment for that crime was more severe
than a slap on the wrist or even a few weeks in the *gaubvachta*—the
brig. Men could be shot for such a crime. Men could lose their lives for
simply not doing enough to stop the mutiny.

All of them locked in the compartment began to realize that they were in deep trouble now. This was no longer an exercise in which passive resistance would do any good. Simply having voted with a black backgammon piece wouldn't be enough to convince a military tribunal that they were innocent officers who had been duped by their *zampolit*.

But the situation was hopeless. They were locked in a belowdecks compartment, and even if they could somehow get the hatch open and rush out into the corridor, there was at least one sailor with a weapon standing guard. They would be cut down before they took two steps. There wasn't a damn thing they could do. They had sealed their fate with the vote in the midshipmen's mess.

Gindin walks to the hatch that opens into the smaller compartment and stares at the pump mechanism in the dark corner.

"My career was spent learning how to fix things," Gindin says. "How to keep a warship's mechanical equipment operating in perfect condition. I'd never dreamed about sabotage, except how to recognize it and how to fix something that had been deliberately wrecked."

"What is it, Boris?" Captain Lieutenant Proshutinsky asks, coming over. "Have you thought of something?"

Gindin looks over his shoulder at the officer, almost afraid of what he's about to suggest. "All our drinking water comes from the main tank in the bow."

"Okay," Proshutinsky says after a beat. "What of it?"

"A ship can't get far without drinking water for the crew."

"That's true."

Gindin nods toward the mechanism in the corner. "That's the pump that draws the water out of the main tank."

Understanding dawns on Proshutinsky all at once. "*Eb tvoiu mat*," he swears softly. "Can you do it?"

"I can do it," Gindin says. "The question is: Should I do it?"

"Of course. Whatever it takes to stop Sablin and the other maniacs you must do, and I will back you up one hundred percent if there are any questions."

Gindin has to laugh inwardly. Proshutinsky still doesn't get it. There'll be questions, for whoever survives this business. And Gindin suspects that none of them will be very easy to answer.

"What can we do to help you?" Proshutinsky asks.

"Just make sure that one of the guards doesn't decide to come in here and find out what's going on."

Gindin rolls up his shirtsleeves and quickly goes through the drawers of tools and spare parts, finding a couple of screwdrivers, an adjustable wrench, and a socket set. It's all he needs.

It takes him about forty-five minutes, working in the dim light, to shut down the pump and disassemble it. From now on there'll be no freshwater anywhere on the ship, and it won't be long before one of Gindin's crewmen figures out what has probably happened and comes to investigate.

Gindin sits back on his haunches and looks at the pump parts spread out all over the place. At least four guys on his crew had the knowledge and skills to come in here and within an hour or two have the pump put back together and running again.

If they could find the parts.

"Are you done in there?" Proshutinksy asks from the open hatch.

Gindin looks up. "No more water for the ship," he says. "I want to keep it that way. Give me a hand, please, sir."

"Sure."

Gindin pulls up a couple sections of the deck grating that opens to the bilges. As Proshutinsky passes him the parts from the pump, Boris drops them into the bilge, tossing some of them farther aft and some farther forward. Now if someone comes to put the pump back together it won't be such an easy job. First he'll have to find all the parts, including a lot of small nuts, bolts, washers, springs, gaskets, C-clips, and gears and impellers. It won't be such an easy job, and it'll take a lot of time.

Time, Gindin hopes, for Sablin to come to his senses, or for someone to come to their rescue.

Someone taps on the forward bulkhead. It sounds to Gindin like a piece of metal, perhaps a pipe, being banged against the steel wall.

"What the hell is that?" Proshutinsky demands.

Gindin holds up a hand for silence. The banging starts again, then stops.

"Someone is trying to communicate with us," Proshutinksy says.

Gindin picks up a wrench and taps a couple of times against the bulkhead.

Almost immediately someone calls out from the other side, "Who is it?"

"My God, it's the captain," Gindin says. "Captain Potulniy!" he shouts. "Can you hear me, sir? Are you okay?"

"Boris, is that you?" Potulniy's voice is muffled but understandable.

"Yes, sir. Are you a prisoner? Have you been hurt?"

"I'm fine, but they've locked me in the forward sonar supply compartment. Are you alone?"

"No, there are nine of us," Gindin replies. Now the others have joined Proshutinsky at the hatch. "We're locked in, and there's no way of getting out. But I disabled the freshwater pump, so there's no drinking water anywhere aboard ship."

"Very good, Boris."

"Ask him what happened," Proshutinsky says.

"What happened, sir?" Gindin calls out. He wants to shout loudly enough so that the captain can hear him, and yet he doesn't want to alert the guards outside in the corridor.

"It was Valery. He told me that some sailors were drinking down here, so I went with him to find out what was going on. Before I could do anything he had me locked in."

"We're on our way downriver, I think," Gindin shouts.

"Yes, I know," Potulniy replies. "Is there a possibility of you getting out of there and releasing me?"

"I don't know, Captain. But we'll try to think of something."

"You'd better hurry, Boris, because I don't think we have much time."

"Sir?"

"Someone must know that we have sailed too early, and they'll be trying to contact us," Potulniy explains. "If Sablin can't give them a good answer, and if he actually makes it out to the gulf, they'll come after us. Someone will give the order to find us and sink us."

No matter what happens, from this point the lives of all the men aboard the *Storozhevoy* will be forever changed, and mostly not for the better.

NINE OUNCES

Life is unbearable, but death is
not so pleasant, either.

KAK IZVESTNO

EXECUTION

Right after the October Revolution of 1917 the tsar's police forces were disbanded and in their place a civilian militia was created. But the militia members were factory workers, some of them peasants, who had no experience being cops.

It didn't take long for the Council of People's Commissars to start a secret political police force, called the Cheka, led by Felix Dzerzhinsky, whose statue was in the courtyard of the KGB's Lubyanka Center in 1975. The main power that was given to the new secret police was the right to hold trials outside the normal judicial system. The Cheka was also empowered to execute anyone it found guilty. No appeals. No second chances. No defense attorneys. No writs of habeas corpus. All of it to protect the revolution.

Over the coming years the Cheka's name was changed to the GPU, the OGPU, the NKGB, the NKVD, and finally the *Komitet Gosudarstvennov Bezopasnosti,* the Committee for State Security, the KGB. But each of these organizations was charged with doing the same things: finding the bad guys, giving them a down-and-dirty trial in secret, and either sending them to a gulag or giving them what was called their nine ounces or, sometimes, their Russian insurance, which was a 9mm bullet to the back of the head at contact or near-contact range.

Over the history of the Chekas and the KGBs, untold millions of Russians—civilians and military—plus a lot of foreign citizens were stalked, surveilled, arrested, and tried by what were called troikas, or triplets, which were special courts-martial in which three judges, but no jury, listened to the one-sided evidence and passed judgment, very often within minutes.

Witnesses and informers did not have to show up in court to offer their testimony. Most of the time they weren't even named.

The accused was very often *persuaded* through his KGB interrogators to cooperate with the court and tell the truth, the whole truth, and nothing but the truth.

All of this was legal under Soviet law, to protect the revolution and later the state from what were called public enemies.

Thousands of mass graves have been found across the Soviet Union, some of the graves containing the bodies of more than one thousand public enemies, each of them with the same wound, a bullet to the back of the head. That's not counting the untold millions killed by the military or the militia on Moscow's orders. These are just the *known* graves of the KGB's victims.

At one point quotas were established specifiying the number of people who were to be arrested, tried, and executed by the KGB. The public enemies were divided into categories, each with its own quota: former members of the royal familes, clergy, military officers, or Ukranians, Germans, and Tatars. Most often the quotas included the children and entire familes of the accused, under what was called NKVD Order 00486.

Very often a purge would have to be organized in order to fill a quota, decided by the Politburo of the Comunist Party in Moscow. For a time engineers became suspect and thousands were arrested and tried and got their nine ounces. It was the so-called Shakhty Case.

Another time it was medical people who were purged in what was called the Doctors' Plot.

Or it would be military officers who might have begun to think they were better than everyone else, and might have thought about over-throwing Stalin's government. This was just before the start of WWII and the vast number of capable officers who got their Russian insurance seriously hurt the Soviet military's ability to fight back.

But there was some poetic justice even in the Soviet Union during Stalin's regime when the officers of the NKVD—the executioners themselves—were purged and executed by the tens of thousands. The bells surely rang in Moscow on those days.

And it wasn't just inside the Soviet Union where executions took place. During the Spanish Civil War the NKVD set up a dozen or more secret prisons in and around Madrid to try and then murder *enemies of the state*.

Until the treaty between Hitler and Stalin went south at the beginning of WWII the NKVD regularly turned over enemies of the state to the Gestapo, and the Germans very often returned the favor, especially in Poland.

Probably the worst of the KGB executions occurred during the winter of 1932–33 in the Ukraine, where Stalin forced millions of independent farmers, called kulaks, into collectives. It was the new Soviet way of doing business. The kulaks objected, so Stalin sent twenty-five thousand Party militants to bring the 10 million farmers into line, executing the tens of thousands who disagreed by shooting them in the back of the head.

But murder on such a vast scale was too slow, so Stalin ordered that in addition to meting out Russian insurance he would take away all the food. All grain, silage, seeds, and farm animals were trucked off. Secret service agents, with the help of the army, sealed off all the roads and rail lines so that not one scrap of anything edible could get in.

Finally, food and fuel was confiscated from every noncollectivized farm in the Ukraine. That winter, while the nine-ounces operation was killing ten thousand Ukranians each week, people began starving to death by the hundreds of thousands. The kulaks ate their pets, then bark from the trees, even their boots and belts and harnesses. Finally they began eating one another. Sometimes parents ate their infant children.

The final tally of deaths by shooting and by starvation is estimated at around 7 to 9 million or more. Fully 25 percent of the entire population had been killed.

When other executions across the Soviet Union were taken into account—the Latvians, Lithuanians, Muslims, Cossacks, and Germans in the Volga region—the number probably rises to 40 million, not counting the 20 million who died in WWII.

On a much smaller and more personal level, executions were a daily occurrence at gulags such as the one in the Solovetski Islands up in the White Sea, close to the Arctic Circle. The camp was established in the early twenties on the site of a monastery and housed, fed, worked, and buried tens of thousands of public enemies.

This was the granddaddy of all the gulags. Solovki, as it was called, was where the Bolsheviks figured out how the system should be run. Like feeding the prisoners who did the most work the most food. This way the poor producers were the first to die. Like repeatedly tossing a prisoner down a long stairway, outside, in the below-zero weather. Sooner or later the poor man would die. Like forcing the prisoners to remain outside during the summer, when mosquitoes would fill a man's bowl at dinner so that the soup was as thick as molasses or pack a man's nose so tightly it would bleed. ". . . and the taste of them," one prisoner wrote, "was sweet, like blood."

It wasn't long after the camp was up and running at full speed when suddenly one day the place was cleaned up, painted, repairs made, trees and bushes planted, and husbands and wives even allowed to live together. This was paradise for the men and women who'd thought they'd been forgotten. At this point all of them firmly believed that they would live out the remainder of their days here and be buried in some anonymous Arctic grave.

The famous Russian writer Maksim Gorky came for a three-day visit. He wanted to see for himself how this model prison camp was being run. Solovki was a Soviet experiment for dealing with what Gorky called counter-revolutionaries, emotional types, monarchists. When he got back to Moscow he wrote that "there is no resemblance to a prison" at that place. Like so many Russians before and after him, he had been thoroughly brainwashed by the system.

As soon as Gorky had left Solovki the guards began digging mass graves, enough for hundreds of bodies. The next day the secret police executioners got drunk and started to work—one bullet to the back of the head of each victim. Most of the time it was enough to cause instantaneous death. But not always. Dead or not, the bodies were tossed in the graves in layers, each layer covered with some dirt.

One prisoner wrote that the next morning the earth was still moving. But the executioners had eliminated what were called the superfluous.

The gulags were not meant to be the same as the Nazis' concentration camps, a place for mass exterminations. Rather, Stalin wanted to keep the Soviet people in an almost constant state of terror. Which he did.

A prisoner who was scheduled for execution often wasn't told about the sentence. But stories circulated among the people, and anyone caught in the KGB's web had to understand that death was not only entirely possible; it was likely.

No appeal could be made, and everyone in the trap knew it. Once caught, the prisoner was totally at the mercy of his captors. Escape was out of the question.

All that was open to the prisoner before execution was imagination. On this evening on the Daugava River downstream from Riga, Sablin and the other mutineers—but especially Sablin—had to be thinking about the price they would have to pay if their scheme failed.

They might be attacked or sunk, or they might be boarded and everyone who wasn't killed in the gun battle arrested. If that happened they would probably all die anyway.

Nine ounces. The entire concept had to be a constant thread running through the *zampolit*'s head. He was a Russian. He'd heard the stories.

Most often the up close and personal executions are not carried out on some windswept hillside, beside a long open-pit grave, but take place at the end of a short corridor that opens to a small, bare room. Cold tile walls, maybe a painted concrete floor that slopes front to back to a narrow trough with a drain in one corner. Often there is a short section of hose connected to a spigot and sometimes, but not always, a chair or a metal stool in the middle of the room, just below a bare lightbulb.

No windows admit the light of day or the stars at night. No radios at the end of the hall play music. No whir of fans or other machinery can be heard. No one is talking somewhere else in the building, the voices barely a murmur. It's not hot, nor is it overly cold.

It is an indifferent place. Anonymous, like the people who pass through it.

But it is the end, and all prisoners who come to this point finally understand that this is the very last place on earth that they will ever see. This is the very last bit of the living world that they will experience. Begging, pleading, bribing, screaming, crying, cajoling, threatening will not have any effect. It's possible that there are miracles, but not in a place like this.

According to a study by the New York-Presbyterian Hospital, almost every victim who is shot in the head and arrives in the ER deeply comatose will die. In these cases very little can be done to try to save the person, because, according to the report, "of the futility of the situation."

One of the common tests is the Glasgow Coma Scale. The higher the score, the more likely it is that the patient will recover, and therefore the more aggressive the treatment should be.

Three tests are given, one for eye opening, in which a score of 4 means the victim's eyes are open and 1 means the eyes remain closed no matter what is said or done to them. Verbal responses run from a score of 4, which means that the victim can talk and make sense, to 1, in which the words make no sense, and finally to 0, where the patient says nothing. Another test is for motor responses, in which a score of 6 means the patient can respond to a command, such as lifting an arm when asked to do so, to 2, in which the patient might twitch, and finally 1, in which there is absolutely no response, even to a pinprick to the bottom of a foot.

Next the ER nurse or doctor looks for some other signs of life or the possibility of survival. What are the sizes of the pupils and their reaction to light? Is there any drainage from the mouth or ears? Does the chest expand evenly? Are the heart tones within limits? Are the lung sounds clear on the right and left? Are wheezes or crackles present? Is the abdomen soft, flat, rigid, or distended? Is the patient incontinent? Does the victim have movement and reactions in the upper and lower extremities? Does the victim have normal movement of the back, or is he or she paralyzed?

If there are any signs of life the victim should be immediately given a normal saline solution for fluid replacement. Blood should be drawn for laboratory analysis.

Above all, if there is to be any chance of survival, the victim should be placed so that he or she is comfortable and can breathe without trouble. He or she should be covered in warm blankets, especially around the head, neck, and shoulders, to prevent shock.

The wound should be cleaned and covered with a sterile dressing.

Drains should be put in place—a nasogastric tube to reduce the risk of the victim throwing up and drowning on his or her own vomit, and a Foley catheter to decompress the bladder and so that the medical staff can check the victim's urine output.

Then there is blood loss that has to be considered. A small man of around 150 pounds has about five quarts of blood in his body. If he loses about three-quarters of a quart, his heartbeat will increase to try to push what's left to all the organs so that they will survive and function. He'll become light-headed and nauseous and will begin to sweat.

If he loses a quart or so, his blood pressure will drop dramatically. The damage to his system becomes almost irreversible unless something is done soon.

Then, with around a 40 percent bleed-out, with loss of nearly two quarts of blood, the damage is complete. The victim goes into shock, which leads to cardiac arrest, and it's game over. Nothing can be done to revive the victim. He dies.

According to Patricia Ann Bemis, RN, CEN, who conducts an on-line nursing course on stab, gunshot, and penetrating injuries: "Penetrating injuries to the brain have a high mortality rate. Missile wounds from high velocity weapons [such as a 9mm pistol at contact range] can penetrate the skull. All patients with brain . . . trauma are assumed to have cervical spine injury until proven otherwise by a negative X-ray or CT."

A brief NewYork-Presbyterian Hospital article on cranial gunshot wounds warns that death will most likely occur if any combination of factors piles up against the victim: a low Glasgow Coma Scale score, an older age, low blood pressure (because of blood loss or other problems), lack of oxygen after the trauma, dilated, nonreactive pupils, and a bullet trajectory that plows through several lobes of the brain or the ventricular system.

All the medical bulletins and monographs agree on a few basic points: A victim of a gunshot wound to the head, especially to the back of the head, probably will not survive without immediate medical help, and even then the prognosis is extremely poor. Shooting someone in the back of the head at close range is a fairly sure way of ensuring the victim will not survive to tell any tale.

It all comes down to the amount of kinetic energy transferred from the bullet to the bone and soft matter of the skull and brain. So long as the projectle remains inside the skull—it does not plow through brain and come out the other side—all the energy of the bullet is transferred to the skull and brain. The damage is maximized.

If a silencer is used and the pistol is fired into the back of the skull at point-blank or near point-blank range, the entrance wound will probably be greater and the damage to the soft tissue even more extensive than with a nonsilenced gunshot wound. Either way, however, such wounds are usually fatal.

When the bullet hits first the bone of the skull, it deforms and sometimes even fragments before it enters the brain. In each case the damage is worse than if the bullet entered the brain intact.

The energy from a bullet entering the brain at the speed of sound will probably cause hyrdraulic shock, which will rupture blood vessels on all sides of the bullet's path. Bits of shattered bone fragments pushed into the brain also cause more damage. And the discharge gases that spew out of the muzzle can also enter the brain through the wound in the skull and act like a blowtorch.

When the pistol is pressed against the back of the victim's head or within an inch of contact, the edges of the wound are seared by the hot gasses, just like a piece of meat held over an open flame will be cooked and turn black from the soot baked into the skin.

The KGB knows all these details, but for men such as Sablin who are caught up in their grand adventure they cannot think beyond the possibility of their arrest and execution. After all, what does it matter how a man dies, so long as it is quick and painless? A bullet to the back of the skull is certainly quick and, for the rare few who get immediate medical attention and survive, almost completely painless.

But the KGB never takes its victims to the hospital. Once they enter the execution room, their next trip will be to an unmarked grave, and just about every Russian knows it. That includes Sablin and his co-conspirators.

THE HUNT FOR FFG *STOROZHEVOY*

There are truths which are not for all men,
nor for all times.

VOLTAIRE

CHAIN OF COMMAND

The thunder spread through the chain of command like shock waves left behind a jet passing overhead at the speed of sound. Fleet Admiral Sergei Gorshkov and his wife had gone out to their dacha about fifty kilometers northeast of Moscow, not too far from Star City, to spend a relaxing holiday with a few friends. He didn't drink much alcohol, unless it was required of him during state affairs. In fact, most of the time he preferred water from fresh coconuts, which he sipped through a straw.

Nevertheless, he stays up until nearly three in the morning, talking and laughing with his friends, before he finally goes to bed, after another long, exhausting day. Perhaps he is finally beginning to think about retirement. He'd been promoted to fleet admiral in 1956 by Nikita Khrushchev and personally seen to the modernization of the entire Soviet navy, which was no mean feat considering the kind of money the Americans were throwing around on their nuclear submarines and aircraft carriers.

On this chilly November morning even all his experience as a naval officer does not prepare him for what he will face in the coming hours when his aide, Senior Lieutenant Yevgenni Markin, scurries down the hall, taps lightly on Gorshkov's door, and enters his bedroom.

The admiral opens his eyes, instantly awake despite the fact he's only had one hour of sleep. He's always imagined that the global thermonuclear war they've dreaded since 1945 would begin this way: a frightened aide coming to his commander with news that a nuclear missile attack had been launched against the Soviet Union.

"*Da,* what is it?" the admiral asks, softly so as not to disturb his wife sleeping next to him.

"No one is sure, Admiral," Markin whispers. "But it's possible that a mutiny may be in progress aboard one of our ships in the Baltic Fleet."

Gorshkov sits up in bed, and by the time he tosses the covers aside and gets to his feet Markin is there with his robe and slippers.

"Would you like tea?"

"Yes," the admiral says, and he marches out of his bedroom, down a long corridor, through a glassed-in unheated porch to his office at the back of the house. During the day it looks down a wooded slope to a small stream from which he has pulled some trout in happier times.

Mutiny. Not in his navy!

He switches on the desk light and telephones Naval Headquarters. The duty officer, a young lieutenant, answers on the first ring.

"What's going on?" Gorshkov demands. He doesn't bother to identify himself. It's up to his people to recognize his voice.

The lieutenant is obviously flustered, but it is to his credit that he maintains his composure. He's reporting directly now to arguably the third most important man in the Soviet Union behind Party General Secretary Leonid Brezhnev and Minister of Defense Andrei Grechko.

"Admiral, from what I have been able to piece together so far, a mutiny may be in progress aboard the antisubmarine vessel *Storozhevoy.* Apparently the *zampolit* enlisted the aid of several officers and a portion of the enlisted crew, arrested the captain, took over the ship, and left their parade formation mooring in Riga."

Gorshkov closes his eyes for just a moment. This is every commander's worst nightmare. An organization, *any* organization, depends on an adherence to a chain of command. When that breaks down, only chaos can result. And when the breakdown occurs within a military unit, a heavily armed military unit, the chaos can turn deadly unless it is stopped.

Markin is there, unobtrusively, with a glass of tea in a filigreed silver holder, which he places on the desk at the admiral's hand. The lieutenant lights a cigarette from a box on the desk and perches it delicately on the edge of a lage marble ashtray, a gift from the president of North Korea. Then Markin leaves, softly closing the door.

"How does this information come to us?" the admiral asks. "Tell me everything." He will have to brief Grechko and Brezhnev, but first he needs answers.

"We're not entirely certain that all the data is accurate, Admiral, but we're told that a senior lieutenant from the *Storozhevoy* jumped ship around twenty-four hundred hours and reported to the captain of an Alpha submarine that his *zampolit* had mutinied."

"Where is that officer at this moment?"

"The KGB has him in Riga."

"What about the submarine captain?"

"He's still aboard his boat, I think," the duty officer says, though he's obviously not sure. "Shall I have him arrested?"

"Not yet," Gorshkov says. "What happened next?"

"The officer was taken ashore, where he told his story to the officer on duty, who in turn reported to the the port security people of Brigade Seventy-eight. It took a half hour for the officer's report to be confirmed before the harbormaster was informed."

Gorshkov closes his eyes for a second. "God in heaven," he mutters. Was the system so bad that it created stupid men who were slow and made stupid decisions? Or were the men so bad that they had created the system? But he knew that every navy was the same, to one degree or another.

"Continue."

"The harbormaster apparently telephoned the Riga KGB *Rezident*, who sent a man down to the dock to interview the officer, and to make sure that this wasn't a hoax. Maybe the officer was drunk, or had gone *samovolka*."

Brezhnev would need to be impressed, but Minister of Defense Grechko would want all the facts.

"How long did this take?"

"From what I gather, about one hour from the time the KGB *Rezident* was—"

"What was the upshot of his investigation?"

"Whether or not the officer was telling the truth is yet to be determined, but it has been confirmed that the *Storozhevoy* sailed without orders and in the process collided with his mooring buoy and very nearly succeeded in running down a gasoline tanker."

"Then what?"

"The ship is presumably still sailing north toward the gulf—"

"How did this come to headquarters, Lieutenant?"

"From Lubyanka, sir," the duty officer says. "The Riga KGB *Rezident* telephoned his boss here in Moscow, who in turn telephoned us."

Gorshkov is about to compliment the lieutenant for acting so quickly, but the duty officer isn't finished.

"Naturally I didn't want to disturb the admiral with hearsay, so I conducted my own investigation."

"Which took one hour?"

"No, sir. Forty-five minutes. And *then* I made the call."

"The *Storozhevoy*'s crew has mutinied and the ship is gone?"

"Yes, sir," the young duty officer says.

Once again Gorshkov closes his eyes for a second. He wants to laugh, but he cannot. If the crew of a Soviet warship has mutinied, men will die.

"Listen to me, Lieutenant, and listen very carefully," Gorshkov says.

"Sir."

"First, I want a reconnaissance aircraft sent to locate the *Sto-rozhevoy*. When the ship has been found, no action is to be taken against him, but I must be personally informed. Immediately. Not one hour later."

"Yes, sir."

"I want the captains of every ship and boat at anchor in Riga to be awakened and ordered to prepare to get under way within the hour on my orders."

"Yes, sir."

"You will personally see to it that nothing of this incident is broadcast to anyone else for any reason. No matter who that might be. Do you understand that order?"

"Yes, sir," the duty officer says unhappily. Like a lot of other people this morning, he is caught between a rock and a hard place and he knows it.

"Now, move it, Lieutenant," Gorshkov says, and he slams down the telephone.

Markin appears at the door. "Will we be dressing in full uniform or civilian attire with medals this morning, sir?"

"A civilian suit. No medals."

THE BRIDGE

A light northwest wind is blowing from the open gulf as the *Storozhevoy* passes the last sea buoy marking the river channel. The fog, which had cleared for a little while, thickens again. Stepping out onto the starboard wing, Sablin can look straight up and see stars, but dead ahead the ship's bows are only a vague outline.

Continuing at this speed out into the gulf blind is tantamount to suicide. It'll be dawn in a few hours, but in the meantime if the *Storozhevoy*, with his sharply flaring, heavily armored bows, collides with another ship, there will be injuries and deaths. That is a certain fact.

Sablin's original plan was to sail out almost due west until they cleared Saaremaa and Hiiumaa islands before shaping a course north and than back east to the narrow opening into the Gulf of Finland and from there continuing the four hundred kilometers to Leningrad, where he would broadcast his tape-recorded speech directly to the Soviet people.

But Firsov has jumped ship and has undoubtedly told the Riga harbormaster about the mutiny. The word will have reached Moscow by now and it will not be long until someone comes after them.

Sablin takes another look up at the stars, then steps back into the enclosed bridge. The two men look up, trying to gauge from the expression on his face how things are going. But he's holding himself in check, making sure he does not show his uncertainty to his men.

"Has anyone tried to contact us by radio?"

Their navigation radar is still off, so Seaman Maksimenko has nothing to do except study the paper charts and listen for radio messages. He shakes his head. "Nothing, sir."

"If they try to contact us, don't answer. No matter what is said, don't answer."

Maksimenko and Petty Officer Soloviev are alarmed.

"Are you leaving us?" Maksimenko asks.

"Just for a minute or two," Sablin says. "I need to get something from my cabin. If anything comes up, page me on the 1MC."

"But, Captain, we are sailing blind," Soloviev says from the helm. "We passed the last sea buoy, and now I am running only on the compass and the fathometer."

The only two pieces of information that the helmsman can rely on at this point are the compass, which shows him that they are heading just slightly west of north, and the fathometer, which shows the depth of the water and that will warn them if they get too close to land. Before they can make their turn to the west to get past Saaremaa Island they must reach Kolkasrags, which is the Latvian headland at the northwesternmost point of the Gulf of Riga. It's more than two hundred kilometers away. It will take another six or seven hours before they get there.

Sablin is thinking at the speed of light. They have passed their first two serious hurdles, taking over the ship and making it downriver to the gulf. They can do this if no one loses his head.

"You may turn on the radar set every fifteen minutes, but only long enough to make sure we're not on a collision course with any other ship."

Soloviev is relieved. "Thank you, sir."

If anyone is looking for them, the moment their radar starts emitting, the game will be up. Sablin just needs his luck to hold a little while longer.

"And don't aswer the radio, no matter who it is," he warns.

Soloviev and Maksimenko nod their agreement, and Sablin leaves the bridge and hurries down to his cabin.

A potentially very large problem they might encounter is uncertainty about their intentions. In order to clear the islands, so that they can make the turn into the Gulf of Finland toward Leningrad, they have to sail directly toward Sweden. If a recon aircraft is sent up to find them or if they are tracked by their radar emissions, it will appear to Baltic Fleet Command that the *Storozhevoy* is trying to defect.

Such an act is even worse than mutiny. It is treason.

The only way that Sablin can think to prove that he is not planning on sailing to Sweden is to broadcast his message right now. Because of the damage Firsov has done to Sablin's plan, he can no longer afford to wait until the *Storozhevoy* reaches Leningrad.

All of the crew not under arrest are at their posts. Sablin has called *boevaya trevoga,* battle station. No one wants to be hanging around their quarters this morning. Too much is happening. Everyone is too keyed up even to find Gindin's stash of *spirt.*

Sablin reaches his quarters without encountering a single soul, which is spooky. The *Storozhevoy* is barreling up the coast toward the open Baltic Sea, his engines spooled up to top speed, and yet the corridors and companionways are deserted. No one is hanging around smoking a cigarette; no music plays from the seamen's mess; no one is making jokes.

Once he has his safe open, he removes the taped message and retraces his steps up to the radio room, where a midshipman and an ordinary sailor are sitting in front of their radio equipment. For the first time Sablin draws a blank on their names. He knows their faces, but he cannot dredge up their names or anything else about them from his memory. And right now he is too excited, too focused, to ask.

Both men look up, alarmed by what they see in Sablin's expression. "Are we okay?" the young midshipman asks.

"We're perfectly okay," Sablin replies. He hands over the tape. "This explains everything."

"Sir?" The young officer is jumpy.

"It's a message I taped. I want it sent out immediately on a civilian broadcast channel. The people need to know what we are doing, and why."

The young officer holds the tape as if it were a wild animal ready to bite him. "When should we send this?"

"Right now!" Sablin fairly shouts. His nerves are finally starting to bounce all over the place. So much is at stake, and he hasn't gotten any decent sleep or rest in the past week. He's been too keyed up, knowing what was coming.

If only Firsov had not jumped ship!

The midshipman just sits there, a dumb expression on his face, like a deer caught in headlights.

"Now!" Sablin shouts. "Send it right now!"

"Yes, sir." The young officer turns, shoots a look at the seaman sitting next to him, mounts the loaded reel on the recorder's left spindle, and threads the tape through the heads to the empty twenty-five-centimeter reel on the right.

Sablin remains only long enough to see this much before he turns and hurries back up to the bridge. He has to make sure that the radar set does not remain on. Everything is coming together now. Everything is coming to a head, and yet there is so much left to accomplish.

Just a little more luck. It's all he asks for.

Midshipman Yevgenni Kovalev has loaded the tape correctly on the machine, his hands shaking. Whatever message their *zampolit* has recorded will certainly be controversial.

The recording is Zampolit Sablin's business, but a radio message from the *Storozhevoy* while Kovalev is on duty is his business.

The crew has mutinied; the captain was under arrest; what made you believe that it was your duty to send such a message en clair so that everyone in the Soviet Union could understand your shame?

Kovalev can hear the question now.

He flips a series of switches on his main transmitter, which will broadcast the tape to anyone with a military receiver monitoring this frequency.

But his hand hesitates at the switch that will start the message.

How will he answer the questions about his role in the mutiny? How will he defend his actions against his duties?

He hesitates a moment longer before flipping another series of switches that enables the encryption equipment to come on line. Only then does he switch the tape recorder on, and the reels begin to turn.

Sablin's message is being broadcast from the *Storozhevoy* all right, but it is encrypted. No one but the navy will be able to understand what is being sent.

Sablin's impassioned message to the people will never reach them.

BELOWDECKS

Gindin sits on the deck, his back to the steel bulkhead, thinking about his father. It is early morning now. In a few hours the sky to the east will begin to lighten with the dawn. But that's topsides. Here, in the small compartment, it could be night or day, except for the numbers on their wristwatches.

Some of the others are asleep on the floor. Their situation is essentially hopeless. They are at the mercy of Sablin and his armed crewmen just outside the door. Yet they must be feeling the pinch of no water by now. Or at least Gindin hopes so.

He can see his father's face in the dim light. It is careworn, with a hint of the illness that has just ended his life. But in happier times he was an animated, happy man.

On the day the letter came announcing that Boris has been accepted into the academy, his father was grinning ear-to-ear as he dressed in his best clothes, his holiday suit. He knotted his tie just so, polished his shoes, brushed his hair, and kissed his wife on the cheek before he left the apartment for work.

Gindin remembers looking out the window as his father started down the street. But the old man didn't get far before he crossed the street to talk to someone he knew. Later Gindin found out that his father was bragging to everyone he met about his son's acceptance into the military school. He was going to be an officer! A Soviet navy officer! It was a red-letter day, in more than one sense. Boris was a good Communist and he was getting his just reward.

At work his father did the same, bragging to anyone who would listen.

Pushkin was a small town, so the word spread quickly that Boris had been accepted to the academy. By the next day he had become famous, the talk of the town, a Soviet hero.

But sitting with his back against the cold steel bulkhead he doesn't feel much like a hero. He has been racking his brain all night to think of some way out of their predicament. He's taken apart the water pump, but beyond that he can think of nothing else.

Earlier they'd banged on the hatch to get Shein's attention. They'd hoped that somehow they could talk him into letting them go. Or maybe they could order him to open the door and then simply step aside. But he kept telling them to keep quiet; he didn't want to listen to their threats or orders.

Gindin looks over at the others, some of them sleeping, heads cradled in their arms. He meets Captain Proshutinsky's eyes.

"Quite a mess, huh, Boris?"

"Yes, sir," Gindin replies.

He keeps going over in his mind what they—he—could have done differently in the midshipmen's mess. Maybe if he'd realized sooner that Sablin was serious, that it wasn't some kind of a political test, Gindin could have rushed the *zampolit* and knocked him on his ass. It would have ended the situation then and there.

Gindin can't help but smile, thinking about his fist connecting with a superior officer's chin.

He looks up and catches Proshutinsky's eye again.

"What in God's name have you got to be smiling about, Boris?" the captain lieutenant wants to know.

But it's gallows humor, whistling past the grave. The old Russian proverb *all the brave men are in prison* seems apt at this moment. But how to explain that to Proshutinsky?

"I was thinking about my dad," Gindin says. "I wish he was here. I'd like to ask his advice."

Proshutinsky nods. "I know what you mean. I was sorry to hear about your father's passing. We all were."

"Thank you, sir."

The *Storozhevoy*'s turbines have settled into a cruising speed, and by the feel of the ship's motion Gindin knows that they are no longer in the river but have made it out into the open gulf. From there it is a matter of just a few hours before they will be out into the Baltic, in international waters. Then God only knew where Sablin would take them.

Sweden? Did their *zampolit* mean to defect to the West?

If that was the case, if Sablin tried to make a dash for the Swedish coast, the navy would not let him get that far. He would be ordered to come about or at least stop. If he refused such an order . . . Gindin lets the thought trail off for a few moments as he tries to figure out exactly what the Russian navy might do. Maybe the KGB would send ships after them. Or perhaps the air force would fly out.

Whatever happened, those ships and aircraft would be armed with live warshots, while the *Storozhevoy* had plenty of weapons but no missiles or ammunition except for the small-arms bullets.

What would his father advise? he wonders at that moment, but it dawns on him that his father wouldn't have been able to give him much advice at all. This was a situation totally beyond the experience of a civilian.

"*Pizdec,*" Gindin mutters. This situation was even beyond the experience of a military officer. Stuff like this wasn't supposed to happen in real life.

He gets to his feet and walks back to the smaller compartment. He has to take a pee, but he can't bring himself to relieve himself in the corner like some of the others had. It stinks in here; he doesn't want to make it worse.

He stares at the dismantled pump, thinking that there must be something else they can do. Something! Anything!

Proshutinsky comes to the doorway. "What is it, Boris? What are you thinking?"

"They'll have to let us out of here sooner or later," Gindin says carefully. The ideas are coming slowly.

"*Da.*"

Gindin turns to face the captain lieutenant. "No matter what happens, we must force the issue. We cannot remain locked up in here."

"Someone could get shot and killed."

"Yes, sir, I know that. But we have to do something. If we can get free we can release Captain Potulniy, and that would be a start. With the captain free we could fight back."

Proshutinsky nods. "First we need to get out of here."

CHAIN OF COMMAND

Well before dawn Gorshkov arrives at the Kremlin, where he is passed through the Spassky Gate by the guards, who have been alerted by the admiral's driver that he is arriving.

Brezhnev and Grechko have been notified that a matter of urgent national interest has unexpectedly come up. If the telephone calls had come from almost anyone else other than Admiral Gorshkov's personal aide, the caller would have already been on his or her way to the prison at Lefortovo to answer questions about his or her sanity. Waking the Party General Secretary and the minister of defense at this ungodly hour is tantamount to suicide.

However, Gorshkov is not a man to be trifled with. If he were to declare that the sun rises in the west and sets in the east, the Communist Party and all Soviet military forces would seriously consider resetting their clocks.

The armed, uniformed guards in front of the Council of Ministers Block come to attention and salute the admiral as he gets out of his car and enters the building, which is all but deserted this morning. Two other long, black ZIL limousines are parked in front, one of them Brezhnev's, the other Grechko's.

Striding down the long corridor on the third floor, Gorshkov's footfalls sound like pistol shots, echoing off the ornate walls and vaulted ceilings. His staff have been awakened and are on their way to their offices here in Moscow. He has received confirmation that the captains of every ship, submarine, and tender in Riga have been notified to light off their engines and stand by to sail on his orders. And the commanders of the various units of the Baltic Fleet Air Wing have been rousted out of their beds as well.

All the way in from his dacha Gorshkov tried to make sense out of the situation. The *zampolit* of a warship had arrested his captain and some of the officers and mutinied.

Some of the officers.

In Gorshkov's mind that can only mean that the other officers must be going along with the insanity. And since the ship actually started his engines, slipped his moorings, and headed downriver to the gulf, a good portion of the crew must also be in league with the traitor.

It beggars the imagination. What does the fool think he can accomplish? Even if the ship actually reaches Sweden and the *zampolit* and the officers and crew who have gone along with his scheme ask for asylum, the Swedes will never grant it. The traitors would be on their way back to Moscow within twenty-four hours of reaching Swedish waters.

Brezhnev's personal secretary, a pinch-faced older man whom Gorshkov has never seen wearing anything other than a dark suit, white shirt, and red tie, comes out of the small conference room adjacent to Brezhnev's office and beckons.

"The Party General Secretary is waiting for you, Admiral."

"*Da,*" Gorshkov says, brushing past the man and entering the conference room where Brezhnev and Grechko are seated at the small mahogany table.

The door is closed and Gorshkov takes his seat across from the two men, who are drinking tea and smoking cigarettes. Both of them appear to be hungover, and in fact Brezhnev is probably drunk. They're both dressed in dark suits, but neither is wearing a tie.

"We're here at your request, Sergei," Grechko says. "What fire has got your ass?"

"We have a mutiny on our hands," Gorshkov says without preamble.

Brezhnev's eyes come into focus. "Mutiny?" he says. "What nonsense are you talking about?"

For the next five minutes Gorshkov explains to the Party General Secretary and minister of defense everything that he knows to this point. Neither man interrupts, but it becomes clear that both of them, especially Brezhnev, are frightened. Theirs is the same initial reaction that Gorshkov had.

Maintaining the status quo depends on a respect for the chain of command. When the system breaks down, the incident becomes like a virus that can quickly spread and destroy the entire body. The mutiny of the *Potemkin*, which led to the grand October Revolution in which the Soviet Union was born, is drilled into the head of every schoolchild; such a little thing to bring down the reign of the tsars.

"Do we know that the *Storozhevoy* has already reached the open sea?" Grechko asks. He has grasped the full implications before Brezhnev has.

"A reconnaissance aircraft is searching."

"Has anyone tried to contact this fool?"

"Not yet. But that's next."

"So at this point we don't know what he's up to," Brezhnev says. "He could be defecting, or he could just as easily be insane and plan on attacking us with his guns and missiles."

"Either is a possibility," Gorshkov concedes. "We don't know yet."

The telephone in front of Brezhnev rings, and he grabs it like a drowning man grabs at a life jacket. "*Da.*" He listens for a few moments, then looks up at Gorshkov. "Bring it in."

"What is it?" Gorshkov asks when Brezhnev hangs up the phone.

"Your *zampolit* has broadcast a message to the people, from the ship."

"Dear God," Grechko mutters, but Brezhnev is actually grinning.

"But it's in code. The idiot sent it in code on a military channel, so no one but our cryptologists can understand it."

A moment later a young senior lieutenant with thick black hair and an impeccable uniform knocks once and enters the conference room. He walks around to Brezhnev, hands the Party General Secretary a thin file folder, then turns and leaves.

Brezhnev has the folder open and he quickly scans the first pages of the document before he looks up. He may be old, he may sometimes become befuddled or even drunk, but he is not stupid.

"Your *zampolit* claims here that he is no traitor," Brezhnev says. "Interesting viewpoint, since he has arrested the legally appointed captain and stolen several tens of million rubles of state property."

Brezhnev flips through several more pages of the decrypted message sent from the *Storozhevoy,* actually chuckling at one passage or another. But when he looks up at his minister of defense and Admiral of the Fleet he is not smiling.

Brezhnev lays the file on the conference table, seems to consider what he might say next, then slams an open palm on the tabletop, the sound sharp.

"Sir?" Gorshkov prompts.

"Find that ship, Sergei," Brezhnev says, his voice low, menacing. "No matter what assets you must utilize, find the *Storozhevoy.*"

"*Da.* Then what?"

"Sink it. Kill everyone aboard."

"Their captain is innocent; so are some of the officers."

"No captain who loses his ship is innocent," Brezhnev flares. He points a stern finger at Gorshkov. "You find that ship, Comrade! You find that ship and sink it. Now, this morning. The damage must be contained before the situation spins totally out of control."

Gorshkov realizes all of a sudden that Brezhnev and Grechko are frightened. It gives him pause. Everything depends upon a respect for a chain of command. That respect does not end with him; it ends with the Party leadership. With Brezhnev.

"As you wish, Comrade," Gorshkov says. He gets to his feet.

Brezhnev looks up at him. "Ultimately this is your responsibility, just as losing the ship is the captain's."

Gorshkov has served the Party too long and too faithfully to be cowed by the rantings even of a General Secretary, but he holds his tongue. Brezhnev is frightened, and frightened men are capable of incredible cruelties.

"The *Storozhevoy* will never reach Sweden," Gorshkov promises.

IL-38 MAY-052

Lieutenant Vasili Barsukhov is flying left stick flat-out at 347 knots, less than one hundred meters above the surface of the river, in pursuit of the *Storozhevoy*, if such a fantastic story as mutiny can actually be believed. His copilot, Warrant Officer Yevgenni Levin, and flight engineer, Warant Officer Ivan Zavorin, monitor the navigational and engine instruments. Flying this fast and this low is inherently dangerous. All of them are dry mouthed. In this fog the slightest mistake could send them into the cold water of the river or the gulf.

The Ilyushin is an ASW turboprop aircraft, powered by four Ivchenko Al-20M engines, that operates from land bases to search for enemy submarines and either launch a torpedo attack or direct ASW surface ships, such as the *Storozhevoy*, where to direct their attack.

In addition to the three-man flight crew, the May-052 usually carries a complement of ten or twelve operational crew who man the airplane's various sensors, including search and attack radars, the Magnetic Anomaly Detector (MAD), and a suite of Electronic Support Measures, some of which are connected to sonobuoys that could be dropped into the water and others capable of detecting and pinpointing any sort of electronic emissions, from either radio transmitters or radar gear.

This early morning only three crewmen have been mustered, because 052 is searching for a surface ship, not a submarine, which is much harder to find. One is manning the Berkut Radar; the other two man the ESM equipment. If the *Storozhevoy* is actually in the river or even out into the gulf they will find him.

Barsukhov keys his throat mike to speak to his crew. "We're just crossing over the mouth of the river; anything yet?"

"Infrared, negative."

"ESM?" Barsukhov prompts.

"Sir, I thought I was receiving nav radar emission about two minutes ago, but it was brief. Soon as I came to it, the transmissions stopped."

"Did you manage to get a bearing?"

"Yes, sir. I'm estimating a bearing of three-five-five."

"Are you picking up any other contacts?" Barsukhov asks.

"Numerous contacts in the Irben Channel, plus the gas tanker we passed eight minutes ago, no other military targets emitting in the gulf, but—"

Barsukhov glances at his copilot, then holds the mike a little closer to his throat. "But what, Oleg?"

"This ship we're looking for must be in some deep shit. Looking aft, I'm seeing emissions from just about every ship at moorings."

"I'm showing heat blooms from every power plant," the infrared operator breaks in. "Soon as we find our target I think the whole fleet means to sail downriver for the gulf. Something's up, Skipper."

"Well, let's do our job and get out of here so that they can do theirs," Barsukhov says. "And God help the poor son of a bitch when the fleet catches up with him, whatever he's done."

It's still pitch-black outside and will be for several more hours before dawn arrives. The fog is thick enough that they cannot make out anything on the surface. They are relying solely on their compass and on their navigation radar. It's like flying over a field of cotton batting, dark gray at this hour.

"Stand by, Lieutenant. I have a possible contact, now bearing three-four-zero," the ESM operator reports from aft.

"Can you say radar type?"

"It's a nav radar. Definitely military, one of ours. Stand by."

The May-052 is flying due north. Barsukhov tweaks the wheel slightly to port, adding a little left rudder, and the big Ilyushin turns gently to the left on a new heading of 340. Considering the top speed of a Krivak-class sub hunter and the *Storozhevoy*'s estimated time of departure from his mooring, this could be the target.

A minute later the ESM operator is back. "They've shut their radar down again, but I'm identifying the target as Bogey-One."

It's the designator for the *Storozhevoy* they've been given.

Barsukhov switches to his tactical frequency and keys his throat mike. "Ground control, this is May Zero-five-two, over."

The ground controller at Riga's Skirotava Naval Airfield comes back. "Roger May Zero-five-two, report, over."

"We're painting Bogey-One, say again, we're painting Bogey-One, and will have a flyover in twelve minutes."

"Say your confidence."

"Confidence is high," Barsukhov replies. "Target bears three-four-zero."

"Roger, May Zero-five-two. Squawk seven-seven-zero-seven."

Barsukhov's copilot resets the aircraft's transponder to 7707 and flips the send switch, radiating a signal unique to this particular aircraft. In this way his ground controller can pinpoint May-052's position and from that locate the *Storozhevoy*.

Their job is nearly done. They will fly out to the actual target and attempt to get a visual verification. But for all practical purposes the ship has been found.

THE BRIDGE

"I think they've spotted us!" someone calls from the CIC, Combat Information Center. He's at the Head net C search radar and he sounds frightened.

"Who has spotted us?" Sablin demands. "What are you talking about?"

"I'm not sure, but when I had the radar on I thought I picked up a target aft and above us. An aircraft. As I was shutting down I got a spike, which I think was one pulse from an aircraft search radar. But I can't be sure."

Sablin has been dreading this moment from the beginning. "Too soon," he says half under his breath. They need more time to get out into the open Baltic, into international waters where they should be safe. If need be, he intends to send his message to NATO. It would be nearly the same as defecting, but if it comes to that, Sablin figures he'll need all the help he can get.

"Is it still there?" Sablin asks. He realizes now that he should have posted lookouts.

"I don't know, sir. Not unless I turn on our radar again."

Sablin considers the options. "Do it," he orders.

It takes precious seconds for the radar operator to comply. "I have something!"

"What is it?" Sablin demands.

"It's too fast for a helicopter. Probably an Ilyushin May reconnaissance aircraft."

"Shut the radar down," Sablin orders. His nerves are jumping all over the place. He is snapping his fingers.

The warrant officer from the communications room suddenly appears at the hatch. "Baltic Fleet is calling," he says. He's out of breath and clearly having second thoughts.

Sablin looks at him and then at the other two men on the bridge before he walks over to the VHF radio on the overhead to the left of the helmsman's position and flips a switch. The radio suddenly comes to life.

"*Storozhevoy, Storozhevoy,* this is Baltic Fleet Command. I repeat, *Storozhevoy, Storozhevoy,* this is Baltic Fleet Command. Respond, over."

Sablin reaches for the mike but hesitates. He turns back to the young comms officer. "When did they start calling us?"

"Just now."

"Nothing from anyone else before this message?"

"No, sir."

The Ilyushin May had spotted them and radioed their position, and now they were being hailed.

"What will we do?" Soloviev asks.

Sablin takes just another moment to gather his wits. After all, isn't this exactly what he had planned for? Hadn't he considered the possibility that their departure would be detected?

He pulls down the mike and presses the push-to-talk swich. "This is the Soviet warship *Storozhevoy*, over."

"Roger, *Storozhevoy*, stand by one, for Vice Admiral Kosov, over."

Sablin's gut tightens. Kosov is the Baltic Fleet's chief of staff and is a reputed son of a bitch. Sablin keys the mike. "Roger, standing by." Now it starts, he thinks.

The admiral is on a moment later. "*Storozhevoy*, this is Vice Admiral Kosov speaking. Let me talk to Captain Potulniy."

"I'm sorry, Admiral, but Captain Potulniy is no longer in command," Sablin responds. He looks over his shoulder as Seaman Shein comes through the hatch.

"They're making a lot of noise," Shein reports. "They want to get out."

"You haven't let them out, have you?" Sablin demands. It's like an electric prod between his shoulder blades.

"No, sir."

"What are you talking about?" Vice Admiral Kosov shouts. "Put the captain on, immediately! That's an order!"

"I'm sorry, sir; I cannot do that."

"Who is this?" Kosov demands.

"Captain Third Rank Valery Sablin, sir. I am temporarily in command of the *Storozhevoy*."

"Mutiny?"

"Sir, I have to announce that the *Storozhevoy* is no longer a part of the Baltic Fleet. This ship is now a free and independent territory, no longer under the authority of the Soviet Union."

Soloviev, Maksimenko, and Shein are staring at Sablin.

"Now listen to me, mister!" the admiral shouts. "You will stop immediately and drop your anchor. This is a direct order. Do you understand me?"

Sablin hesitates again before he keys the microphone. Until last night and this morning he's never disobeyed a direct order. He's preached the Party line his entire career. He has been a good Communist. "Sir, I'm sorry, but I cannot comply with that order."

"Report your situation, Sablin."

"Respectfully, sir, I cannot do that, either."

"You will do as you're told—"

Sablin keys his mike, stepping over the vice admiral's transmission. "Sir, since this ship is no longer a part of the Baltic Fleet, I am no longer under your command. I am no longer accountable to you. I have sent my message to the Soviet people, and now it is up to them to respond."

"Sablin!" Vice Admiral Kosov shouts.

"*Storozhevoy,* out," Sablin radios. He replaces the microphone on its bracket and turns off the VHF radio. There will be no further communications.

Soloviev disagrees. "Maybe it's not such a good idea to switch off the radio, sir," he says.

Sablin looks at him.

"We don't have to answer. But if someone who wants to help tries to reach us, we should be ready to acknowledge."

Soloviev is right, of course, and Sablin reaches up and switches the radio on, but he turns down the volume.

CHAIN OF COMMAND

Gorshkov is seated at a desk in a small office adjacent to Brezhnev's conference room, connected by telephone to Vice Admiral Kosov. The transmissions to and from the *Storozhevoy* have been patched to the telephone circuit. The Fleet Admiral has heard everything.

"It's definitely mutiny," Kosov says. "The man must be insane."

"*Da*," Gorshkov replies dourly. This is not like the old days, when his officers obeyed their commands without hesitation. He's heard that the Soviet navy is trying to learn a lesson from the Americans and British. The Soviet navy is supposed to become the "thinking man's" navy, whatever that means. It's a mystery to him, where the time has gone, and he has to wonder if the incident now unfolding aboard the *Storozhevoy* is a portent of the end of the Soviet regime, just as the mutiny aboard the *Potemkin* signaled the beginning of the end for the tsars.

"What are your orders, sir?" Kosov wants to know.

Gorshkov thinks that this will be a big responsibility for a mere chief of staff. But in this incident at this moment in time the responsibility will be given to any officer willing to take it. "The order is to hunt for the *Storozhevoy* and sink him before he reaches Sweden."

"What about the officers and crew? Surely not all of them have gone along with this insanity. Captain Potulniy is apparently under arrest. And there are others."

"The mutineers have given up their right to our consideration, and Captain Potulniy should never have allowed his ship to be taken from him. Find the *Storozhevoy*, Admiral, and kill him. That order comes directly from Secretary Brezhnev."

Kosov is momentarily taken aback. "He knows?"

"Yes, and in the next few hours half of Moscow will probably know," Gorshkov says. "Carry out your orders, Admiral. Quickly."

"Yes, sir," Kosov replies, and the connection is broken.

Gorshkov puts the phone down. Now that the order has been given he could drive back out to the dacha, return to his apartment on Arbat Street, or go to his office. But if there is to be an assault on the Kremlin, he wants to be here.

For the first time he'd seen genuine fear in the eyes of the Party General Secretary, and it was disquieting. It was like this during what the Americans called the Cuban Missile Crisis, when the fear was in Khrushchev's eyes. And the reasons were the same: Both men were afraid of making the one mistake that not only would cost them their jobs but also could cost the Soviet system its very existence.

Russians are a passionate people. It had been decades since crowds had marched in protest in Red Square, but it could happen again. A military command structure is only as good as the willingness of its officers to obey orders. And any government, even one so powerful as the Soviet Union's, is only as strong as the confidence of its citizens in the status quo.

The young mutineer aboard the *Storozhevoy* meant to destroy this confidence, by seizing the ship and sending his message to the people.

Thank God it had been broadcast in code.

But Sablin could very well discover that error and retransmit the message, this time en clair. That was the major reason Brezhnev had ordered the *Storozhevoy* found and destroyed, before the message was sent again.

BELOWDECKS

It's after six in the morning. Some of the officers are curled up on the deck, asleep, and Gindin wishes that he could be like them. He is bone weary, but he can't shut down his thoughts about what happened last night in the midshipmen's dining hall.

Sablin's incredible speech, unbelievable then, is even more unbelievable now. Their only chance is to reach Swedish waters before Fleet Headquarters sends a force out here to either stop them or sink them.

Kuzmin, who's been lying in a corner, gets up, comes over, and sits down on the deck next to Gindin. He looks just as worried as Gindin feels. "I can't sleep," Kuzmin says.

"Neither can I," Gindin replies.

Kuzmin looks over at the hatch to the corridor. "It feels like we're in the open sea."

"I think so."

Kuzmin nods toward the hatch. "Anything from those pricks with the guns?"

"Not for the last few hours."

"Do you think maybe they're gone?" Kuzmin asks. "I don't mean from just out in the corridor, but maybe they decided to abandon ship. We could be down here all alone."

"I don't think so, Sergey. They'd have to slow down first, but the engines have run steady all night. Means somebody is driving the ship and some of my guys are running the engines." It's a bitter thought for Gindin, that the men he trained had so easily betrayed him.

"I wonder what Sablin offered them so that they would go along with the mutiny," Kuzmin muses. It's almost as if he is reading Gindin's mind.

"I was just thinking the same thing," Gindin says. "My guys wouldn't have gone along with the crazy scheme unless there was something in it for them." Gindin shakes his head. "Not that it makes much difference to us now."

"Maybe if we can find out what it was, we can make them a better offer," Kuzmin suggests.

The two of them get up and go to the hatch, where Gindin places his ear against the steel door. The only sound he hears is the distant hum of the turbines. He looks up and shakes his head.

Kuzmin slams the heel of his hand against the door. Once, twice, three times, and Gindin puts his ear to the door again. Still nothing.

"You out there!" Kuzmin shouts. "Open this door! We want to tell you something!"

The other officers are waking up, because of the noise.

"What's going on, Boris?" Proshutinsky asks.

"We're trying to get their attention," Gindin answers.

"*Da*, we can hear that. But why? They're not going to let us out of here."

"They might if we can find out what Sablin offered them to go along with the mutiny. Maybe we can make a better offer."

"I don't think so," Proshutinsky says.

"Sir?"

"I can guess exactly what he offered the enlisted crew. The only thing they care about is getting out of the navy and going back home."

"Sablin doesn't have that authority," Gindin says.

"True, but those boys probably don't know that," Proshutinsky points out.

Kuzmin has been listening at the door. He looks up and shakes his head. "It doesn't matter. Nobody's out there. They've gone."

He and Gindin share a glance, and each knows for a fact what the other is thinking at that moment. If the guards are no longer guarding this hatch, what will happen if the ship is attacked and sinks? No one will be down here to open the door.

They would all drown in these two tiny compartments.

BALTIC FLEET HEADQUARTERS, KALININGRAD

Kosov arrives at his office in a rush, not bothering to wait for his driver to open the car door for him, or return the salute from the guard at the front entrance.

Everything Kosov has done to this point has been by telephone from his house and the mobile radio in his car. He has not bothered encrypting any of his orders; there is no time for that. Party General Secretary Brezhnev has ordered the *Storozhevoy* found and destroyed immediately.

The first part has been accomplished, and now will come the most difficult assignment of Kosov's long and illustrious career. In effect, his head has been placed on the chopping block. If he succeeds with this business, if the fleet actually catches up with the mutineers before they reach Sweden and if his forces actually stop or destroy the *Storozhevoy*, he might get a medal and a promotion. But if he fails . . .

He lets that thought trail off as he hurries down the fourth-floor corridor to the operations center, where most of the staff has already arrived. The fleet commander is away on holiday, which leaves Kosov the senior officer. He might wonder if it's by chance or by design that he has been placed in such a delicate, difficult situation.

Chief of Operations Captain Third Rank Viktor Badim looks up from the plotting table as Kosov walks in. "Admiral on deck!" Badim shouts.

The eight staffers on duty stiffen to attention.

"As you were," Kosov grumbles. He glances at the large table on which is a detailed chart of the Baltic, including all of its islands, inlets, rivers, and bases, as well as those of Sweden and other bordering nations.

Every warship that the Soviet navy is tracking is represented as a tiny wooden model on the table, and talkers, connected by headsets with the electronics sensors section, move the pieces around the table as if they were chessmen in a deadly, real game.

Kosov takes his position at the command console that looks down on the table, and one of the ratings brings him a glass of sweet tea, with one small piece of lemon, just as he likes it.

Badim comes up. "The fleet at Riga is under way," he reports to the admiral. "But there are a lot of questions."

"Are they clear on their orders?" Kosov demands. He's not in a very good mood. But then that's to be expected. No one can be cheerful when he knows that his career is on the line. God help Potulniy if he survives.

"Yes, sir," Badim says. "They're to catch up with the *Storozhevoy* and stop him by any means possible."

"The orders have changed, Viktor. We're to hunt down the *Storozhevoy* and kill him."

Badim visibly reacts as if he's been slapped in the face.

"I spoke with Gorshkov. The order comes from Brezhnev himself. Under no circumstances will the *Storozhevoy* be allowed to reach Swedish waters."

"But, sir, according to the encrypted transmission, they aren't defecting. They mean to lay off Leningrad and make more broadcasts. They're fools, but they're not defecting."

Kosov leans forward. "Is there anything unclear about my orders, Captain? Or should I repeat them?"

Badim backs down. "No, sir."

"Very well. Order as many units of our air wing as you think necessary to help with the hunt." Kosov has started to spread his responsibility. The more officers under him he can commit to making decisions on their own, the more he will be insulated from retribution in the end.

Badim undersands this game as well, but there's no countermove he can make. "Yes, sir," he says, resigned.

"Make it happen now," Kosov orders.

Badim goes off to order the air wing into action, as Kosov sits back with his tea and watches as the talkers push the fleet that was at anchor in Riga down the river toward the Baltic. The *Storozhevoy* has at least a five-hour head start, and it's not likely that the fleet will catch up with him before the air wing does.

Sablin and his mutineers will never come within sight of Sweden before they are sent to the bottom, probably in the next few hours.

It's too bad, Kosov thinks. The *Storozhevoy* was a good-looking ship.

TU-16 BADGER FLIGHT-01

The flight of ten Badger recon/bomber aircraft from Skirotava Naval Airfield outside of Riga rose up through the fog and burst into the star-studded sky well after 0600. Flight Leader Colonel Gennadi Kabatov keyed his throat mike.

"Ground control, this is Zero-one Flight Leader at flight level five. Our ETA for formation is zero-six-twenty. Do you have an update on Bogey-One's position, course, and speed?"

"Roger Zero-one Flight Leader. We have a visual. Target bears three-zero-five degrees, range two-one-seven kilometers, and opening at three-zero knots. Target's estimated course is now three-two-zero degrees."

"Acknowledged," Kabatov radioed. "Zero-one Flight Leader out."

The big twin-engine jet bomber was more suited to long-range nuclear bombing missions or, closer to Soviet waters, could be used effectively as a strike platform for anti-aircraft carrier operations or attacks against ships much larger than the *Storozhevoy*.

When the alert klaxon sounded, bringing Kabatov out of a sound sleep, he'd not had any deep thoughts. He'd been trained to react first and think later. But in the pilots' briefing room when he'd been told the target and given his flight's orders he did a lot of wondering. The best he could figure was that someone in Moscow was shitting in his trousers to order such a massive strike force against a lone, unarmed ASW ship.

With a length of just under forty meters, the Tu-16 was more than one-third as long as the warship he was hunting. Powered by a pair of massive Mikulin AM-3 turbojets, the bomber had a maximum speed in excess of 1,000 kilometers per hour, a range of 7,200 kilometers, and a service ceiling of nearly 13,000 meters. He was capable of carrying conventional and nuclear bombs weighing as much as nine thousand kilograms and was armed with a half-dozen 23mm cannons.

Instead of carrying bombs this early morning, each aircraft had been loaded with either one AS-2 Kipper antiship missile or one AS-6 Kingfish missile.

This was more firepower than was needed to take out an American nuclear-powered aircraft carrier.

To Kabatov's way of thinking, this was overkill taken to a ridiculously dangerous level. American warships sometimes operated in the Baltic and, along with Swedish radar installations that had undoubtedly detected the flight as soon as it took off, would have to wonder what the hell was going on.

Wars had begun just like this, he thought. Or at least battles had.

He switched to his command frequency, not bothering to use an encrypted channel. He wanted anyone listening in to know that this wasn't the beginning of an attack on NATO. "Flight One, this is Flight One Lead. Report, over."

One by one the commanders of the other nine Badgers reported their positions and altitudes, inbound on Kabatov's aircraft.

"All operators keep a sharp eye for threat radars. I want to know what's aimed at us out there."

"My scope is clear," Kabatov's own Yen-D search radar operator reported.

"Roger," Kabatov acknowledged. He glanced over at his copilot, Lieutenant Demin, who shared the same feelings about this morning's mission and raised an eyebrow.

"We've got our orders, Gennadi."

"*Da*," Kabatov said. "No matter how stupid they are, those are our guys down there. Russians."

"Mutineers," Demin pointed out.

"At lot of those boys are going to die before lunch if we follow our orders."

Demin nodded. "Whatever you want to do, I'll go along with you."

"Could mean trouble later on," Kabatov warned.

Demin grinned, his wide, dark eyes lighting up. "What can they do? Shoot us?"

Kabatov nodded. "They might do just that."

THE BRIDGE

It's still too foggy to see much of anything beyond their bows, so Sablin walks out onto the port wing and cocks an ear to listen. Vice Admiral Kosov has probably sent ships out after them and possibly a couple of attack aircraft from Skirotava or maybe even Mamonovo Airfield outside Kaliningrad.

But besides that, this is the open Baltic, an area normally heavily traveled by commercial ships flying flags from a dozen different countries, the occasional warship, sometimes U.S. but most often Swedish or West German, and of course KGB patrol boats.

They are blind and they are going too fast. Sablin can almost sense the presence of other ships out there, although he can't hear anything over the noise of the 30-knot breeze blowing across the deck and sending an icy spray over the bows when they plow into a trough.

He ducks back onto the bridge. Shein is still there, and under the circumstances Sablin doesn't think it matters if a guard is stationed below to make sure Potulniy and his officers get out. Besides, Shein looks nervous, even frightened, as well he should be.

"Turn on the radar," Sablin orders.

Soloviev is clearly relieved, but Maksimenko isn't sure.

"Won't they see us?" he asks.

"The fleet already knows where we are," Sablin says. "The moment we were overflown, our position was pinpointed down to the meter. But now we need the radar; we can't continue blind like this. If we collide with another ship, someone will get killed. Then we would be in serious trouble, and I don't want that on my conscience."

All three crewmen look at their *zampolit* as if he were crazy. How much more trouble can mutineers get into?

Maksimenko turns on the Palm Frond navigation radar and as soon as the set warms up the screen comes alive with targets.

"*Eb tvoiu mat,*" Soloviev swears half under his breath.

They are nearly out of the Irben Channel and around the Sōrve Peninsula at the southwestern end of Saaremaa Island. From here they are about one hour from international waters, where Sablin believes they will be safe.

If they can make it that far.

"What's out there?" Sablin demands. "Talk to me."

It takes an agonizingly long time for Maksimenko to sort out what's being depicted on the radar screen.

"Ahead of us is nothing but commercial traffic, so far as I can tell," he says. "We're not on a collision course with anything, but that'll change in the next half hour." He looks up, and at that moment he could be a deer at night caught in the headlights of an onrushing truck.

"What else?" Sablin prompts.

"We're in trouble."

"What do you mean?"

"A small ship is coming up fast off our starboard quarter. Less than five hundred meters out now. It's probably a KGB patrol boat. And just coming out of the river, it looks as if every ship that was moored with us is heading our way."

The KGB patrol craft probably couldn't do much damage to them, and long before the fleet catches up the *Storozhevoy* will be out of Soviet waters. What really matters is what aircraft Fleet Headquarters has sent after them. But he does not want to call CIC again for another radar search.

The trick will be to somehow survive the next hour.

Sablin is taking it as an article of faith that the *Storozhevoy* will not be attacked once he reaches international waters.

BIG EARS

Sweden and Russia have been at war with each other for three hundred plus years by this chilly morning of November 9. True, no shots are being exchanged at this moment, and haven't been for a very long time, but Sweden does not ignore threats.

At times during the history of these two nations, Sweden has been the dominant power, while at other times, like right now, Russia, the Soviet Union, has been the vastly superior force. So when the Russians start moving their warships and military aircraft around the Baltic the Swedes definitely sit up and take notice.

The Swedish National Defence Radio Establishment, *Försvarets radioanstalt,* or the FRA, is responsible for signal intelligence and works closely with the Swedish intelligence service, the S1 regiment. Ever since the middle of WWII, the FRA has been electronically eavesdropping on its neighbors, most especially the Russians.

The sophisticated organization's headquarters is at Lovon, just west of Stockholm, but it maintains listening posts at such places as

Ostergarn on Gotland Island, which is just two hundred kilometers to the west-southwest of the mouth of the Gulf of Riga.

At this moment the *Storozhevoy* is about 125 kilometers away, on a heading that would appear to be taking him directly toward Stockholm.

Doris Sampsonn, a radar intecept and evaluation officer at the FRA's Ostergarn station, suddenly sits up at her console. The room is small and dimly lit in red. A half-dozen other Electronic Intelligence (ELINT) officers man their consoles; only the murmur of the air-conditioning fan and the muted hum of low conversations mar the almost churchlike silence.

Sampsonn is receiving a strong shipborne radar signal from the southern edge of the Irben Channel, and it's definitely a military set. A Soviet military set.

The FRA, which is a civilian organization, works under the umbrella of the Ministry of Defence. They'd been warned early this morning of some unusual activity in the Gulf of Riga, on the surface and in the air. Also, they'd been given the heads-up that the Russians were filling the airwaves with all sorts of wild, frantic messages.

Something big is in the works, and all of Sweden's military and civilian ELINT capabilities have been placed on high alert. It's possible, no matter how unlikely, that the Soviet Union is making its long-feared run on NATO. But they have to be sure before they sound the alarm.

Sampsonn adjusts a few controls on her console and brings up a list of Soviet warships. Each ship's radar suite broadcasts a signal that's different from every other ship.

She is an experienced intecept operator, but it takes her the better part of a half hour to finally come up with a positive identification and exact location.

A hotline phone connects her directly with the ELINT duty operator at FRA Headquarters at Lovon. "Sir, this is Doris Sampsonn, intercept officer at Ostergarn Station."

"Go ahead," the duty operator replies crisply. It's been a busy morning.

"I've identified the lead Soviet ship that just came out of the Irben Channel. She's an ASW frigate, the *Storozhevoy*." Sampsonn makes another adjustment to her console. "She is on a course of three-two-zero degrees, making thirty knots."

"The bastard is heading right at us," the duty operator said. "What's her present position?"

Sampsonn picked it off her screen. "Fifty-seven degrees, fifty-three minutes north latitude, twenty-one degrees, ten minutes east longitude."

"Anything else?"

"Yes, sir. She's just the lead ship. There are at least one dozen military sets radiating behind her, moving out of the gulf. I think the Russians are chasing after the *Storozhevoy*. Or maybe it's an exercise."

"Let's hope you're right about the latter," the duty operator says. "Keep a sharp eye."

"Will do," Sampsonn says. It's been a long morning already, and it doesn't look as if the situation will ease up any time soon.

Although it's not part of her job to listen in on Russian military communications frequencies, Sampsonn's ELINT console is capable of not only detecting and identifying radar signals but also intercepting Russian military traffic. Anyway, one of her many talents is a near-perfect fluency in Russian. She was raised by her grandmother on her mother's side, who was from Leningrad. From time to time Sampsonn does a little eavesdropping on the side.

She dons a set of headphones and switches to one of the main ship-to-ship channels that Baltic Fleet Headquarters uses. Normally most broadcasts are encrypted, but this morning they are broadcasting in the clear.

The channel is choked with what sounds like the frantic messages from frightened men. Sampsonn sits forward and presses the head-phones a little tighter to her ears, her heart starting to accelerate.

"What the hell is going on?" she mutters.

THE BRIDGE

"*Storozhevoy, Storozhevoy,* this is the coastal patrol vessel *Smirnov* off your port quarter," the VHF radio on the overhead blares. "Immediately shut down your engines and prepare to be boarded."

Soloviev and Maksimenko are looking at Sablin, waiting for him to respond, to say something or do something, anything.

But in Sablin's estimation there is nothing they can say or do, except continue on their present course and speed. As soon as they reach international waters they will be relatively safe. But as soon as they can clear the Ristna peninsula on the western side of Hiiumaa Island they can start to make their turn away from Sweden and make directly for the Gulf of Finland, at the end of which is Leningrad.

Once they make it that far, no one in Fleet Headquarters or in Moscow will be able to misunderstand Sablin's intentions.

Sablin doesn't reach for the radio. Instead he goes over to the hatch that opens outside to the port wing, but he doesn't go outside. Only KGB patrol boats have names; all the others merely have numbers. The navy considers it a little pretentious to name such small vessels. Such a sentiment does not bother the KGB.

The *Smirnov* is a Pchela-class fast-attack hydrofoil boat capable of much higher speeds than the *Storozhevoy* can manage. He's only twenty-five meters on deck, with a crew of twelve, but he is armed with four 23mm cannons, with which the gunners could take out the *Storozhevoy*'s bridge. He's also equipped with depth charges that could be laid out ahead of the *Storozhevoy*.

More important, the KGB boat has sophisticated radar and communications equipment. By now every military unit in the Soviet Union knows, or at least thinks it does, exactly where the *Storozhevoy* is headed: to Sweden, where Sablin and his mutineers mean to defect.

It's galling to Sablin that he cannot make them believe he's no traitor. But he knows that nothing he can say will convince them. He simply has to suvive long enough to make the turn toward Leningrad. But that seemes like a million light-years from here.

"*Storozhevoy, Storozhevoy,* this is *Smirnov;* respond," the order comes over the radio.

"Maybe we should answer them," Maksimenko suggests fearfully.

"There'll be no further radio messages from this ship," Sablin says, not taking his eyes off the KGB boat.

He can see the *Smirnov*'s skipper and two others on the bridge and several crewmen on deck, two men manning each cannon. They mean business.

"Captain, we have two more patrol boats coming up fast from astern," Maksimenko says from the radar set.

"How soon before they reach us?" Sablin wants to know. Another KGB crewman has come up on deck. He raises a light gun and begins signaling. It's in Morse code, something Sablin was good at in the academy.

S-T-O-R-O-Z-H-E-V-O-Y, H-E-A-V-E T-O. P-R-E-P-A-R-E T-O B-E B-O-A-R-D-E-D.

Even three small patrol boats don't worry Sablin much. It's the aircraft probably on their way that bother him.

He looks up into the sky, but nothing is heading their way at that moment.

Perhaps his message broadcast to the Soviet people is finally having the effect that Sablin intended. For the first time since the radio message from Fleet Headquarters, Sablin truly believes they will succeed.

It's a heady feeling.

A couple of KGB parol boats can't do a thing to a warship the size of the *Storozhevoy,* and the fleet steaming through the Gulf of Riga will never catch up with them. He wants to dance a jig or clap his hands.

Wait until Nina finds out that he has succeeded. All of the Soviet Union will thank him, but what is even more important is his wife's approval.

CHAIN OF COMMAND

Brezhnev and Grechko are keeping their distance from Gorshkov. The navy belongs to the admiral; in fact, it was he who almost single-handedly invented the modern Soviet maritime force, so that's no stretch. But Gorshkov is on his own in this situation. It's almost as if he has contracted the bubonic plague and no one wants to help him lest they become infected, too.

He has had no time to move from the small Kremlin office adjacent to Brehznev's conference room. The general staff has answered the recall, but all Gorshkov needs is the telephone that connects him with Navy Headquarters, with KGB Headquarters, and with Vice Admiral Kosov at Baltic Fleet Headquarters in Kaliningrad.

"I have recalled the Tu-16s," Kosov is saying.

Gorshkov knows this, because fleet communications have been patched to his phone. "Why did you give that order?" he demands, though he has a fair idea of the answer.

"The Tupolevs are not needed. They're too big, and not accurate enough for a ship as small as the *Storozhevoy*."

"What are you sending in their place? The fleet will not catch up in time before the bastards reach Sweden, and they've ignored lawful orders from the KGB patrol boats."

"A squadron of Yak-28s will be taking off momentarily. They'll reach the *Storozhevoy* in about fifteen minutes' flying time."

Gorshkov thinks for a moment about the consequences of sending so many warships and fighter-bombers out into the international waters of the Baltic. Should one of the fighters fire on the wrong ship, a civilian, commercial vessel or, God forbid, a warship from another country, the situation could spiral totally out of control.

"Who will be in charge of the flight?" Gorshkov wants to know.

"The air wing commander Sergei Guliayev is personally taking charge," Kosov says. He has been handed the responsibility for stopping the *Storozhevoy,* thus easing some of the burden from Gorshkov. And in turn Kosov has transferred some of the burden to an air wing commander. It's called covering your ass, and Soviet commanders are consummate professionals at the game.

Defense Minister Grechko walks in at that moment and sits down across the table from Gorshkov. Grechko is sweating, though the room is cool.

"Keep me informed," Gorshkov tells Vice Admiral Kosov.

"Yes, sir."

Gorshkov puts down the phone and looks at the defense minister.

"Is the situation under conrol yet, Admiral?" Grechko wants to know.

"Vice Admiral Kosov is a good man. He assures me that he has everything under control, and that the *Storozhevoy* will be neutralized within the hour."

Grechko sits forward all of a sudden and slams his open palm on the table, the noise fast and sharp. "Not neutralized, Admiral, destroyed!"

THE BRIDGE

The KGB patrol boat *Smirnov* has used semaphore flags, international signal flags, and red flares from a Very pistol. Just now an officer is on the port deck, just below the bridge, shouting orders through a bullhorn, his voice so highly amplified that it is distorted beyond all understanding.

Sablin stands at the port wing hatch. The officer with the bullhorn and the skipper and helmsman on the bridge can see his face in the window, just as he can see theirs. Less than fifty meters separates the two vessels. And now that the fog has lifted momentarily he can see the two other KGB patrol boats trailing one hundred meters aft.

It must be frustrating for them, Sablin thinks. They have been given the job of stopping a ship, but nothing they have done has had the slightest effect. He wonders what they will eventually put in their reports and how they will answer the questions from their superiors.

"Why did you fail to stop the mutineers?"

"Where was your initiative?"

"You are trained officers of the KGB; why is it that you didn't carry out your orders?"

In some small measure Sablin may feel sorry for the men on the three patrol boats. After all, they are good Russians, just like the *Storozhevoy*'s officers and crew. He sincerely wishes that there were some way for him to help absolve the patrol boats' crews for their failure this morning. But nothing like that is possible.

"Bljad," Maksimenko swears softly. He's done a lot of that in the past hour.

Sablin turns away from the window. "What is it now, Oleg?"

The same kid calls from CIC: "We should surrender now, Captain," he says.

"You turned the radar on again?" he shouts into the handset.

"I'm sorry, sir, but I had to make sure. I'm showing war planes heading our way. Very fast."

"Can you tell what kind of aircraft these are?"

"Yak-28s."

"I know this name," Sablin says. "I think NATO calls them Brewer. Are they jet fighters?"

"They're bombers. Meant to attack ships like ours. They're coming out to sink us. We're all going to die."

"We're not going to die," Sablin says sharply. "I promise you that no one will die this morning."

"If we don't follow their orders, if we don't heave to right now and let the KGB board us, they'll drop bombs until we sink to the bottom and drown."

"If someone was going to attack us, the KGB boats out there would already have put warning shots across our bows." Sablin looks out at the KGB vessel alongside. "They could also put a few cannon rounds through our windows and destroy us and the bridge, but they haven't done that, either." He looks over at Shein. "I'm telling all of you that no Russian will fire on this ship."

"I don't know . . . " The CIC operator trails off.

"If the tables were reversed would we shoot at another Russian ship?" Sablin wants to know.

"If we were ordered to do it," the midshipman says.

"Even if we were ordered to do it, Captain Potulniy would never pull the trigger."

"He's not here," the boy says defiantly. "I say that we stop right now."

"Well, I'm here," Sablin retorts. "And we will maintain our course and speed."

"What happens when the bombers arrive and start attacking us?"

"That's not going to happen."

"But what if it does?"

"Then we'll deal with that problem," Sablin says lamely. But he is counting on his belief that no Russian naval officer will fire on another Russian ship.

YAK-28 SQUADRON

Captain Yuri Zhernov is squadron leader for the flight of twenty Yak-28s based at Mamonovo. He and most of the other pilots were at first surprised and then deeply troubled at their mission briefing. They were to fly north into the open Baltic under guidance from their air-based controller aboard an Il-38 circling at flight level eighteen, find the ASW frigate *Storozhevoy,* and open fire.

"You are ordered to sink that ship as quickly as possible," the boss of the Baltic Fleet Air Wing, Colonel Sergei Guliayev, told them.

Zhernov got to his feet. "Sir, shouldn't we first order them to heave to and surrender before we open fire?"

"They've already been given that order, Captain, and they have ignored it. They are mutineers and traitors who are trying to defect to the West, where they will turn over their ship and his classified equipment to NATO. Do you want such a thing to happen?"

"No, sir," Zhernov said. But he'd not been sure of anything then. And now, approaching the *Storozhevoy* at more than 1,000 kilometers per hour, he is even less sure.

"I have the target in sight," his weapons officer flying second seat reports over the aircraft's intercom system.

Zhernov hesitates.

"You are in position, Captain Zhernov," the voice of the air wing commander suddenly comes over the tactical frequency. "Prepare to destroy the target."

"Roger," Zhernov replies automatically.

Still he hesitates.

THE BRIDGE

The Yak-28 squadron is directly overhead, coming in at a low altitude, but still no shots are being fired.

Sablin has turned down the volume on the VHF radio; there are so many voices screaming at them to stop, to heave to, to surrender, that it's become impossible to think over the racket.

From the open bridge door to the corridor below he can hear the sounds of the morning crew coming on watch. They sound excited. Exercises were canceled for the morning, no officer showed up to conduct them, but Sablin can smell the odors of breakfast.

Sablin grabs a bullhorn from a locker and steps out onto the port bridge wing. The *Smirnov* is still there, and the fog is beginning to lift even more.

Overhead, the Yak-28s have passed and are making a long, sweeping turn to come back for a second run.

Sablin raises the bullhorn toward the KGB patrol boat and presses the talk switch. "*Smirnov,* we do not mean to fire any shots. We are not defecting. We are en route to Leningrad, where we will address the Soviet people. Do you understand?"

Several armed crewmen with grappling lines are standing by on the patrol boat's deck.

The KGB officer raises his bullhorn. "*Storozhevoy,* heave to at once and prepare to be boarded."

Sablin goes back inside, puts the bullhorn down, and calls the gunnery division. One of the midshipmen whose name he cannot recall at that instant answers. The boy was one of Vinogrodov's crew.

"This is Captain Sablin on the bridge. I want our cannons turned towad the small patrol craft that's just off our port quarter."

"But, sir, we have no shells."

"I don't care!" Sablin shouts. "Do it now!"

YAK-28 SQUADRON

Zhernov is lined up for his run on the *Storozhevoy,* and his squadron is fanned out behind him. They will make their attack in five waves of four aircraft each.

"Control, we are commencing our attack," Zhernov radios. "Have they surrendered yet?"

"Does it look like it?" Guliayev shouts. "Follow your orders!"

"On my lead," Zhernov radios his squadron, and he pushes the stick forward.

His aircraft is an older model, designated Yak-28I, equipped with the Initiativa radar bombing system, and it still has its 30mm cannons, which have been pulled out of some of the newer Yaks. Powered by a pair of Tumansky R-11 afterburning turbojets the aircraft carries conventional bombs large enough to take out the *Storozhevoy.*

"I have the target," his weapons officer reports.

"Roger," Zhernov responds. "Report weapons lock."

"Roger," the weaps reports. A moment later he is back. "I have a primary weapons lock. Do I have permission to fire?"

Zhernov makes his decision at the last possible moment. He wants to frighten the stupid fools into surrendering, not kill them all. "*Nyet, nyet!*" he shouts. "I'm firing with our cannon on the first run. On the deck, forward of the bridge, and then aft along the weather deck."

His controller above in the Ilyushin is shouting in his headphones, as are at least two others, one of them probably Guliayev, but Zhernov ignores them.

Two of his wingmen drop their bombs, but they have aimed wide of the mark. Purposely? Zhernov wonders.

The *Storozhevoy* looms large outside his canopy, and he can even imagine that he is picking out individual faces through the bridge windows when he fires his cannon, the shells tearing up the foredeck and then along the hull as he screams past, leaving the ship in his wake.

Off to port Zhernov spots a flash and sudden plume of smoke and he turns his head toward it. One of the bombs dropped by his wingmen has found a target. But the wrong ship!

It's the fog. It's the lousy orders.

"Break off! Break off!" he orders his squadron.

BELOWDECKS

When the first shots hit the deck forward of the bridge they sound like the distant blows of a jackhammer.

Gindin and the other officers locked in the compartment look up in alarm.

"They're shooting at us," Kuzmin says.

Almost immediately cannon shots rake the side of the ship, and this time the noise is deafening. Up close and personal. Deadly. For the first time every man in the room understands that they could die down here in a matter of a few more minutes.

Kuzmin starts pounding on the door again, and Gindin joins him.

CHAIN OF COMMAND

Gorshkov has switched the telephone to speaker mode so that Grechko can also hear the communications relayed from Baltic Fleet Headquarters. Both men are having trouble believing what they are listening to.

"Am I correct in understanding that your pilots refuse to drop their bombs?" Gorshkov demands.

"Three have been dropped so far," Kosov replies. He sounds shaky.

"Has the *Storozhevoy* been destroyed?"

"No, sir. Two of the bombs missed their target, but the third struck the wrong ship."

"What ship?" Grechko demands.

"One of ours," Kosov responds. "Another Krivak class, just like the *Storozhevoy*."

"Casualties?" Gorshkov wants to know.

"I have no reports yet. The situation is very confusing at the—"

"But the *Storozhevoy* has not been stopped. He is still sailing to the west?" Gorshkov asks.

"Yes, sir, I'm afraid so," Kosov admits. "But not for long."

Grechko suddenly switches to another line. A moment later it is answered by an aide.

"What is the nearest air force base to the *Storozhevoy*?" Grechko demands.

"Tukums, in the Pribaltiysk Military Region."

"Didn't we just send them a couple squadrons of Sukhoi attack bombers?"

"Yes, sir," the aide replies.

"Order them into the air immediately!" Grechko shouts. "Tell them to sink that ship!"

"Yes, sir," the aide replies as calmly as if he had been ordered to bring the minister's limousine around to the front door.

Grechko breaks the connection. "The navy doesn't want to shoot at one of its own ships, so now we'll see what the air force can do," he says to no one.

SU-24 SQUADRON, TUKUMS AIR FORCE BASE

Sukhoi-24 Squadron Leader Captain Ivan Makarov arrives at the pilots' briefing room shortly after breakfast. The runner who summoned him said that something very big was in the wind, and he was ordered to "move your ass."

Two dozen crewmen have already assembled, and even before Makarov can take his seat Air Regiment Commander Colonel Nikolai Teplov walks in and charges to the podium at the head of the room.

Everyone jumps to attention, but Teplov, who normally is a stickler for military courtesy and etiquette, waves them down.

"Your aircraft have been fueled, and ordnance is being loaded at this moment. In addition to ammunition for your cannons you will be carrying laser-guided bombs. You are to take off as soon as you can get to your aircraft. Captain Makarov will be in overall command once you're in the air." Teplov gives them a hard stare. "Dismissed."

Makarov jumps to his feet as Teplov steps away from the podium and strides toward the door. "Colonel, where are we going?"

"The Baltic!" Teplov shouts. "Once you're in the air and assembled you'll be given the coordinates of your target."

"Yes, sir. What target?"

"A ship, which your squadron will stop," Teplov says. He raises a hand to silence Makarov's next question. All the pilots are looking at Teplov, some of them with their mouths half-open in astonishment. "This is not war, I assure you. Your mission is to prevent a war, and the orders come from Minister of Defense Grechko himself. Do I make myself clear?"

Makarov nods. "Yes, sir," he says, though Teplov's order is anything but clear.

THE BRIDGE

"Sir, it looks as if all the ships that were following us have fallen back," Maksimenko says.

"Thank God," Sablin says softly. Like everyone else aboard, he is deeply shaken. He had convinced himself that no Russian would fire on them. Yet the foredeck and starboard side are chewed up by cannon fire from one of the Yaks. And it looks as if one of the ships trailing them was hit by a bomb.

It's insanity. What could those pilots be thinking?

"What about the aircraft that fired on us?" he demands, and he can hear the unsteadiness in his voice.

"They're circling overhead," Maksimenko responds. His voice is shaky, too. "They actually shot at us."

"It was just a warning," Sablin assures Maksimenko and Soloviev and Shein. "If they had meant to stop us or even destroy us they could have done it easily. But they didn't."

"I think we should stop now and surrender," Soloviev says.

"Are any of the airplanes or ships making an attack run toward us at this moment?"

Maksimenko shakes his head. "No, sir. But I agree; I think that we should surrender before something worse happens."

Sablin has been trying not to listen to the garble of radio traffic they're picking up on the VHF set. But it's impossible to ignore. Someone who identified himself as Minister of Defense Grechko has repeatedly warned the *Storozhevoy* not to sail beyond the twentieth meridian or they will be attacked.

But they're still nearly one hundred kilometers away from that position. In any event, Sablin plans to make his turn to the north and then the northeast by then, to shape his course up into the Gulf of Finland and, from there, Leningrad.

If they can survive that long. Just a couple more hours.

He walks to the port wing and steps outside. The KGB patrol vessels are somewhere behind, lost in the fog that has persisted even though the sun is up. It's very cold, and he thinks that he can smell the odors of exploded ordnance and hot jagged steel plating where the shells hit.

No major damage has been done, but looking toward the chewed-up foredeck he knows that Potulniy will go ballistic when he sees what has been done to his ship.

One reasonably clear voice comes over the VHF radio. It is a ship, and it must be close. "*Storozhevoy, Storozhevoy,* this is Patrol Vessel . . ." The name of the ship is garbled. ". . . now or you will be destroyed."

Sablin and the others look up at the VHF radio as if it were a bomb on the verge of exploding.

"This is Captain Neipert from Liepaje; stop now, or we will fire on you."

Sablin had never heard of this captain, but Liepaje was a Soviet naval base in Latvia. Sablin takes the microphone off its bracket and keys the push-to-talk switch. For just an instant he doesn't know what to say. But then it comes to him.

"Listen to me, my friend. We are Russians together. We are not traitors to our Rodina. We will be changing course very soon, to the north and then the northeast. We are not heading to Sweden. We are heading to Leningrad."

"Stop now."

"I cannot do that."

"Then change course now."

"I will as soon as we reach the shipping channel," Sablin radioed.

"Bridge, CIC," the intercom blares.

Sablin grabs the hand set. "What?"

"I'm painting at least twenty aircraft approaching at a high rate of speed. I think they might be the new Sukhoi-24s."

Sablin replaces the microphone, ending his conversation with captain Neipert, his heart in his throat. "I don't know this airplane."

"I don't, either, but I heard one of the officers talking, maybe it was Lieutenant Firsov, saying that the navy might get the new jet." Maksimenko looks up. "They're ship killers."

A shiver runs up Sablin's spine. He turns to Soloviev. "What is our present course?"

"Two-nine-zero, sir."

That's almost directly toward Stockholm. But it's still too soon to make the turn to the north. He has to make a decision, and make it fast, before those jets reach them.

Russians might shoot up their foredeck or even fire a few cannon shells into their side. But no Russian will destroy a Russian ship and kill fellow Russians.

It is an article of faith that will soon be put to the test.

"Steady on that course," Sablin orders.

SU-24 SQUADRON

Captain Makarov glances over at Lieutenant Aleksandr Ryzhkov, his copilot/weapons officer flying right seat. This mission is totally impossible, and Makarov can see that Ryzhkov feels the same way.

Ten minutes ago they received their final orders. They were given vectors to the *Storozhevoy* heading toward Sweden. When they reached the ship they were to bomb him and send him to the bottom with all hands.

Even if the crew had mutinied and was trying to defect to the West, it would only be a matter of a few hours before the Swedes would send the ship home. If the *Storozhevoy* could somehow reach the United States it might be a different story. But Sweden would never go head-to-head with the Soviet Union.

"They have ship-to-air missiles," Ryzhkov said on the way out. "What happens if we're targeted and they shoot at us?"

"It won't happen," Makarov had replied gruffly.

"*Da,* Ivan, but what happens if they do?"

"In that case, we would have to drop our bombs. We wouldn't have a choice."

"Do we have a choice now?" Ryzhkov asks.

THE BRIDGE

Although Sablin can see the blue sky straight overhead, the dense fog near the surface of the water persists. It must make it difficult for the aircraft pilots circling above them. Mistakes have already been made, and more are likely.

He's gone back out on the port wing, and he can see the thick column of smoke rising up into the sky from well back. It was the ship hit by mistake. He sincerely hopes that there were no casualties, although he doesn't know how that is possible.

It astounds him that Russians could fire on fellow Russians. It has seriously shaken his belief that they have a chance of pulling this off, and for the first time since this morning he is seriously considering stopping and surrendering.

He has been considering what sorts of arguments he can use so that he will be the only one punished. But he has come to the sad conclusion that everyone will be blamed for the mutiny, even Potulniy for losing his ship.

It's the Soviet way.

"Captain!" Maksimensko calls from the inside. He sounds even more shaken up than he has all morning.

Sablin goes back onto the bridge. "What is it now?"

Soloviev nods toward the VHF radio. "Listen, sir."

For several seconds Sablin has a hard time separating individual voices from the garble. But then it starts to become clear that he is hearing transmissions between the Su-24s and their controller back at Tukums Air Force Base, and between the squadron leader in the air and the pilots of the other aircraft.

". . . leaving one thousand meters. We have to get lower; from up here we can't tell one ship from the other."

"You are cleared for low-altitude flight operations at your discretion," another voice comes clear.

"Able Section, we go first, acknowledge."

Several aircraft respond in rapid order.

"Control, Squadron Leader, request permission to release weapons."

"Squadron Leader, Control, you have permission to release your weapons."

"Able Section, arm your weapons. We have permission to release."

Maksimenko's eyes are as wide as saucers. "They're going to attack us for sure this time."

Sablin is at a loss as to what to do.

"Captain, what are your orders?" Soloviev asks. He, too, is frightened.

SU-24 SQUADRON

"Listen to this," Ryzhkov says excitedly. He's momentarily switched to Baltic Fleet's tactical channel.

Makarov is about to push his stick forward to commence the attack run when he hears someone identifying himself as Minister of Defense Grechko.

"*Storozhevoy*, you will stop immediately. Do you understand?"

The squadron is approaching the point where Makarov must either start his attack run or do a fly-by and come around.

The *Storozhevoy* does not answer.

"*Storozhevoy*, this is Minister of Defense Grechko. You will stop immediately. Acknowledge."

There is no answer from the ship.

"Captain Makarov, can you hear me?"

Makarov keys his helmet microphone. "Yes, sir."

"You have my authorization to begin your attack run. Do it now!"

"Acknowledged," Makarov says, and he slams his stick forward and to the right, sending his aircraft into a steep turning dive.

THE BRIDGE

"They're attacking us!" Maksimenko shouts, stepping away from the radar set.

Sablin has heard the radio messages, as well as the warning and orders from the minister of defense, with his own ears, yet he still cannot accept what is about to happen. Russians attacking Russians goes against everything he has ever believed.

Attacking traitors or officers guilty of treason is something completely different from what is happening here. The *Storozhevoy* is unarmed. He has no ammunition and no missiles with which to defend himself. The crew is helpless.

All Sablin wants is to send his message to the Soviet people and let them decide their future. Is that too much to ask the Kremlin? One voice among millions. Nothing more than that.

Something hits the starboard side of the ship with a tremendous bang that nearly knocks Sablin and the others off their feet.

Almost immediately more sledgehammer blows hit the ship, this time on both port and starboard sides.

Sablin looks up in time to see at least six jet aircraft bracketing either side of the *Storozhevoy*, bright pinpoints of lights coming from beneath the aircraft as they fire their cannons. The shells slam into the ship now so fast that it becomes impossible to think, let alone issue an order.

As the jets roar past just a few meters above the level of the bridge the banshee scream of the jet engines all but blots out even the noise of the incoming shells impacting against the ship's hull.

"They're attacking!" Soloviev shouts, needlessly.

Sablin wants to get on the radio to tell the pilots that they are making a dreadful mistake. But he cannot move.

The jets were so low and close that he was certain he could see the faces of the crew. Two men in each cockpit.

But the jets are gone now, and the shooting has ceased.

"Is it over—," Makismenko starts to ask when a tremendous explosion slams into the ship somewhere aft.

This time the blow is so massive that Sablin is actually knocked off his feet.

"It was a bomb!" Maksimenko cries. "Captain, they're bombing us!"

More jets appear out of the fog, shooting their cannons into the *Storozhevoy*'s hull, the ship actually shuddering with each hit as if he were a mortally wounded animal.

The ship suddenly begins to turn to the left. Soloviev is fighting the wheel, but it's having no effect.

Sablin scrambles to his feet. "Come back on course!" he shouts.

"I can't," Soloviev says. "I think the rudder has jammed."

"Captain, we need to stop and surrender before it is too late!" Maksimenko shouts. "We're going to die here!"

"Nobody's going to die!" Sablin shouts back, and he reaches for the radio as a second laser-guided 250-kilogram bomb hits the stern, shoving the ship twenty meters off his track.

BELOWDECKS

Gindin and the others locked in the sonar compartment can smell smoke coming through the ventilators. Besides cannon fire, the ship has taken at least two indirect hits by bombs somewhere toward the stern.

They suddenly made a turn to port but have not straightened out. The rudder has probably been hit and put out of commission. They are like sitting ducks now.

None of them has any doubt that word has gotten to the Kremlin and the order is to find the *Storozhevoy* and send him to the bottom with all hands.

"We have to get out of here!" Proshutinsky shouts over the din of the bombs and cannon shells slamming into the ship.

Gindin and Kuzmin have found a couple of screwdrivers and wrenches, and they are desperately trying to dismantle the hinges on the hatch to the corridor. But it's no use. The job is impossible. What they need is an acetylene torch.

"Can you get the hatch open?" Proshutinsky demands.

Gindin turns to him and is about to shake his head when they hear someone out in the corridor. It sounds like someone shouting something, but Gindin can't make out what he's saying over the noise of the attack.

Gindin pounds on the hatch. "Let us out!"

Kuzmin also slams an open palm against the hatch.

Something heavy, maybe a pry bar, falls away and clatters on the deck out in the corridor. The dogging wheel begins to turn.

"Watch out; they probably have guns," Proshutinsky warns.

At this point Gindin doesn't care. If the attack continues, the *Storozhevoy* will sooner or later be struck a mortal blow and sink to the bottom. He'd rather face a few men with pistols than remain locked up down here to drown.

He and Kuzmin step back and prepare to launch a charge the moment the hatch is opened.

"Good luck," Kuzmin says.

"*Da,*" Gindin replies as the hatch swings open.

There are three men there, Petty Officer 2nd Class Kopilov and two seamen. Gindin launches himself out into the corridor, slamming into the petty officer and knocking the man backward against the bulkhead.

Kuzmin is right behind Gindin at the same moment another tremendous explosion comes from somewhere aft. The ship is violently shoved sideways.

Kopilov is just a kid and obviously frightened out of his skull. "You have to help us, before he kills us all," he shouts. "They're attacking us. We'll all be killed."

The other officers and midshipmen are scrambling out of the sonar compartment. "First we need to release the captain," Proshutinksy orders.

Kopilov leads the way forward to the other sonar compartment. The hatch has been braced shut with a large piece of dunnage, a heavy wooden beam fifteen or twenty centimeters on a side and two or three meters long. It takes Gindin and the sailors to prise the beam away from the hatch and pass it back to the others.

"Captain, it's Boris; we're opening the hatch for you!" Gindin shouts. He undogs the hatch and yanks it open.

Potulniy is right there, his face screwed up into a mask of rage. Gindin doesn't think he's ever seen a man so angry.

"I'll kill the bastard!" the captain shouts. He looks at the others, mentally cataloging the faces of everyone with him. "Do we have any weapons?"

Kopilov pulls a Makarov pistol from his belt under his tunic and hands it to Potulniy.

"I'm going to the bridge to put an end to this," the captain tells them. "The rest of you get to one of the the armories and see if you can find some other weapons. I want half of you to cover the ship from somewhere aft and the other half to go forward. But be careful; I don't want you getting shot up."

"I'll take the stern," Proshutinsky volunteers.

"Good," Potulniy says. He turns to Gindin. "Get down to the engine room, and see what you can do to talk some sense into your men. We're probably going to have company real soon, unless they mean to sink us."

"Captain, I don't think Captain Sablin is a traitor," Gindin says. "I think he somehow got his head up his ass. He's naive, not a criminal."

"Naive or not, the bastard's going to get us all killed."

Another bomb hits somewhere aft, and the ship shudders from stem to stern.

"Go!" Potulniy orders, and he turns on his heel and heads for the bridge as fast as he can move.

Heading down to the engineering spaces, Gindin has to think, God help anyone who tries to get in the captain's way now. And God help Sablin.

THE BRIDGE

On the way up from deep within the ship, Potulniy encounters a half-dozen sailors but no officers and no one with any guns. The kids are all clearly frightened and have no idea what they're supposed to do.

The murderous rage continues to build inside him. He wants very badly to lash out at someone, something, for what is being done to his ship. But not these kids.

"Return to your duty stations," he orders.

The attacks seem to have stopped, at least for the moment, when Potulniy reaches the bridge deck. He pulls up short just around the corner from the open hatch. From where he's standing he can see one of the seamen by the radar set and can hear Sablin talking frantically on the radio, but it's difficult to make out who the *zampolit* is talking to or what he's saying. But he sounds just as frightened as the rest of the crew.

As well as the bastard should be, Potulniy thinks. Naive, my ass.

His own naval career is finished. He will never be able to explain to a court-martial board how he came to lose command of his ship. Or why he wasn't able to stop the destruction of his vessel.

But Sablin has another reason to be afraid. Potulniy means to kill him. Right now.

The captain thumbs the pistol's safety catch to the off position and steps around the corner and onto the bridge.

The seamen at the radar set and the two standing at the now useless helm all look up, first in alarm and then in relief.

"Captain," Soloviev says.

Sablin begins to turn as Potulniy raises the pistol, his finger tightening on the trigger. But then the man holding the microphone is just Valery, married to Nina, with a son, Misha. Sablin is a fellow officer, misguided, foolish, and, *da*, naive, but not a criminal.

"Captain—," Sablin blurts.

Potulniy lowers his aim and fires one shot, catching the *zampolit* in the left leg, just above the knee.

Sablin cries out in pain and falls to the deck. He reaches for the pistol in his belt holster, but Potulniy gets to him and takes the gun away.

For a long moment the two men stare at each other across a chasm of more than just a meter or so. What Sablin has done is treason. It goes against every fiber of Potulniy's being.

He wants to ask why, but he knows that if Sablin tries to convince him that the mutiny was the right thing to do, he might fire again and this time kill the *zampolit*.

"*Eb tvoiu mat*," Potulniy swears softly. "Take this bastard to his cabin and see that he remains there," he tells the seamen. "If he tries anything, kill him."

All three of them jump to it immediately. They help Sablin to his feet and between them hustle him out the hatch and belowdecks to his cabin, leaving Potulniy alone on the bridge of his wounded ship for the moment.

He looks out the window and can see dozens of jets circling overhead like angry bees. A group breaks off from the swarm and starts its final attack run.

Potulniy snatches the handset for the ship's comm from its cradle and calls Engineering.

"Boris, are you there?" he shouts. But there is no answer.

ENGINE ROOM

Gindin has managed to arm himself with a pistol as he races belowdecks to his engine room. He can actually see daylight coming through a series of baseball-sized holes in the hull from the cannon fire.

Sailors are everywhere, running down corridors and up companionways like ants boiling out of their disturbed nests. But nobody notices the officer with the pistol racing past. Sometimes he has to shove his way through a knot of frightened kids, but even then no one tries to stop him.

He slams open the hatch and barges into the engineering space where the main control panels are located.

Five of his crew are there, running the engines, checking the control panel, and Gindin's blood boils. He trained these men. He stood up for them when the captain complained about missing potatoes, when they didn't want to get out of bed, and when they got Dear John letters from their girlfriends. He even got them early leaves when they finished installing the five new diesel engines at the last refit.

This is how they have repaid him.

He raises his gun and points it at the ones near the control panel.

At this point he is drenched with sweat, and he thinks that it won't take much of a push to start him firing.

"Get away from the panel!" he shouts over the din of the turbines.

All the sailors look up when they hear his voice.

"Get away from the panel!" Gindin shouts again. "Over by the wall. Move it!"

All five immediately follow his orders, with relief, now that an officer is in charge again, mixed with fear.

As soon as they are standing facing the wall, Gindin leaps to the control panel and starts shutting down the engines. Immediately the whine of the turbines begins to decrease and the deafening noise winds down.

Keeping the pistol trained on his five sailors, he snatches the ship's comm handset from its bracket. "Bridge, Engineering."

Potulniy answers immediately. "Is everything okay down there?"

"Captain, I've shut down the engines."

"Any casualties?"

"No, sir," Gindin says. "Not yet. What about Captain Sablin?"

"He's been neutralized, and I'm in command again."

"Have you contacted Fleet Headquarters yet?"

"There's no time! We're under attack!"

"You have to call them, Captain!" Gindin shouts. "Before it's too late!"

"Stay at your post, Boris," Potulniy orders. "I may need the engines in a big hurry."

"Yes, sir," Gindin replies, and he replaces the handset.

He's in a quandary just then. He can't run his engines without the help of his crew, yet he can't trust them. They've stabbed him in the back.

He wants to lash out with frustration. Like Potulniy, he suspects that his naval career is over. There's nothing any of them can do now to change what has happened.

Gindin glances toward the overhead. He hopes that the captain can convince the fleet that he's back in charge and to stop the attack.

Potulniy is their best hope for survival.

SU-24 SQUADRON

"Do you mean to sink him?" Ryzhkov asks.

Makarov looks over at his copilot/weapons officer and nods. "We have our orders."

They're flying low and slow, a few hundred meters above the waves, at around 400 knots. They cannot miss. The *Storozhevoy* is on fire and circling to port a couple of miles to the west. Perhaps the ship is slowing down, but at this speed and angle it's hard for Makarov to be sure. Anyway, what he's told his weaps is true; they do have their orders to stop the traitors.

If it means sinking the ship and killing the officers and crew, then so be it. The air force did not create this situation.

Makarov keys his helmet mike. "Unit Three, on my lead, let's finish this."

They are the next wave of attack jets that have not dropped their laser-guided bombs.

This time the *Storozhevoy* has no chance whatsoever to survive.

Within a few minutes he and his crew will be at the bottom of the Baltic.

"Fighter squadrons attacking the *Storozhevoy*, this is Captain Anatoly Potulniy."

Makarov slams his stick hard right and full forward, ignoring the urgent voice in his headset, and his jet peels off to starboard in a steep dive toward the ship he means to kill.

In thirty seconds it will be mission accomplished.

THE BRIDGE

It's obvious that the commander of the strike force heading toward the *Storozhevoy* either didn't receive Potulniy's radio message or has chosen to ignore it. Either way, five Su-24s are heading right at his bows and will be in a position to release their bombs in a matter of seconds.

His rage toward Sablin has been replaced with fear for his ship. Not fear for his own life but a genuine concern for the *Storozhevoy* and all who've sailed him—including the mutineers.

He keys the VHF radio again. "Baltic Fleet Headquarters, this is Captain Anatoly Potulniy. The mutiny has been put down. Cease fire; cease fire! I am in command of the ship!"

"Who is this?" the radio blares.

Potulniy recognizes the voice of the chief of staff. "Admiral Kosov, it's me: Potulniy. Can you recognize my voice?"

The radio is silent for several ominous seconds. Potulniy is staring out the windows, the jets looming ever larger.

"Report your situation," the admiral demands.

"The mutiny has been put down, and I have regained command,"

Potulniy says in a rush. "My engines have been shut down and we are slowing to a stop. Call off the attack!"

Again the radio is ominously silent.

The jets are less than one hundred meters out.

SU-24 SQUADRON

"Break off the attack! Break off the attack!" a voice is shouting in Makarov's headset.

"Ready for weapons release," Ryzhkov reports.

Seconds.

"Break off the attack!" The same voice is in Makarov's headset.

He keys his mike. "This is Sukhoi-24 Squadron Leader Captain Makarov. Identify yourself," he demands.

"This is Vice Admiral Kosov. Break off the attack now!"

They have reached the *Storozhevoy*. Makarov can see a man on the bridge, looking up at him.

"Weapons release now possible," Ryzhkov reports.

"*Nyet*," Makarov replies. "Unit Three, Unit Three, break off. I repeat, break off." He hauls the heavy jet hard over to starboard and pulls back on the stick, sending them climbing into the crystal-clear blue sky. They have accomplished their mission. Time now to go home.

THE BRIDGE

The *Storozhevoy* finally comes to a complete halt in the middle of the Baltic, nearly all the way to Swedish waters. It's a little past 10:30 in the morning, local time, and a sudden hush has descended on the warship.

Once the jets broke off their attack, Potulniy had time to study the images on the radar screen. It looks as if the entire Russian navy has them surrounded.

Now it begins, he thinks.

He keys the VHF radio. "This is Captain Potulniy. We are standing by to be boarded. Which side do you prefer?"

"Port," the terse reply comes back.

Potulniy gets on the 1MC. "Attention, all hands, this is the captain speaking. If you have weapons, put them down. We will be boarded in a couple of minutes. Anyone caught with a weapon will be forcibly disarmed and placed under immediate arrest."

"Bridge, Acoustics," Proshutinsky calls on the ship's comm.

"Yes, Nikolay?" Potulniy replies. At the moment Proshutinksy is the second-ranking officer aboard.

"Shall I order a damage control party?"

"*Nyet*," Potulniy says. "That will be up to the KGB when they come aboard." Even as he speaks the initials a chill comes over him. It's unknowable how this will all turn out. But it will not end well for any of them.

FEAR HAS BIG EYES

Once a word is out of your mouth
you can't swallow it.

KAK IZVESTNO

VLADIVOSTOK

This summer afternoon nearly two years after the mutiny the gentle Pacific breezes blow unusually warm in the harbor. A lot of people are out and about along the Korabelnaya Naberezhnaya Ulitsa, the main thoroughfare right on Golden Horn Bay. The winter was long and bitter, so no one wants to stay indoors unless absolutely necessary. Vendors are selling everything from ice cream to kvass, a mildly alcoholic drink, like watery beer.

The ships and submarines are lined up in precise rows at their docks on the Pacific Fleet base, their flags snapping crisply even in the light breeze, activity bustling on nearly every deck.

Gindin has been demoted one rank to lieutenant and has been assigned to work at the navy fire department in Kaliningrad. He was accused of being a coward, a disgrace to the Rodina, for not doing a better job training his men, for allowing himself to be arrested and locked up, for not making a better effort to stop the mutiny, for not willingly giving his life to save the ship.

The captain and all the other officers who had voted with the black

backgammon pieces were demoted to sailors, got the same sort of punishment, except for Firsov, who was blackballed. Most of the enlisted
men got exactly what Sablin had promised them: They were held for
several months but then were discharged from the navy and allowed to
go home. Only Alexander Shein was given an eight-year sentence at
hard labor and a small fine.

Immediately after the incident, when they were taken back to Riga
for their initial questioning, Gindin met his roommate, Vladimir
Firsov, at the KGB's Riga headquarters. The meeting was short and
awkward, although the two men embraced warmly.

Standing on the dock now, looking at the warships, Gindin wonders why he didn't ask his friend what had happened that night. Why
had he voted to go along with Sablin's mutiny, and then later why had
he jumped ship?

Even though Gindin called Vladimir's parents in Leningrad and
asked that a message be passed along, he hasn't seen or heard from
Firsov since then. Perhaps it's for the best.

After the dust had settled from thirty days of interrogations,
Gindin and the others were made to sign a classified document promising never to talk to anyone about the mutiny. It was a KGB order, so
everyone, including Gindin, took it seriously and signed without hesitation.

He has been assigned to be a fireman; it is a dead-end career in the
navy that will lead to nothing as a civilian. All of his plans, all of his
hard work at the academy and out in the fleet, have gone down the
drain. Blotted out by the insane act of one man.

Gindin has taken a leave and come out here to the Far East to visit
with his sister, Ella, and her husband, Vladimir Simchuk, his brother-in
law just a few years ahead of him who had recommended the academy.

No one knows why Boris has been reassigned from his job as an
engineer aboard a ship to a job as a commander of a small fire station,
but rumors are still flying through the fleet about an *incident* aboard a
Baltic Fleet ASW ship.

Gindin can't explain his side of the story, of course, but if his brother-in-law knows or suspects something, he's shown no sign of it. In fact, Vladimir has been just as open and kind and loving toward Boris as his sister has been. Family ties are very strong here.

Vladimir, who is a captain third rank, with a Ph.D. in military engineering, has invited Gindin to come to the base and take a tour of the ships. He's left Boris's name with the guards at the gate, to whom Gindin shows his military ID. He's been allowed inside and has been directed to the docks.

But he's standing, slack jawed, his heart in his throat, his stomach burning, looking up at a ship. No pride has been taken by the captain or crew. Rust weeps from fittings here and there. The paint has faded in big splotches, and nothing has been done about it. Patches have been sloppily welded into the steel plating of the hull. And his flags don't seem to be as bright or snap as crisply as those on the other ships.

For just a moment Gindin was happy to see the ship.

"For that second or two it was like a reunion of old friends," Gindin recalls. "We were happy to see each other after so long a time separated us."

But then everything comes back in a sad, hopeless rush, and Gindin wants to turn away, but he can't. He's mesmerized by the ship and by his memories.

The numbers have been changed, but the name on the hull near the stern is the same. *Storozhevoy.*

No one had been hurt in the attacks that morning, except for Sablin, who received the gunshot wound in his leg. And after everything was over, Gindin had heard by rumors that Sablin had been tried and found guilty of treason and gotten his nine ounces from the KGB.

So now it was truly over.

A lieutenant comes to the rail and spots Gindin staring at the ship. "Hey, you, *pizda,* what are you looking at?"

Gindin slowly shakes his head. "Nothing, sir," he says, and he turns and walks away without looking back.

AFTERWORD

With the book finished, Boris Gindin admitted that he'd experienced a mixed bag of emotions on the project, especially at the ending, when in Vladivostok he came across the rust bucket that the *Storozhevoy* had become.

"It was strange and unsettling to have to relive the incident," Gindin said. "Sometimes I had nightmares about the KGB coming after me and my family for going public with the story."

Even today he sometimes gets a cold feeling between his shoulder blades, and he stops a moment to look over his shoulder to make sure that no one is coming after him.

The death in London of the former KGB spy Alexander Litvinenko weighs heavily on Gindin's mind. The man was poisoned with a highly radioactive isotope of polonium, a method of assassination favored by the Soviet secret service. Russians have long memories and don't treat people they consider traitors very kindly.

But it's more than thirty years after the mutiny, and the real story that inspired Tom Clancy to write his first novel did not end on a sad note on the docks at Vladivostok. It was more involved than that, more complicated, with a happy ending.

After the KGB's interrogation, during which one of the investigators even shared a bottle of vodka with Boris in the military prison where the crew was held, Gindin was demoted one rank and sent ashore to work at a fire department, as mentioned earlier. He hadn't done enough to stop the mutiny. He was worthless. He was a traitor. He was a Jew.

Two years later he sent a letter to the Ministry of Defense requesting permission to resign his navy commission and return to civilian life. Such requests were rarely granted, and then it usually took a year or more for an answer to come from Moscow.

But within three weeks Gindin got his permission to resign and went to the only place he knew he'd be safe, home in Pushkin, to be with his mother.

It was only a one-bedroom apartment, and within a few weeks after Boris got home his sister, Ella, got a divorce and moved back with her two children, Vladik, ten, and Julia, three.

"The adjustment was tough," Gindin remembers.

There was no privacy, no quiet time for him to figure out what to do next. And yet being surrounded by family, by a sense of normalcy in a world that, for him, had gone insane, was just the ticket to help him deal with the pain of a bright future that had gone up in smoke.

Ella worked as as Russian literature teacher at a trade school, where she got Gindin a job teaching auto mechanics. Their mother was receiving a pension of forty rubles a month from the state, which was impossible to live on, so Ella and Boris contributed most of their income to help run the household.

After a few months the shock of leaving the navy finally started to wear off and Gindin began to think about meeting a girl, getting married, and starting a family. But with almost no money left over at the end of each month and with no real prospects for any sort of a meaningful career ahead of him a marriage was not likely. It was the reality of living in Russia as a nobody.

"I had to deal with it, one day at a time, so that my wounds could heal."

Nevertheless, three months later his uncle Boris on his mother's side introduced him to Yana Shnaydman. Boris was twenty-eight and she was nineteen, in her second year studying economics and finance at the St. Petersburg State University of Economics and Finance.

"It was love at first sight for both of us," Gindin says. "I couldn't keep my eyes off her. She was tall, and she had dark long curly hair and brown eyes. She had that lethal combination of beauty and brains. She was fun to be around, easygoing, always smiling. I wanted to impress her and give her a good life, which wasn't so easy under the circumstances."

He took a construction job in the evenings and taught during the day at the trade school, which left him and Yana only a couple of hours first thing in the mornings to go on dates. It wasn't anything fancy. He would take a train to Leningrad, where they would walk through the busy streets until it was time for him to return to school in Pushkin.

They dated for only six weeks before they got married and moved into an apartment in Leningrad with another couple. A year later their son, Vladimir, was born, and shortly after that they finally got permission to get their own apartment, a tiny studio in the city, and they were in seventh heaven.

Yana took one year off from school to stay with the baby, while Boris moved from job to job, trying to find something decent enough so that they could live.

By the time Vladimir was three, Yana had graduated with her master's in economics and got a full-time job—her parents helped with babysitting duties. Boris landed a position as maintenance supervisor at an elevator company, and they were able to move into a two-bedroom apartment and take an occasional vacation.

"Though our lives started to become financially steady, it was still a constant struggle to get basic stuff like groceries. Store shelves were almost always empty. Everyone was looking to make friends with someone in the grocery or clothing business, so that they could trade favors for a piece of meat or cheese or something imported to wear. Whatever was manufactured in Russia at the time was ugly and disgusting.

"People drank a lot. Liquor stores opened at eleven in the morning and long lines of people were waiting every morning to get in. People dealt with the pain of hopelessness by drinking vodka, which was cheap and plentiful.

"Russia was the perfect place in which to rot until you died."

But not everything was so black-and-white. Leningrad was a major cultural center. Boris and Yana went to the theaters, took long walks down the streets and boulevards during the White Nights, and visited the beautiful parks scattered throughout the city's suburbs. As their son, Vladimir, was growing up they were able to show him the beauty of Russia's most European city.

"These were the greatest moments of our lives, when we could escape from our reality," Gindin recalls.

But then they began to hear about the exodus of Jews from the Soviet Union. At first it was mostly rumors, which seemed unreal. But after a while even the rumors couldn't be ignored. A new mood of a kind was spreading across the country, as Jews were being blamed for everything from the lousy food to the acute shortage of decent jobs. Kids who heard their parents talk about being a Jew as if it were some sort of disease brought their hatreds to the schoolyards.

"Why don't you go to Israel, you hebes, and leave the good jobs for us?"

"Why don't you get out of here, you bastards, and stop taking the apartments we need?"

"Stop eating our food!"

"Stop poisoning our vodka!"

"Die!"

Boris and Yana decided that it was time to leave. But there was a serious problem. He had resigned his commission in 1978, and by law he would not be allowed to leave the country for ten years. There was no way around it. They would have to tough it out for another five years, with the odds against them and Jews getting out every month. The Soviet Union was sliding into chaos, and the Jews, not Moscow, were being blamed.

On top of that, Gindin wasn't at all sure what sort of a firestorm the KGB might bring down on him if he applied for emigration papers.

And there were even more roadblocks against getting out of the country. Leaving the Soviet Union has never been easy, especially not for Jews—even though they were never wanted in the first place. The Soviets would rather have exterminated them all than admit that anyone would actually *want* to leave the country.

The Gindins stuck it out until Boris could legally apply to leave the country, but that's when the real difficulties began.

First he and Yana had to quit working. No one with a job could even ask for an exit visa. And the application process to OV&R, the Department for Visas and Registrations, took at least five or six months, which meant they had to survive that long without an income.

When they were given the green light they had to pack everything they could take with them and sell everything else, then fly to Moscow to pick up the visas, which in their case turned out to be handwritten, not typed, documents, which would later cause them a lot of trouble on the outside.

"Of course during the three months while we waited for our approvals to come from Moscow, Yana was kicked out of Komsomol; our neighbors and co-workers turned against us, calling us traitors and other names," Gindin recalls. "Even our friends disapproved, and in some ways worst of all was the condemnation we got from other Jews who still weren't ready to leave."

The Gindins decided to go to the United States, not Israel, because of the stories they were beginning to hear about opportunities. It was a bit of irony that a man who'd pledged himself to fight the evil capitalists by becoming a naval officer ended up taking his family to America. But their eyes were fully open by then to the harsh realities of life in the Soviet Union.

On top of that, Russia was becoming a dangerous place for Jews. By the summer of 1988 a lot of them were leaving for the United States, so an ultranationalist group calling itself *Pamyat* (Remembrance) rose up with the purpose of eliminating all Jews. Not by deportation, but by extermination. It was the old pogroms all over again, which seemed to be a part of the Russian soul.

It was right after that difficult summer that the Gindins finally got their exit visas and in October booked a flight to Vienna, as a waypoint to the United States. Boris's uncle Vladimir, who had emigrated to the States in 1979, offered to help get them settled once they arrived. The Hebrew Immigrant Aid Society (HIAS), the New York Association for New Americans (NYANA), and the Jewish Agency for Israel, Sohnut, also pitched in to help, because by Western standards the Gindins were poor to the point of destitution.

But before they could actually board the aircraft, the Soviet system took one last swipe at them. All their luggage was searched for contraband, they were patted down to make sure they weren't hiding something illegal beneath their clothing, and Yana's engagement ring was confiscated because it was worth more than the 250 rubles allowed to be taken out of the country.

In Vienna they were housed in a big building with ten or fifteen other families who'd left the Soviet Union and were heading either to the United States or to Israel.

"We stayed there for eighteen days, and the city was shocking to us, to see the luxuries in every shop window. It was clean, beautiful, and charming.

"We were free. A huge load had been taken off our shoulders, even though we knew that we'd be facing a lot of new challenges."

At that point Boris didn't even speak English.

The Sohnut representative gave them a small amount of money so that they could live until they reached the next stage of their journey in Rome. But their trip almost ended right there, when they showed their handwritten exit visas. No one wanted to believe the documents were real. They had to be forgeries. It was possible that the Gindins were smugglers or thieves or perhaps even wanted for murder back in Russia.

"It took us sixteen hours that day to convince our interrogators that the visas were real, and that it wasn't our fault they were hand-written."

The Gindins were finally placed on a train that was to take them to Rome by the next morning, but in the middle of the night the train was stopped out in the countryside, in the middle of nowhere, and all Jews were told to get out with all their belongings.

Terrorists were planning on attacking the train and killing all the Jews.

"Armed soldiers were everywhere," Gindin says. "We did what we were told to do, and we were taken by bus to a small hotel in Rome where would we have to stay for the first week until we could find an apartment. It would be several months before our U.S. visas arrived, and in the meantime we had to somehow make a life for ourselves."

In the hotel the HIAS organization fed all the immigrants. It wasn't much: bread, oatmeal, soup, a small pat of butter, and one piece of fruit three times a day, but it was better than nothing.

The Gindins were interviewed again, and the same question came up: Why are you leaving Russia? This time Gindin hinted that his reasons for getting out had to do with his service in the navy.

It got the attention of the CIA. Gindin wasn't exactly a superstar, but he was what the Company called a person of interest. Field officers interviewed him several times in Rome and then again in the United States, piecing together not only his military knowledge but also the story of the mutiny.

Rome was a tough three months. The Gindins found a small apart-ment in the suburb of Santa Marinella, but there was no heat, so at night they slept with all their clothes on.

Among the few things they'd taken out of Russia were some sou-venirs, nesting dolls, caviar, and silk and linen sheets, which they'd planned on selling or bartering for food. They took to the streets in Rome's largest bazaar to peddle their goods so that they could have money for food. What they were doing was illegal without a license, which they couldn't afford, so they kept on the move from spot to spot, always trying to keep from being noticed by the police.

The biggest worry was their visas. It was at this time that the United States started clamping down on allowing Russian Jews into the country. Every day the Gindins heard stories about other families who'd come out of Russia and been denied entry to the United States. For them the prospects of a bright future was gone.

But in February the long wait was over; the Gindins got their visas and flew to New York, where Uncle Vladimir met them at the airport.

"This is how we started our lives in America," Gindin remembers, smiling. "I spoke almost no English, and we had only three suitcases of belongings and five hundred dollars in cash."

He got a job as a mechanic at an elevator company, earning eight bucks an hour. Yana went to school to learn English and another school where she learned bookkeeping, and she got a job.

Eventually they landed nice positions with big companies and bought a small house in Connecticut, a short train ride from Manhattan, and their only child, Vladimir, graduated with a master's degree in finance.

Only now and again will Boris stop to cock his head and listen for sounds from across the fog-bound Daugava River, smell the chill, damp air that night before the mutiny. Only now and again will he think of the base at Baltiysk and the *Storozhevoy* and his crewmates, especially Captain Potulniy and Sablin and Firsov and the seamen in his gas tur-bine section. Only now and again will he relive the mutiny, but then he grins; it's time to get on with his new life in America.

Eternal Father, strong to save,
Whose arm hath bound the restless wave,
Who bidd'st the mighty ocean deep
Its own appointed limits keep,
Oh, hear us when we cry to Thee
For those in peril on the sea!

A NAVY HYMN

BIBLIOGRAPHY

Backous, Douglas D., MD. *Temporal Bone Gunshot Wounds*. Bobby R. Alford Department of Otolaryngology—Head and Neck Surgery, August 5, 1993.

Barron, John. *KGB: The Secret Work of Soviet Agents*. Reader's Digest Press, 1974.

"Battleship Potemkin Uprising." Wikipedia.org., October 1, 2005.

Bemis, Patricia Ann, RN, CEN. *Stab, Gunshot and Penetrating Injury*. Nursingceu.com, August 16, 2006.

Chipman, Dr. Donald. "Admiral Gorshkov and the Soviet Navy," *Air University Review,* July–August 1982.

"Cranial Gunshot Wounds." Cornell.edu, August 16, 2006.

Dutton, Denis. "A New Russian Revolution." *The Press,* denisdutton.com, May 12, 1990.

"Gunshot Wounds." Med.utah.edu, "Firearms Tutorial," 1987.

"HMS Bounty and Pitcairn Island." lareau.org, "Bounty on the Internet," April 25, 2006.

"Illuyshin Il-38." Wikipedia.org, September 19, 2006.

"Inside Brezhnev's Office." *Time,* June 25, 1973.

BIBLIOGRAPHY

"KGB, History." Wikipedia.org, July 18, 2006.

Margolis, Eric. "Remembering Ukraine's Unknown Holocaust." Ericmargolis.com, "Archives," 1998.

Marxist.com. "A Leninist Hero of Our Times: In Memory of Valery Sablin: The True Story of *Red October*." January 26, 2006.

Miller, David, and John Jordan, *Modern Submarine Warfare*. Military Press, 1987.

Miller, David, and Chris Miller. *Modern Naval Combat*. Crescent Books, 1986.

Moore, Capt. John, RN. ed. *Jane's Warsaw Pact Warships Handbook*. Jane's Publishing Company, 1986.

"Mutinies." Wikipedia.org, February 4, 2006.

"NKVD, History." Wikipedia.org, June 15, 2006.

"Patterns of Tissue Injury." Med.utah.edu., "Firearms Tutorial," 1987.

Remnick, David. "Seasons in Hell: How the Gulag Grew." *The New Yorker*, April 14, 2003.

Russia, Ukraine & Belarus. Lonely Planet Publications, 1996.

"Sakharov, Andrei." Wikipedia.org, January 8, 2006.

Solzhenitsyn, Aleksandr I. *The Gulag Archipelago, 1918–1956*. Harper & Row, 1973.

"Soviet Navy History, 1696–1991." Wikipedia.org, February 21, 2006.

"Soviet Navy History to 1917." Expo 96, January 26, 2006.

Soviet Union. Fodor's Travel Publications, 1989.

"Soviet Union History, 1917–1975." Wikipedia.org, March 22, 2006.

"Sukhoi Su-24." Wikipedia.org, September 19, 2006.

"Swedish National Defence Radio Establishment, FRA." Wikipedia.org, August 20, 2006.

Taylor, John W. R., and Kenneth Munson. *History of Aviation*. Octopus Books, 1975.

"Tupolev Tu-16. Wikipedia.org, September 19, 2006.

"Wound Ballistics." Firearmstactical.com, August 16, 2006.

"Yakovlev, Yak-28." Wikipedia.org, September 19, 2006.

Young, Gregory D, and Nate Braden. *The Last Sentry*. Naval Institute Press, 2005.

ABOUT THE AUTHORS

DAVID HAGBERG spent his early career as a cryptographer for the U.S. Air Force, where he traveled in the Arctic and in Europe at the height of the Cold War. For the past four decades he has studied America's enemies and their militaries, especially the Soviet Union—its history, its secret intelligence services, and its navy—writing more than seventy novels, as well as novellas, short stories, and journalism. *Mutiny: The True Events That Inspired "The Hunt for Red October"* is his first book-length nonfiction. He has been nominated for the American Book Award, three times for the Mystery Writers of America's Edgar, and has won Mystery Scene's Best Mystery three years in a row. He and his wife, Laurie, live in Sarasota, Florida.

BORIS GINDIN resigned his commission in the Soviet navy within two years of the incident. However, he remained in the Soviet Union until 1988 when he immigrated to the United States with his wife, Yana, and their son, Vladimir. They all became citizens, and have highly productive careers. Boris and Yana live in Stamford, Connecticut. Vladimir got married to Dana and lives with their daughter, Alexandra, in New York.